ACKNOWLEDGMENTS

My Sugar Biscuits, love y'all, where are we going this month for dinner?

The This Is How We All Got Cancelled Crew—no comment. Just no comment.

Theatre Centrale, can somebody get Amy an iPhone, please?

Lisa Portale, 12:34.

Sami Klein, forever my friend. Forever.

Lavonne Joseph.

Laurie Shannon.

All of my Eutaw family, ROLL TIDE.

The Queens of Buda and your world-traveling men, whatever it is…Jordan will eat it.

Gavin, Danielle, Sydney, Caleb, Ben, Remy, thank you for welcoming me into your world.

The King family.

Chelsea Nachman and Jessica Phillips, you are my favorite thing about NYC, and I really love NYC.

Jimmy and Molly, thank you for being there.

Karen Hunter and the family at SiriusXM Urban View.

Dr. Tan, thank you for saving my life.

Dr. Barocas, thank you for making sure that Dr. Tan could correctly save my life.

Dr. Niels Vass Johnsen, thank you for saving all the lives that I could possibly create in the future?

Jeff Cobble, we all need a good physical therapist. For real, good looking out. I haven't forgotten.

Las Vegas, Nevada, thank you for infusing me with a certain work ethic and continuing to inspire me.

Scotts Valley, California, thank you for teaching me how to dream.

Nashville, Tennessee, thank you for taking the time to grow me all the way up.

Vanderbilt hospital, I hate that I ever have to see you, but I'm so thankful that you are there to be seen!

The Hachette/Worthy team, thank you for believing that my stories are worth telling to the world.

Beth Adams and Daisy Hutton, let's go change the world (again), shall we?

Jen Patten-Sanchez and the Hachette Audio team, thank you for curating the Tyler Merritt Cinematic Universe.

My manager, Amanda Hendon (and the amazing Toks Olagundoye).

My agent Cookie McCray.

My agents at the Houghton Team.

My agents at Talent Plus.

My speaking agent, Jayme Boucher.

My literary agents at Folio. Erin Niumata, I ALWAYS want you on my side, PLEASE!!!! Josh Shipp, you know without you there's no book(s). Thank you, brother.

Dave Tieche, dude, who lets us write books? And also, do you think they'll let us write another one? 'Cause it's kind of the most fun thing to do ever!

The Theater Bug, y'all have my heart.

The Las Vegas Academy of the Arts, I'm nothing without you. Keep making the world shine!

The Tyler Merritt Project community, online and on the ground, thank you for your boldness and love. It means the world. Let's keep going!

ITMCB Virtual Book Club, my day ones!

love, and humor, as much as God is also within these difficult experiences of pain and initiation. And that no matter what we are walking through, we always have the option to do it with humor and laughter. He's taught me that. He's also taught me, as a writer, how to bring my own truth and voice into the words I share. To bring all of me—even the musical theater part of me that my dad thought was annoying when I was a kid. In fact, I think my favorite excerpt from the book might be when Tyler compares Scottie Pippen to Audra McDonald and gently acknowledges, 'I know that you don't care about sportsball, my Musical Theater People.' Yup. That's the truth. (And I deeply needed that reference, so thank you very much for taking care of all your fellow musical theater nerds, Tyler!!) Tyler Merritt is a national treasure and I'm so grateful that he finds the time, courage, and joyful abundance in sharing himself and his writing with the world. Because his work makes me even happier to be part of it."

—Autumn Reeser

"Tyler Merritt is doing the impossible job of investigating and exploring America, using his life as the road map. His good humor and vulnerability make it a bouncy and joyous—but also a tender and honest—ride."

—W. Kamau Bell, Peabody Award and Emmy Award winner, *New York Times* bestselling author, and stand-up comedian

"*This Changes Everything* is a profoundly moving and unexpectedly humorous exploration of life's deepest challenges, written by a man who has faced more than his share. Tyler Merritt invites us into his world with raw honesty as he navigates the emotional landscape of his life. His reflections on living with terminal illness—where isolation, fear, and anger threaten to overwhelm—are nothing short of inspiring. Tyler's resolve to let go of unforgiveness and bitterness is a powerful lesson for us all. In a world where dying may seem easier than the courage it takes to keep living, Tyler reminds us of the transformative power of love, resilience, and grace. This is a book that will change how you see life, urging you to make the most of each day."

—Barb Schmidt

"*This Changes Everything* may be the first book I read in one sitting. It was captivatingly human. It is Tyler's story, but it is also all of ours. Finding a way to live, to truly live, in the midst of pain, sorrow, and grief is something Tyler demonstrates through every page. Unlike other books that border on denial and toxic positivity, Tyler doesn't look away from the fear that tries to stop us. This book is a dance between joy and fear. Happiness and grief. Laughter and lament. Pain and relief. All exist and are part of us. But Tyler shows us how we can let love lead and keep moving, no matter what dance partner life throws our way."   —April Ajoy, author of *Star-Spangled Jesus*

"The whole time I was reading *This Changes Everything*, I couldn't help but wonder why Tyler Merritt had never taken me out for dinner. I don't normally like to make things all about me, but honestly, what is he thinking not getting to know me? We would be best friends. But that's really the magic of who Tyler is, isn't it? He barges in and makes himself comfortable in your world, in your head, and in your heart. You see yourself hanging out with him, crying with him, rejoicing with him. I hope this book changes everything (see what I did there?) for anyone who has received the same devastating news. I have no doubt it will. Tyler, I think I'm in love."
                    —Melissa Radke, author of *Eat Cake. Be Brave.*

THIS CHANGES EVERYTHING

A Surprisingly Funny Story About Race, Cancer, Faith, and Other Things We Don't Talk About

Tyler Merritt

with David Tieche

New York • Nashville

Worthy

Hachette Book Group

1290 Avenue of the Americas, New York, NY 10104

worthypublishing.com

twitter.com/worthypub

First Edition: January 2025

Worthy is a division of Hachette Book Group, Inc. The Worthy name and logo are registered trademarks of Hachette Book Group, Inc.

The publisher is not responsible for websites (or their content) that are not owned by the publisher.

Worthy Books may be purchased in bulk for business, educational, or promotional use. For information, please contact your local bookseller or the Hachette Book Group Special Markets Department at special.markets@hbgusa.com.

Unless otherwise indicated, Scripture quotations are taken from THE HOLY BIBLE, NEW INTERNATIONAL VERSION®, NIV® Copyright © 1973, 1978, 1984, 2011 by Biblica, Inc.® Used by permission. All rights reserved worldwide.

Scripture quotations marked ESV are taken from The ESV® Bible (The Holy Bible, English Standard Version®), copyright © 2001 by Crossway, a publishing ministry of Good News Publishers. Used by permission. All rights reserved.

Print book interior design by Bart Dawson

Library of Congress Cataloging-in-Publication Data

Names: Merritt, Tyler, author.

Title: This changes everything : a surprisingly funny story about race, cancer, faith, and other things we don't talk about / Tyler Merritt.

Description: First edition. | Nashville : Worthy, 2025.

Identifiers: LCCN 2024033729 | ISBN 9781546006961 (hardcover) | ISBN 9781546007333 (ebook)

Subjects: LCSH: Merritt, Tyler—Health. | Cancer—Patients—United States—Biography. | African American actors—Biography.

Classification: LCC RC265.6.M46 A3 2025 | DDC 616.99/40092 [B]—dc23/eng/20241022

LC record available at https://lccn.loc.gov/2024033729

ISBNs: 9781546006961 (hardcover), 9781546007333 (ebook)

Printed in the United States of America

LSC-C

Printing 1, 2024

These words and stories are dedicated to the medical professionals out there doing the darn thang! More specifically, to those who are out there but often get overlooked and undermentioned! Like the surgical first assistants, scrub and surgical techs, all y'all operating room nurses, respiratory therapists, anesthesia techs, and anesthesiologists! All y'all residents, sterile processing technicians, patient care techs, food and nutrition services, oh, and housekeeping. Don't sleep on housekeeping! I see y'all out there keeping us alive, and I can't thank you enough. This book is dedicated to you.

Oh, and also to ALL the Black people. All y'all! Every single last one of us! I see you, family. Keep your head up.

All right, we good? Leggo!

CONTENTS

CONTENTS

CHAPTER 1

IT'S ALL HAPPENING

The first thing they told me when I woke up from the anesthesia is that the surgery didn't go as planned.

That's never a good thing to hear. You never want to hear a barber, a pilot, or a surgeon say "Uh-oh."

"Uh-oh" from a British bake-off judge means there was too much powdered sugar on your apple tartlet. "Uh-oh" from a pilot means "Engine four just fell into the ocean."

That's a big difference.

And apparently, during the surgery, my metaphorical fourth engine fell into the metaphorical ocean.

It was pretty touch-and-go for a minute, and—real talk—I almost didn't make it out.

Obviously, I did.

I mean I'm here writing these words. Talking to you.

But there was a catch.

Later, I'd find out that the doctors didn't get all of it.

Six months—I'd have to come back every six months, they said. They said they'd "do a scan and see where we are."

See where we are?

See where we are?!?

My doctor said it's not a matter of if, but when they will need to go back in and attempt another surgery.

Attempt?

Attempt?

That's the word we're choosing to use here? Can a brother get something that conveys a little more confidence? I don't know, a little more urgency. Something a little more stable and reassuring?

"Mr. Merritt. We're going to go in and make this surgery our bitch."

Yeah. That's more like it! Say it with yo chest, Doc!

(Look. I know that's aggressive. But *that's* the kind of reassurance your boy needed in that moment. Don't judge me, people.)

When the news hit me, I tried to be a good patient. Besides, I am a strong Black man. So it was officially time to go into Strong Black Man Mode.

But the truth is, all I could think was "I almost didn't make it out of the *last* surgery, right? God. I can't go through that again."

And it was at that moment when I first felt the countdown.

I'd never felt it before. But now, not a moment goes by when I don't.

Tyler, mark the date on your calendar. That's when you will find out how much this thing has grown.

And if it's time for surgery. Time to go back under the knife. Again.

Six months.

180 days.

525,600 minutes... divided by two.

Half a season of love.[1]

I have never been big on dates and times. I mean, I know my mom's birthday, of course. I'm not an animal.

All that changed on December 15, 2020.

Now it seems like all I think about are dates and times.

How did I get here?

Well.

Let me explain.

DATE: Monday, November 23, 2020

Like most things in my life, it all started with a biscuit.

It was the Monday before Thanksgiving. My best friend Shannon and I were sitting at a table at Puckett's, a dope little country-themed restaurant here in Nashville. We were celebrating. Just the day before, I had submitted the final manuscript for my first book, *I Take My Coffee Black*. Finally, the 108,000 words I'd sweated and poured my life force into were going to go out into the world.

By the way, if you haven't read my award-winning first book, *I Take My Coffee Black*, you really should check it out. And by "award-winning" I mean my mom really liked it, and she probably would have printed me out a certificate if I had asked her to.

But back to the biscuits.

So there I was, about to enjoy a buttery biscuit with blackberry jam. Now, I love me some blackberry jam, not just because the berry

---

1. If you didn't come here for musical theater references, you're going to be very disappointed in this book. Eighty-six percent of my thoughts are in musical theater lyrics. I'm nonstop. The heat is on in Saigon. 24601. So anything else that you get that's not that, consider yourself lucky. Man, I love *Rent*, though.

name has positive racial overtones, but also because of deliciousness.[2] But if I'm being honest, it is because BLACKberry jam best seems to understand my people. As if raspberry can possibly understand what we went through. And raspberry is always hanging out with white chocolate. WHITE chocolate. That's always felt a little suspect to me. What the hell, raspberry?

But I couldn't concentrate on the deliciousness of the jam nor the light flakiness of the biscuit.

The only thing I could focus on was that I could *not* seem to swallow it. It felt like it was getting caught midway down my esophagus.

I must have made a concerned face, because Shannon made a concerned face right back.

"Is it happening again?" she said.

I nodded.

This was the third or fourth time this had happened recently. Whenever I ate, it felt like things weren't right inside. I thought maybe it was indigestion, but then it started happening even on an empty stomach.

When I got home from my biscuit misadventure, I called my doctor's office and hounded her enough to get her to send me to a local clinic for some tests.

DATE: Tuesday, November 24, 2020

The doctor sent me to get an ultrasound, and perhaps because the week of Thanksgiving was slow, there was an appointment the very next day.

---

2. I have this standing joke whenever I see a jar of blackberry preserves. I grab it, hold it up, and say to whoever is in earshot, "What? No way. This is my *jam*!" Haha. Get it?

So there I was, shirtless, lying on my right side on an exam table, and this young lady started spreading cold, translucent gel over my abdomen. I decided to make some jokes because that's what I do when things get super awkward. And a young lady spreading what feels like cold gravy all over my belly counts—in my book—as, well, awkward.

"Whoa, Beyoncé," I said. "That's cold. Warn a brotha. I was not ready for that jelly."

"Haha!" She laughed because I am hilarious. "I am just doing my job trying to get some good images."

Now at this point, I need to tell you a little about the ultrasound process. This young lady was the ultrasound technician. She sets up and operates the machine. Then she sends those images to a doctor, who reads the official images and reports back to you what they mean. **But to my understanding—and this is important—*the technician isn't supposed to tell you what the images mean.***

Even if there is a clear outline of a black-and-white baby right in the middle of the ultrasound screen, and the baby is doing the Macarena, and spreads its legs and you can clearly see the baby's... uh...well, Macarena, and you say, "Wait a second! Is my baby a boy?" Even then, the ultrasound technician is not supposed to, under any circumstances, say *anything* about anything. No signs. No tells.

If, because of that analogy, you now have "Macarena" stuck in your head, that's on me. My bad. Also, did you know that in 1996, "Macarena" bumped "One Sweet Day" by Mariah Carey and Boyz II Men off the top of the charts? That actually happened, people. Google it.[3]

---

3. This was the second biggest travesty of 1996, the first being that the Cleveland Cavaliers drafted Vitaly Potapenko from Wright State University (!) with future NBA Hall of Famers Steve Nash *and* Kobe Bryant still available.

But back to the biscuits.

Wait. No.

Back to the ultrasound. Yeah, that's where we were. The ultrasound.

"I'm just going to take this probe and move it around," she said.

"Listen, I wasn't told anything about a probe," I said, once again making a level-ten hilarious joke. This was some of *the best* comedy work I had ever done while being shirtless and covered in medicinal Smuckers.

She laughed and moved the wand over the jelly, left and right, up and down. I could hear the *wum-wum, wum-wum* of the machine.

"You got any peanut butter and white bread over there?" I said. "Because if so, we got lunch all ready to go."

Another hilarious jelly joke. At this point, I was the LeBron James of jelly jokes.

The tech, though, wasn't laughing. She had stopped moving the wand and was staring at the screen. She wasn't smiling anymore.

She abruptly stood up.

"Mr. Merritt, I will be right back."

And she left.

Suddenly. I was alone in the room.

The wand dangled off the device so that it swayed rhythmically with the hum from the machine.

Wum-wum.

Wum-wum.

Wum-wum.

A few minutes later, the technician returned with an older woman, wiser, with dignified gray hair. She introduced herself as the senior technician. The younger woman pointed to the screen, and the older woman furrowed her brow. She took the wand and moved it over my side, stopping at the same place the younger woman had.

She clicked some buttons. I couldn't see the screen. She kept looking back and forth, between me and the screen. Then she said it.

"Mr. Merritt," she said. "Are you feeling okay?"

What?

Am I feeling okay?

What the hell kind of question was that? Was this lady even supposed to be asking me that? *Why* was she asking me that? Was she seeing something on her black-and-white sonogram screen that would indicate that I should *not* be feeling well? That I should not be feeling okay? If so, what? What did she see?

Shit. *Was* I pregnant?

"Well, umm," I stammered. "I am having some gastro issues."

The room was quiet, except for the gentle humming of the machine.

Nobody said anything.

And nobody was joking anymore.

DATE: Thursday, December 3, 2020

About a week later, I was in a hospital preparing for a CT scan of my abdomen. This would provide the doctors with more detailed information, they said.

I walked into the hospital. It was cold and sterile, and the tile echoed underneath me. The CT scan tech appeared to be a few years younger than me.

The situation with CT techs is pretty much the exact same as the ultrasound folks. They don't comment on what's in the image.

This time, I wasn't shirtless being covered with goo, but I was in a blue hospital gown. Again, a little awkward. Again, I broke out the jokes.

"Is this radiation going to turn me into a mutant or something?" I asked the dude. "Because if I could come out of this with superpowers, that'd be great."

"Haha!" the tech said. "What powers would you want?"

"Maybe transporting myself from place to place, like poof," I said. "Easier to rob banks."

The tech laughed.

"Bank robbing, eh?" the tech said.

"How else am I going to pay for this medical bill?" I said, "So if you could dial up some teleportation back there, that'd be great."

"Just lie right here on your side," the CT tech said to me, pointing to the table. I made another joke. Something about adjusting my Sleep Number because I was a side sleeper. The tech laughed again, because—and I hesitate to have to say this to you again—I am unbelievably funny.

I had to lie still for a few minutes while the machine whirred and clicked. Finally, it stopped.

"So what's the process now?" I said as I slid my legs off the table.

I turned toward the CT tech. He was out from behind his bunker and was in the exam room with me. His face was blanched white. He wasn't smiling anymore.

"Uh, Mr. Merritt," he said slowly.

And then he said it.

"Are you feeling okay?"

There it was again.

That question.

What were these ultrasound and CT techs seeing on my scans?

These technicians look at dozens of images every day. They have some sense of what's going on.

What were they seeing?

And more important, what was it they were seeing that they couldn't tell me?

I took a deep breath.

I held it.

LATER THAT DAY: Thursday, December 3, 2020

Now at this point, I'm going to introduce you to a few names.

- Sara
- Janet Kuhn
- Janet's husband, Jed Kuhn (actual name John E. Kuhn, MD)
- Dr. Marcus Tan

I want you to remember these names, because in the span of about four hours, these four people saved my life. At lunch, I told Sara about my appointments, and how weird they'd been. She called Janet, who talked to Jed. Together, they worked to get me in front of a specialist (Dr. Tan) at Vanderbilt University Medical Center, easily the most prestigious and well-respected research hospital in the region (and one of the most respected in the world).[4]

I'll tell you that whole story later. It's a doozy, involving the NHL, one of Nashville's most famous residents, a binding legal

---

4. Did you know that Vanderbilt University ranked thirteenth overall out of 1,800 US colleges in *US News and World Report*'s Best Colleges rankings? Thirteenth. In the nation. Tied with Brown. That's Ivy League level, people.

document, a grizzly bear, and forty pounds of cocaine. Okay, I made that last part up. But how cool would it be if there was a cocaine bear in this story? You find me *one single* story that would not be better with a cocaine bear. Go ahead. I'll wait.[5]

Regardless, because of the efforts of these four people, twelve days later, on December 15, 2020, I had an appointment with Dr. Marcus Tan at Vanderbilt University Medical Center.

DATE: Tuesday, December 15, 2020

That Tuesday morning, I drove to the address given to me by Dr. Tan's office. I asked Shannon to come with me. I was worried, and I didn't want to do this alone. Shannon was not only the closest thing I had to family here in Nashville, but she was also literally the closest. She lives right around the block from me.

Honestly, I know I am a grown man, but this is one of those times in my life when I was starting to feel like I just needed my mom. I love my mother more than my own life, and just the sound of her voice is like cocoa butter to the skin of my soul. But she lives in Las Vegas, so that wasn't feasible.

Shannon and I drove to downtown Nashville, past the famous Music Row, as Google Maps directed us through the maze of buildings at the Vanderbilt University Medical Center. We looped past the ER. Past the Children's Hospital. We arrived at the parking lot at the address. Shannon read the sign as I drove by.

The Vanderbilt-Ingram Cancer Center.

---

5. Okay, so *Schindler's List* is iffy, but tell me a cocaine bear ripping up Nazis wouldn't be epic.

"Cancer center?" she said to me. "You didn't tell me this is where we were going."

"I didn't know this was where we were going," I said. "This is the address I was given."

Earlier that year, in April, Shannon had buried her beloved father (and one of my favorite former professors) because of cancer. I knew the wounds were still fresh.

"Were you keeping this from me?" she said.

I tried to find a parking spot.

"Shannon, I'm finding this out at the exact same time you are."

Suddenly, it was getting weird.

We went into reception, and I was ushered into Dr. Tan's office. I nervously bounced my leg up and down as I waited for him.

When he opened the door and walked in, I stood up to greet him and almost laughed.

First of all, Dr. Tan was maybe five feet tall.

And I am about six feet two inches.

It was like Chewbacca standing next to Prince.

"Hello there, Mr. Merritt," Dr. Tan said.

Now I really almost laughed.

Here was this tiny Asian man speaking with a *thick Australian accent*.

It was as if ChatGPT had been given the assignment to create a person who destroyed all racial and national stereotypes. Have you ever met an Asian man with a thick Australian accent? I had not.

"Mr. Merritt, have you seen your scans yet?" Dr. Tan said.

"Do I need to see them?" I said, again defusing the awkward with my jokes. "I mean, I know my sexiness is more than skin de—"

"No, Dr. Tan, we haven't," Shannon said, interrupting.

"Well, then, let me show you," he said.

He turned his computer screen around and showed me a large scan. It was blue and black. I saw my name in the upper left-hand corner.

MERRITT, TYLER (MILTON)
M
44 years.

I realized I was staring at a top-down image, as though Superman were hovering directly above me and staring down at me with his X-ray vision. There was a thick half circle, like an upside-down "U." That was my skin and a layer of insulating fat that formed the barrier of my abdomen. Honestly, that barrier was probably a little thicker than it needed to be, because, well, biscuits.

I could see the oblong shape of my stomach. I could see a cone-shaped organ, just to the side of that. That was my liver. Also, in blazing white on the screen were what looked like thick, bubbled ropes. I realized those were my intestines. They were off to the edge, strangely, as though they were being pushed off to the side by something.

And there, taking up most of the picture was . . . darkness.

I couldn't figure out what I was looking at.

It was just black and empty.

Oh, man, there's a Candace Owens joke in there somewhere, but like her integrity and intellectual honesty, I just can't seem to find it.

Sorry.

Not a time for jokes.

Honestly, the picture reminded me of a time when I flew into

Chicago at night. You could follow the contours of the city, the bright yellow lights outlining the skyline and the streets and the hustle and bustle of this massive, sprawling city. But as you looked down, the lights suddenly stopped, and there was only blackness on one whole side because of Lake Michigan.

The darkness of the lake contrasted against the brightness of the city.

My CT scan was like that.

There was a giant black, empty spot in my abdomen. What *was* that?

"And if you look here," Dr. Tan said, circling the dark lake with his finger, "this is your mass."

"His mass?" Shannon asked.

"Yes, and here you can see how it's pushed aside all his organs."

"It looks large. Is it?" Shannon asked.

"Well, we don't really know for sure, but I've done some measurements." Dr. Tan clicked some buttons, and some faint orange lines appeared on the screen, bisecting the mass in the photo. "It's at least twenty-seven centimeters by thirty centimeters, and I estimate it's twelve point zero three kilograms."

I cursed myself, wishing I'd paid closer attention in third grade when we first covered the centimeter-to-inch conversion scale. I was frustrated, like when I read my Bible and it says that something is 300 cubits high. Seriously, Bible? Cubits? Really? I'm gonna need that in feet. Or years. Or whatever the hell a cubit is.

"Sorry, Doc, I know you're from Australia, where I assume they have the metric system," I said quickly, "but can you translate those numbers for me?"

"Sure," he said. "So this mass is about ten inches by about twelve inches. And it's about twenty-seven pounds, give or take."

I couldn't breathe.

I heard Shannon exhale, almost involuntarily.

"Twenty-seven pounds?" she managed, for the both of us.

"Yes. And the growth is wrapped around your right kidney, nearly entirely, and probably has encroached on some of your intestines," Dr. Tan said. "The good news is we can go inside and take it out."

"Like a surgery?" I said. "I have to have surgery?"

"We like to operate as soon as we can to remove this kind of cancer," Dr. Tan said.

Whoa. Did I hear him right? Did he just say *cancer*?

"Cancer?" I said. "I have cancer?"

"Oh, Mr. Merritt," Dr. Tan said. "You're chock-full of the cancer."

Okay, that's *not* what he said. I'm sure he said something more doctor-y. But in that moment, that's what I heard.

Damn. Cancer.

This…changes…

You know, both of my parents are still alive. I don't know what it's like to lose one of your parents. I don't know what it's like to stand over the grave of your mother or sit next to the bed as your father takes his last breath. But I have friends who do.

With that, I don't know if you've ever sat across from your doctor and heard the word "cancer" come out of their mouth. I don't know if you know what that's like. I know some of you reading this right now have had that moment. And I'm so sorry. I'm just so sorry. This feeling is unexplainable. It's an unhappy fraternity that nobody wants to belong to. It's awful.

It was as though my life was suddenly delineated, like history, between two epochs.

Before I knew I had cancer...

And...

After I knew I had cancer.

I also don't presume to know how everyone who has gone through this has experienced it. And I'm certainly not going to pretend to know everything about every form of cancer.

But what I do know is my own story.

And I'd be honored if you let me share that with you. Who am I kidding? You already bought the book. So, if you think about it, you're kinda stuck with me. Eh. Whatevs. Here's my promise to you, though. If you trust me enough to walk with me through these next few chapters, I promise to be as real, honest, and transparent as I possibly can. And look, I don't know what's going to happen here. But my hope is that when you close this book, you and I will be a little bit closer. I believe that having proximity to someone that maybe you don't even know is the key to bringing the world together. Because I also bet that as I share my story, you will relate to more of it than you can imagine. Even if you're not a six-foot-two, super-sexy Black man who is arguably sexier than Denzel. A fact that's well documented.[6]

So back to my story. If I had to choose one word to describe my personal emotional state when I heard the news, I know which one I'd choose. I know what I felt, because I had never felt it like this before.

Fear.

Fear descended on me, almost like an incredible panic, as though there were a bomb inside me, threatening to go off. It *had* to be defused. Someone *had* to defuse it before it took me out.

---

6. Go ahead. Google that. I'll wait.

Look, I know I joke a lot. Some might even say too much.

But I joke because I'm afraid.

As a Black man in America, I think about death a lot. I am forced to. I can't help but see every step and course of my life through the lens of Blackness, because that's who I am and it's how God made me. The idea of death and the fear of death is not something new to me. So many times, being a Black man in America, it feels almost inevitable that my life is going to end sooner than it should.

The bleak history of my people is that not every Black man gets to grow old.

This isn't always just a Black thing. It's also a human thing.

And there was something else.

Dr. Tan told me that they'd have to operate, but that there was a catch. With this form of cancer, there was no way that they could possibly get all of it. There was just too much inside my body. Who knows where else it might be hiding.

And, to complicate matters, this particular form of cancer just so happened to be immune to radiation and chemotherapy treatments.

It just . . . sits there.

And grows. Like some sort of sleeping Godzilla deep in my bones.

After breaking the news to me, Dr. Tan told me I needed emergency surgery before the cancerous mass wrapped itself around more of my vital organs.

"Is your office going to call me tomorrow, or something?" I said weakly.

"No," Dr. Tan said. "We need to get this on the books today."

"Today," he said. "Today."

And that, my friends? That is how we got here.

Tick.
Tick.
Tick.
<Exhale>
This changes everything.

CHAPTER 2

CAN I BE REAL A SECOND...
FOR JUST A MILLISECOND?
(HOW I LEARNED TO LAMENT, PART 1)

Wow, y'all.

That was a *really* intense first chapter. What a ride. Incredible writing, really. Whew!

Is it just me, or do you feel like we need to take a breather here? That was intense, like an episode of *24*.[1] Just call me Jack Bauer. No! Call me Black Bauer.

Jack Black Bauer.

I like it.

Anyway, where was I? Oh yeah! So, when I was a kid, Darth Vader lived in my closet.

Now, it's possible the Dark Sith Lord didn't *live* in my closet, but rather had some sort of portal that opened inside my closet. However he got in there, this was not ideal.

---

1. Wow. That reference is really dated. Whatever.

Having Darth Vader as a quasi-permanent nocturnal resident of my bedroom closet was even worse than the fact that Jaws—yes, Jaws the shark from the movie—lived under my bed. How is that possible, you ask? Was there an ocean under my bed? A large body of salt water? Look, I don't know. I was five, okay?

What I do know is, when I came back from the bathroom in the middle of the night, I had to long-jump from three feet away to get back into bed. Otherwise, the *Jaws* theme song would play, and that'd be the end of my ankles and probably the rest of my little Black butt. That's it. That's how my story would end.

At any rate, as a five-year-old, I discovered there was an easy way to protect yourself against Darth Vader (and under-bed-dwelling apex ocean predators). You just pulled the covers over your head. Bam! Voilà! Safe.

If you don't look at him, he's not there.

Did you know that you can do the same thing with cancer? Just ignore it and it goes away. It totally works.

Yeah. Well. At least a brotha can try.

As I sit here, no matter how hard I try to pull the covers over my head, I can't seem to make my brain forget that there are five months and twenty-four days left until my next appointment with Dr. Tan and Dr. Barocas. Five months and twenty-four days until I see if whatever cancer is left inside me has grown or simply stayed put, like a sleeping tiger. Five months and twenty-four days until Dr. Tan and Dr. Barocas...

Wait. You know Dr. Tan, but you don't know who Dr. Barocas is.

Sorry. He's important to the story.

Let's rewind and go back to the first time I met him.

DATE: DECEMBER 15, 2020
(LATER THAT SAME DAY)

So I sat there in Dr. Tan's office, having just been told I have cancer. Suddenly, there was a series of urgent questions in my mind that I had to have the answers to. Who is this Dr. Tan character? Is he good at his job? Is he like Dr. Meredith Grey in season one, or Dr. Meredith Grey in season 142?

BECAUSE THOSE ARE DIFFERENT PEOPLE, DAMMIT.

I mean, the last thing I want is a highly compromised Dr. Meredith Grey, like when she was stabbed in the shoulder with that dirty blade by the homeless guy in season seventeen, episode thirteen, and she contracted acute ocular syphilis, which affected not only her vision and her fine motor skills but also her right fallopian tube. What? You don't remember that? Okay, that's not really an episode, but at this point, can we all agree that Shondaland is just making up diseases?

Now. Some of you reading this might think to yourself, "But, Tyler, of course, Dr. Tan is great at his job. You're at Vanderbilt University Medical Center, a world-class research hospital."

Look, I didn't know this dude. And okay, fine, it's possible that I might have been slightly afraid. Just a little afraid. Just a skosh. And that—just like the acute ocular syphilis in Dr. Meredith Grey—was messing me up a little bit.

"Dr. Tan," I said. "Do you know anything about sports?"

"Sports? Why sure," Dr. Tan said, a bit surprised.

I still *could not* get over the heavy Australian accent coming from this tiny-framed Asian man. I cannot tell you how disorienting this was for me. It'd be like if you met Kristin Chenoweth and she opened her mouth and sounded just like Barry White. Or if Morgan Freeman suddenly sounded like Dolly Parton. Or how Mike Tyson sounds in real life. That'd mess you up, right? Right? Back to Dr. Tan.

"All right, then, what is your favorite sport?" I asked.

I expected him to say something like "basketball" or "football" and then I would say, "Okay. So for my own peace of mind, I want to know that you're the Michael Jordan or the Tom Brady of this type of cancer operation. Have you done it before?" Etc. That's what I was trying to do.

"My favorite sport? Easy. Cricket," Dr. Tan said.

Cricket?

Cricket?!

Da hell?

Now I was screwed. Do you know how many famous cricket players I know? Zero.

"Uh," I stammered. "Okay, so who is the best cricket player in the world?" I asked. I was going to have to go the long way around for this metaphor.

"Well, there's The Don," Dr. Tan said.

"The Don?" I said. Was this about the mafia or...worse... Donald Trump?

"Donald Bradman, the Australian cricketer," Dr. Tan said. "You know, he still holds the record for most consecutive centuries."

That sentence made as much sense to me as it currently makes to you. What is a century? I thought it was a unit of time. Dang it! My metaphor plane had just run into a flock of frozen geese, both my engines were now on fire, and I was going to have to Captain Sully this thing right into the Hudson River.

"Okay, do you know who Michael Jordan is?" I asked urgently.

"Of course!" Dr. Tan said.

Thank God.

"So are you like the Michael Jordan of this cancer?" I asked. "Do you have a lot of experience with this kind of cancer?"

"Well, I did four operations on this particular type of cancer..." Dr. Tan started.

"Four?" I thought to myself. It's not a lot, but it's better than one...

"...and that was yesterday," he finished.

"Just yesterday?" I said.

"People fly in from around the world to get treatment here," Dr. Tan said.

Oh, snap! My dude! Now 👏that's 👏what 👏I'm 👏talking 👏about.

"So you *are* the Michael Jordan of this cancer?" I said.

"I mean, no one is Michael Jordan," Dr. Tan said, speaking the *truth*. "But this is my specialty."

What I didn't know at the time, but know now, is that Dr. Tan was underselling himself. He kind of *is* the Michael Jordan in his field. In fact, he might be the very best doctor in the entire world with this particular cancer. You could say he's the Donald Bradman of abdominal liposarcoma operations. In fact, I think I'm going to make him a small plaque for his desk.

DR. MARCUS TAN
"The Donald Bradman of Abdominal Liposarcoma"

That has a nice ring to it, doesn't it? No. No, it doesn't.

I breathed deep. I wasn't worried.

No.

I wasn't worried.

I JUST CALLED … TO SAY … I HAVE CANCER
I JUST CALLED … TO SAY … THAT I MIGHT DIE

In his office, Dr. Tan told me that I needed to have emergency surgery to remove this mass. But it was already mid-December, and the holidays were fast approaching. Dr. Tan told me that I could proceed with the surgery in eight days on December 23, or I could push it out until after the New Year. He never really said this explicitly, but I could tell by reading between the lines that he thought the wiser option would be to operate sooner rather than later.

"Do it now," Dr. Tan said, "I would do it now."

Okay, actually, looking back on it, maybe he *did* say it explicitly. But I was torn. Every year since I had moved away from home I had flown back to Las Vegas to spend Christmas with my mom and dad. I mean, I am an only child, so not going back home for the holidays was never really an option.

But then I found out I had cancer.

So I called my mother. Now, for those of you who read my last book, you know not only what a tour de force my mother, Jerrie Merritt is, but you also know her particular role in my life. I have a deep conviction that everyone's life would get a little bit better if they met my mama. So, if I was going to cancel Christmas on her, I was going to talk to her and see what she thought first. My mom answered her phone. I told her what I'd just found out.

"Mom, I need you to be my mom right now," I told her. "I can have the surgery now, but that will mean I can't come home for Christmas. Or I can postpone it until after the New Year. What should I do?"

"What do you mean, what should you do?" she said.

"I'll be honest, Mom," I said. "This is a decision I don't feel like I can make. I'm worn down. Just tell me what to do, and I'll do it."

"Why are we talking about this?" my mother said. "Tyler, you are a grown man. Whatever you decide, decide."

And with that, she politely excused herself and hung up the phone.

I stared at my phone in disbelief.

My mom hung up on me.

My mom hung up on me!

Looking back at that moment, it was pretty unfair of me to do to my mother what I did. There she is, at work, and her son calls her, out of nowhere, telling her that he has a twenty-seven-pound cancerous tumor inside him and that he needs emergency surgery. That's a pretty big emotional weight to dump on a mother in the middle of her workday.

It's tough for any parent, but especially mothers, to see their children go through suffering.

So I guess I understand why my mom hung up. Why she had to, at a psychological level, just get away from that moment.

It's like me in my Darth Vader–infested bedroom. If you pull the covers over your head, maybe Darth will go away. If you hang up the phone, maybe the cancer will go away.

But—and I checked with Dr. Tan the cancer specialist about this—this technique never works.

THE LOSS OF LAMENT

This brings me to the word "lament." Now we don't use the word "lament" much. It's an old-fashioned word that's gone out of style. Lament means "to wail" or "a sad, mournful cry." It's an expression of grief that erupts from a human being when life turns tragic and is deeply painful. I'm not an expert on this, nor am I a trained counselor, but for a lament, at least two things have to be in place. And here's the first one.

HOW TO LAMENT

STEP 1: You must **fully face** the **reality** of what's going on—no matter how awful.

I'm gonna be honest. This is *not* how I deal with most grief, suffering, and pain in life. I busy myself with myriad details. I numb out. I run away. But mostly, I make a ton of jokes and try to pretend like it's always sunny in Philadelphia.

Just lock all those emotions away.

I started wondering if I was the only one who was not very good at lamenting. I had a hunch that I am not. So I did some research into mental health and found out that, statistically, not only are Americans not great at this, but Black folk, in particular, aren't good at lamenting. Here are some statistics that hint toward that reality.

Get ready to be edumacated.

- As of 2018, 11.5 percent of Black Americans (versus 7.5 percent of white Americans) did not have any form of health insurance.[2]

---

2. Latoya Hill, Samantha Artiga, and Anthony Damico, "Health Coverage by Race and Ethnicity 2010–2022," KFF.org. https://www.kff.org/racial-equity-and-health-policy/issue-brief/health-coverage-by-race-and-ethnicity/.

- The US Surgeon General found that from 1980 to 1995, the suicide rate for white kids ages ten to fourteen increased 120 percent. During that same time, among Black kids ages ten to fourteen, it increased 233 percent.[3]
- Black adults in the US are more likely than white adults to report persistent symptoms of emotional distress, such as sadness, hopelessness, and feeling like everything is an effort.[4]
- Only one in three Black adults who need mental health care receive it.[5]
- 63 percent of Black people believe that a mental health condition is a sign of personal weakness.[6]
- 26 percent of Black people felt that discussions about mental illness would not be appropriate even among close family.[7]

Like so many things in the world, paying attention to one's interior life—one's emotional health and well-being—seems to be a luxury that not everyone can access. Life is too tough. Life is too hard. Too difficult. You simply have to move on.

3. "Mental and Behavioral Health—African Americans," US Department of Health and Human Services Office of Minority Health, n.d. https://www.minorityhealth .hhs.gov/omh/browse.aspx?lvl=4&lvlid=24.

4. "Mental and Behavioral Health—African Americans," https://www.minority health.hhs.gov/omh/browse.aspx?lvl=4&lvlid=24.

5. "2019 NSDUH Detailed Tables," Substance Abuse and Mental Health Services Administration, September 11, 2020. https://www.samhsa.gov/data/report/2019 -nsduh-detailed-tables.

6. "Mental Health in Black Communities: Challenges, Resources, Community Voices," National Alliance on Mental Illness California, n.d. https://namica.org /mental-health-challenges-in-african-american-communities/.

7. Monica T. Williams, "Why African Americans Avoid Psychotherapy," *Psychology Today*, November 2, 2011. https://www.psychologytoday.com/us/blog/culturally -speaking/201111/why-african-americans-avoid-psychotherapy.

But as bad as we Americans are at lamenting, and as bad as we Black folk, in particular, are at lamenting, there is an interesting paradox.

LAMENT PARADOX

Because the history of Black people in the United States contains so very much suffering, tragedy, and loss, some of the very best resources to deal with suffering and lament have emerged from the Black community.

It is Black leaders and artists who have shown the nation, and the world, that the way forward in life is not to run from the pain, or ignore the reality of the awful, but to gather up the courage and properly lament.[8] Even though the Black community is, statistically, worse at talking honestly about mental health and trauma, our own community has been on the front lines and has offered up some of the best resources to deal with suffering.

Including one of the most powerful lessons about lament ever given to our nation.

And it came from a strong Black mama, just like mine.

THE TIMES, THEY ARE A-CHANGING

In 2022, I got an email from my acting agent for a new TV show that was being produced on ABC called *Women of the Movement*. She was asking if I knew of any young Black boys, around the age of twelve to fifteen, who might be able to play the role of Emmett Till. I passed along some names, and pretty soon, I had all these young

---

8. Even Alanis Morissette, who doesn't seem to understand the definition of "ironic," would say that this is ironic.

Black actors calling me, asking for help with their auditions. One young man called me, and before he could even ask anything, I said, "Is this for Emmett Till?"

"Yeah," he said. "How'd you know?"

"It's a big role that they're looking all around the nation to fill," I said.

There was a pause.

"Hey, Unc...who is Emmett Till?"

My initial response was "Whoa. I thought everybody knew about Emmett Till!"

I realize that a lot of people are familiar with the tragedy of Emmett Till, but it has always had particular meaning to me because it happened just 160 miles away from where my parents were from. I don't want to assume that everyone reading this knows the whole story, so if you don't mind, I'd like to share it, as it is one of the most impactful stories about lament that I've ever encountered.

So, my parents were both from a small, rural town called Eutaw, Alabama, located along the banks of the Black Warrior River waterway. About 160 miles away is another tiny rural farming town called Money, Mississippi. Now, if Eutaw was small and rural, then Money was even more small and even more rural, with about 400 residents total, most of whom were there because of a local cotton mill.

In late August of 1955, a fourteen-year-old freshman in high school from Chicago named Emmett Till was sent by his mother to visit her family down in Money. He stayed with his great-uncle, Mose. But Emmett was from a school up north that was integrated.[9] It had white kids and Black kids together in the same class. He didn't

---

9.   "28 August: Emmett Till Abducted and Murdered in Mississippi Delta," A History of Racial Injustice, https://calendar.eji.org/racial-injustice/aug/28.

understand that in the South, to paraphrase Bob Dylan, the times were *not* a-changing.

One day, while in town, Emmett showed a group of his cousins and their friends pictures of him and his white classmates. They were astonished. "You talk to white people?" they asked. Because he was a fourteen-year-old boy, Emmett went a step further, making up a story that one of the white girls in the photo was his girlfriend. They all whooped and hollered.

This is how Curtis Jones, the cousin of Emmett Till, described what happened in the 1987 PBS documentary *Eyes on the Prize*:

> *So, one of the local boys said, "Hey, there's a girl in that store there." He said, "I bet you won't go in there and talk to her," you know. So, he went in there to get some candy. So, when he was leaving out the store, after buying the candy, he told her, said, "Bye, baby." And the next thing I know, one of the boys came up to me and say, "Say, man, you got a crazy cousin. He just went in there and said 'bye' to that white woman." And that's when this man I was playing checkers with, this older man—I guess he must have been around about sixty or seventy—he jumps straight up and say, "Boy, say you all better get out of here." He say, "That lady will come out of that store and blow your brains off."*[10]

The store in question was Bryant's Grocery and Meat Market. And the white woman in question was twenty-one-year-old Carolyn Bryant, who owned the store with her husband, Roy Bryant, who

---

10. PBS, "Awakenings (1954–1956)," *Eyes on the Prize, The American Experience*, aired April 4, 2021.

was twenty-four. And the phrase in question, "Bye, baby," was said by a braggadocious, silly fourteen-year-old boy.

But this went against the Southern racial caste system. You have to understand, this system is something that Emmett just would *not* have picked up on *because he was from Chicago.* Little did he know, those two words would cost him his life.

A few nights later, Carolyn's husband, Roy, and his friend J. W. Milam kidnapped Emmett Till at gunpoint from his great-uncle's home. Are you hearing me? They took a kid from his family's home. At gunpoint. That takes a certain type of darkness. But it gets worse.

NOTE: If you're a sensitive soul, like me, you may not want to read the next paragraph, if for no other reason than for the sake of your heart. And there's no judgment here. Even reading these descriptions can feel defiling: we're not supposed to—as humans—stare at this measure of violent inhumanity. So if you need to skip down to the next subchapter heading, I get it.

The two men drove Emmett to a storage shed on Milam's property, where they took turns beating him, torturing him, and mutilating him. Then, they forced him to load a seventy-four-pound fan from a cotton gin into the back of their pickup truck. The men then drove Emmett to the edge of the Tallahatchie River, ordered him to remove his clothes, and shot him in the head.[11] Then, Bryant and Milam chained the fan to his corpse with barbed wire and rolled it into the river.

Listen. I've grown up with this story. I've read about it. I *know* this story. But when I stop—when I really stop to think about what these men did to a young boy—a young boy whose skin color looks

---

11. "Remembering Emmett Till," United States Civil Rights Trail, n.d. https://civil-rightstrail.com/experience/sumner/.

like mine—it's almost unbearable. Sometimes, being an empathic person doesn't seem to be worth it. It's too much for your heart. This is what makes what Emmett Till's mother did so astounding to me.

REALITY USED TO BE A FRIEND OF MINE

Emmett's mother, Mamie Till Bradley, learned about the death of her son on a Sunday morning. She then made two very, very brave decisions. And I submit to you it was because she had the strength and courage to lament well.

Mamie Till Bradley was not a trained psychologist, but she knew something deep and true. She knew that you can't pull the covers over your head and make the bad things go away. You have to face them. Head-on.

Lament (v)

to fully face the reality of what's going on—no matter how awful.

First, there was going to be a murder trial for the two men who had killed Emmett. The chief defense strategy was that the body the police recovered from the river was so disfigured that it was impossible to even identify that it was Emmett. So Mamie Till Bradley would have to travel down to Mississippi and officially verify that the body in question was the body of her son.[12]

---

12. Allison Martin, "This Week in History: Mamie Till-Mobley Testifies for Her Son," *Chicago Sun-Times*, November 25, 2021. https://chicago.suntimes.com/2021/11/25/22799210/mamie-till-mobley-emmett-till-murder-trial-testimony.

I cannot imagine how she managed to face this. I cannot imagine the horror of what she went through. Being in a cold coroner's office and being presented with the mutilated, bloated, tortured body of your little boy? I think that most of us wouldn't have blamed Mamie if she said, "I just can't do it." Some truths are too painful to stare at.

But Mamie was brave. She studied "the hairline, nose, lips, chin—there is not a shadow of a doubt," she told investigators[13] and later, the court, as she testified as a key witness.[14]

But that's not the only brave decision Mamie made. And it was this second decision that really changed history. She insisted that her son's body not be buried in Mississippi, but be brought home to Chicago. There, she insisted on an open-casket public funeral service, held at her church, "so all the world can see what they did to my boy."[15]

If lamenting means that you have to face reality, then Mamie faced reality in a way that very few could have.

Tens of thousands of people[16] attended the funeral or viewed Emmett's open casket, rallying Black support and white sympathy across the entire country.[17] And then Mamie made an even more

---

13. Martin, "This Week in History: Mamie Till-Mobley Testifies for Her Son."

14. Mamie also pointed to the ring found on the body, the one Emmett had been wearing when he left Chicago, which had belonged to his father, who was killed while serving in the military during World War II. The ring was engraved with his father's initials.

15. "Historian Recalls Moment Emmett Till's Accuser Admitted She Lied," *CBS Mornings*, CBS News, January 31, 2017. https://www.cbsnews.com/news/the-blood-of -emmett-till-carolyn-bryant-lied-timothy-tyson-new-book.

16. Katie Nodjimbadem, "Emmett Till's Open Casket Funeral Reignited the Civil Rights Movement," *Smithsonian*, September 2, 2015. https://www.smithsonianmag .com/smithsonian-institution/emmett-tills-open-casket-funeral-reignited-the -civil-rights-movement-180956483/.

17. "Emmett Till's Funeral," *The American Experience*, PBS.org. https://www.pbs.org /wgbh/americanexperience/features/emmett-tills-funeral/.

courageous decision. She allowed photographers to take pictures of the body of her son. A Black publication, *Jet* magazine, and the *Chicago Defender* (a Black newspaper) published the photo[18] of this young man's corpse…you know what…check that…Emmett wasn't even a young man yet. He was a fourteen-year-old teenager. He was a kid. Emmett Till was a *kid*.

Even today, there's a whole generation of Black people who remember the galvanizing horror of that photo. It forced the US to stare, long and hard, not only at Emmett, but at something deeper— the entrenched racism and racial caste system that still existed in so many hearts and parts of the US.

Time magazine later listed that photo as one of the most influential and important photographs of all time, writing, "For almost a century, African Americans were lynched with regularity and impunity. Now, thanks to a mother's determination to expose the barbarousness of the crime, the public could no longer pretend to ignore what they couldn't see."[19]

A mother's determination. Damn. Maybe Mamie Till Bradley was showing us that facing the reality of the world is part of lament. It's critical. Again, here is Mamie Till Bradley, in her own words:

> *I believe that the whole United States is mourning with me,*
> *and that the death of my son can mean something to the other*

---

18. "Taking a Look Back at Emmett Till's Brutal Murder on the Anniversary of the Historic Jet Cover," *Ebony*, September 15, 2022. https://www.ebony.com/taking-a-look-back-at-emmett-tills-brutal-murder-on-the-anniversary-of-the-historic-jet-cover/.

19. "100 Photos: Emmett Till," *Time*. Archived from the original on November 19, 2016. Retrieved June 25, 2017. https://web.archive.org/web/20161119053502/http://100photos.time.com/photos/emmett-till-david-jackson.

unfortunate people all over the world. Then for him to have died a hero would mean more to me than for him just to have died.[20]

Mamie Till Bradley was mourning and lamenting, and in the process, she was helping everyone else. She was helping Black folks traumatized by the terror of racial violence that had plagued our nation. She was helping white folks whose hearts were grieved at this injustice and who longed to help create a different world. She was helping everyone stare at the reality, as ugly as it was. As cruel as it was. Mamie's ability to lament had a positive impact that I don't think even she could have imagined. It was helping.

I can't help but think that the reason that Mamie leaned in and faced the ugly realities of what happened to her son was because she knew that if she didn't, this incident might just be another nameless tragedy. Call it a mother's intuition, but she probably had a feeling that the two men who killed her son wouldn't have to face legal consequences. The South is gonna South. But a Black mama is gonna Black mama. So she did something. Even if the judicial system couldn't.

(And by the way, she wasn't wrong.)

The trial of Roy Bryant and J. W. Milam was held in September of 1955 and lasted for five days. On September 23, the all-white, all-male jury acquitted both defendants after a sixty-seven-minute

---

20. "AFAM 162: African American History: From Emancipation to the Present," Lecture 14, Open Yale Courses. https://oyc.yale.edu/african-american-studies /afam-162/lecture-14.

deliberation. One juror said, "If we hadn't stopped to drink pop, it wouldn't have taken that long."[21]

A few months later, both men, protected by double jeopardy laws, admitted the whole story of how they kidnapped and killed Emmett Till to *Look* magazine for $4,000 (or about $40,000 today).[22] Let me give you just a glimpse into the darkness of J. W. Milam's heart, and what they paid this man $40,000 for. Here he is—revealing who he really is[23]—in his own words:

> *Well, what else could we do? I like n****rs—in their place—I know how to work 'em. But I just decided it was time a few people got put on notice. As long as I live and can do anything about it, n****rs are gonna stay in their place. N****rs ain't gonna vote where I live. If they did, they'd control the government. They ain't gonna go to school with my kids. And when a n****r gets close to mentioning sex with a white woman, he's tired o' livin'. I'm likely to kill him. Me and my folks fought for this country, and we got some rights. I stood there in that shed and listened to that n****r throw that poison at me, and I just made up my mind. "Chicago boy," I said, "I'm tired of 'em sending your kind down here to stir up trouble. Goddam you, I'm going to make an example of you—just so everybody can know how me and my folks stand."[24]*

---

21. Harold K. Bush, "Continuing Bonds and Emmett Till's Mother," *Southern Quarterly Hattiesburg* 50, no. 3 (Spring 2013): 9–27. https://www.proquest.com/docview/1436022903.

22. "Emmett Till," History.com, December 2, 2009, updated October 12, 2023. https://www.history.com/topics/black-history/emmett-till-1.

23. See Matthew 12:35–37.

24. https://web.archive.org/web/20230429191201/https://xroads.virginia.edu/~public/civilrights/0161.html.

So to recap: these two white men kidnapped a boy, tortured him, killed him, threw his body in a river, were acquitted of all wrongdoing by a jury after an hour of deliberation, then made $40,000 by admitting their guilt to a national publication.[25]

But here I am, almost seventy years later, telling you this story. And I'm able to do that for one single reason—because Mamie Till Bradley knew how to lament. She taught our nation how to mourn, how to stare at the dark reality of the world, and feel, with impunity, all the emotions that came with it.

Thank you, Mamie, for facing the reality of what was going on. No matter how awful.

Thinking about the story of Mamie, and how difficult lament is, I realized how ridiculous it was for me to call my own mother up out of the blue and drop that kind of emotional weight on her. I was basically calling my mom to make her pick what day I was going to face a surgery that had a good chance of killing me, her son. Without any warning! It wasn't fair. No wonder she'd hung up. I couldn't blame my mom.

I began to think, "I guess I'll just have to figure this out by myself."

I sighed.

Then my phone rang.

(Because of course it did.)

THE CALLBACK

I answered my phone.

It was my mother.

---

25. Good luck on the Day of Judgment, gentlemen. You think Mississippi is hot in the summer? Boy, do I have news for you.

"Do it now," she said matter-of-factly. "Do the surgery now."

"But…" I began to protest.

"I am going to fly out," she said. "I will be there. I will be right there."

What I didn't know as I sat in Dr. Tan's office was that my mother was drawing up her own courage. In that previous phone call, when she'd hung up, she had short-circuited emotionally. Every self-protective instinct railed up in direct conflict with her other mama-bear instincts. Or maybe it's the other way around: maybe her fiercely protective mama-bear instincts short-circuited her own emotions. Or maybe I don't know what the hell I'm talking about, and my mother's just a human being confronted with awful news who needed a minute to process it.

In that moment, I don't think my mom was able to face reality, or what was going on inside her. Again, fully facing the reality of what's going on—no matter how awful—is not easy. But my mom closed her eyes. She took some deep breaths. And if I know my mama, she prayed.

My mom had course-corrected. She had lamented. There was no avoidance of reality with her. She was going to fly out to meet this threat face-to-face. This tumor was about to meet Dr. Tan, and behind him, it was going to see my mom there. Probably holding a shiv and mouthing some threats.

My mom had faced reality.

But now it was my turn.

DATE: Tuesday, December 22, 2020, 3:30 p.m.

Before I knew it, my mom and I were sitting in Dr. Tan's office. We had decided on a date for the surgery, December 23. The day before the surgery, on December 22, my mom went to the presurgery appointment with me.

"Tyler, I wanted you to meet a surgeon who will be assisting me with the operation," Dr. Tan said. "His name is Dr. Barocas."

A tall man, six feet four inches or so, with salt-and-pepper hair entered. We made introductions.

"I'm Daniel," Dr. Barocas said.

"I'm Tyler," I said. "You are tall. Did you play basketball?"

"Yes," Dr. Barocas said. "Best sport in the world."

My man! Finally! This was a guy who was going to super-understand my Michael-Jordan-of-surgery metaphor. Unlike Dr. Tan and his tiny cricket-loving ass.

"Okay, so I was talking to Dr. Tan and I told him I needed him to be my Michael Jordan," I explained. "Which means, I need you to be my..."

"...Scottie Pippen," Dr. Barocas said, completing my sentence.

"MY DUDE! YES! EXACTLY!" I whooped.

"I will do my best," Dr. Barocas said.

It was then I realized I didn't really understand how surgery worked. Why were there two doctors involved?

"So...I guess I don't understand," I asked. "Are you a surgeon, too, or how does this work?"

"Oh, there's probably going to be ten people in that room tomorrow," Dr. Barocas said.

Ten people? Wait. What?

"And I'm the urologist," he said.

Urology? What did that have to do with abdominal cancer?

What Dr. Barocas said next was much more doctor-y because he speaks fluent doctor, but I'm going to translate for you what I heard him say. Dr. Barocas explained that yes, Dr. Tan was indeed the Michael Jordan of this type of liposarcoma removal. But this was a massive tumor, with tendrils and growth everywhere. Dr. Tan was going to have to cut into my body cavity, and try to disentangle the tumor from my body and my organs. This wasn't a simple operation. It wasn't like removing a marble embedded in Jell-O. It was more like trying to remove an invasive, evil vine that had grown up around a rosebush—a vine that had been there a long while, twisting and combining and choking the healthy plant.

"We have scans of the tumor, but we won't really know what we're up against until we're in there," Dr. Barocas said. "Dr. Tan is going to have to pull through a lot of fat. It's highly likely he won't be able to save your kidney."

I found out later Dr. Tan knew there was no way he was going to be able to save that kidney. He didn't tell me. But the doctors knew.

"We're going to be around a lot of complex systems, a great deal of nerves and blood vessels and tissue, and Dr. Tan may have to cut something, and I am there to keep it from going south."

Keep it from going south?

Going south?

That moment was the first time that I *truly heard* what these doctors had been trying to tell me, but I was unable to hear. This was the first time that I was able to fully face what was really going on inside me with this cancer.

And it was awful.

This tumor was massive, this cancer was deadly, and this surgery was dangerous. I could lose my kidney. I could wind up without the ability to use the bathroom on my own. I could lose part of my bowels. I could have nerves severed that would never grow back. I could spend the rest of my life with a urostomy pouch collecting my urine. I could lose the ability to stand or to walk. There were implications that even the two best doctors in this entire region couldn't predict. Including this one:

I could die.

For the first time, I felt all of it hit me, and I felt like the building was collapsing on top of me.

And that?

That, my friends, was when I truly started the process of lamenting. I saw reality. Let it in. Stared at it.

And that was the first time that I cried.

I sobbed into my hands.

I thought about my five-year-old self. I can assure you, back then, I'd never thought I'd long for the days of Darth Vader in my closet.

CHAPTER 3

MAYBE I'M JUST LIKE MY FATHER

(HOW I LEARNED TO LAMENT, PART 2)

You know what I wanna know? I want to know who was the first person to use the phrase "Fear is a funny thing."

Is it, though?

Is fear funny?

Who was the guy, who, I don't know, was fishing in the Everglades and got charged by a fourteen-foot alligator who nearly dragged him into the river, and then, after reaching safety on the shore, just started—wait for it—giggling.

"Ha, ha, ha," he said to himself. "Now, *that's* funny."

Nobody.

Nobody, that's who.

But to be fair, you imagined a white guy in that scenario, didn't you? You did. And I did set the hypothetical scenario in the Everglades, which is in Florida, which means, at some point, dammit, I bet this actually *did* happen. I can see the headline now:

Florida Man Chuckles after Close Call with Alligator
"Fear Is Funny," Local Man Says[1]

Do you remember the first scary movie you saw that absolutely terrified you? I do. And if you're my age reading this right now, we should all have the same movie. Let's all say it out loud on the count of three.

One.
Two.
Freddy's coming for you.

That's right, people!
A Nightmare on Freaking Elm Street.
I will give you a pass if you said *Poltergeist.* That movie also scared the heck out of me. Remember that scene where a tree came alive, broke into one kid's bedroom, grabbed him, pulled him outside and attempted to *eat him.* That's the scariest ish ever. Even now, as a fully formed, rational adult, I want to go out and cut down all the trees near my house. Screw you, climate change. At least I am safe from hungry demon trees.

Back to *A Nightmare on Elm Street.*
This is a terrible movie, for so many reasons. If you're not familiar with this film, congratulations, someone in your life loves you and protected you from this trauma. The film is about a villain named Freddy Krueger who has knife blades on his fingers. I want to

---

1. My favorite "Florida man" story is about a guy who held up a Wendy's drive-thru while threatening the cashier with a live alligator, and then threw it through the window in an attempt to rob the place. He was charged with assault with a deadly reptile. https://www.jacksonville.com/story/news/2016/02/10/florida-man-threw-live-gator-wendys-drive-thru-window-police-say/985469007/.

stop there. Knife blades as fingers. This is not okay. So Freddy goes around killing unsuspecting teenagers by tracking them down in their dreams. And if Freddy killed you in your dreams, you died in real life.

Now I know what you're thinking. You're thinking, "Tyler, what kind of lawless, Wild West, Gen-X world did you live in that parents let kids watch that kind of stuff?" First of all, I don't appreciate your tone. Second of all, no one was *allowed* to watch this film. No one's parents were like, "What's that? You want to watch a slasher horror film as a thirteen-year-old. Sure, sweetie! Would you and your friends also like some crack cocaine on a Ritz cracker?"

Look, people, I don't know how crack works. Is it in a pipe? Do you take a rusty spoon and…can you even put it on a cracker? Is crack ingestible? I don't know! Look. I don't know.

The point is, that never happened. But…

At any rate, there's always that one kid. This kid would have procured a hidden, secret VHS tape of *A Nightmare on Elm Street*. You know the kid. The one whose parents were too busy going through the messy divorce to pay close attention, the one whose pants were filled with Now and Laters he effortlessly lifted from the corner 7-Eleven, the one with the "troubled" older brother. If you don't immediately know who this kid was at your school, then let me just say I'm so glad you're finally getting your life together. I hope this book helps you through your thirty-day residential program.

Now, for the record, we weren't blameless in all this. Our interest would build like an avalanche, and we'd have a sleepover, and after the parents went to bed, we would huddle together and watch a terrifying movie about a supernatural monster who kills you if you fall asleep.

At a sleepover.

Folks, the tagline of this movie was "Don't Fall Asleep." And we watched this *at a sleepover*. And then, after watching this film, hopped up on terror-induced adrenaline rushes, we would huddle together in the dark in fear of…

You guessed it, people!

…Falling asleep.

Knowing that if we fell asleep, we would be killed.

I will remind you that sleep is *biologically unavoidable*. It would be like if you made a film where the monster killed you if you urinated. And then you and your friends sat around trying to hold it.

"Oh, God! I knew I shouldn't have drunk that second Pepsi!"

Second Pepsi? You drank the first one and thought, "This *Pepsi* is so good! I'll have another?" I don't care that you're eleven. You deserve to pee and die. Do better.[2]

What I'm trying to say here is, that's the film that most people my age would say is the first scary movie they ever saw.[3]

But the central lesson from this film is actually pretty deep. The main character, Nancy, realizes that Freddy is powered by fear, so if she just faces her own fear and deals with it, he vanishes and is powerless.

You gotta face the emotion of your fear head-on.

So yeah, Florida Man, fear really isn't that funny to me. It's such a powerful emotion. I've seen what it does to folks, how it short-circuits different people in different ways. I've seen people

---

2. If you're reading this footnote, wondering if I am going to take a hard stance on the controversial question of Coke or Pepsi, then let the record show, you're clearly a communist who hates freedom and America. Only pinko communists drink Pepsi. This is a fact. So is this: Coke is the drink choice for those who love democracy.
3. FUN FACT: Did you know that in 2021, the Library of Congress selected *A Nightmare on Elm Street* for preservation in the United States National Film Registry by the Library of Congress as being "culturally, historically, or aesthetically significant"? That is some nonsense. That movie does not need to be preserved. It needs to be destroyed. For the sake of the children!

shut down. I've seen people numb out. And I'm not talking about drugs or alcohol. I've seen people so afraid, they start companies and relentlessly climb corporate ladders. I've seen people pretend. Just stick their head in the sand and ostrich for years. Decades, even.

Yes, fear is a very powerful emotion.

I've even seen grown men do everything in their power to avoid it, even when it's right there, staring them in the face.

Damn.

That's something I know *personally*.

THE SECOND PART OF LAMENT
DATE: DECEMBER 22, 2020, 3:30 p.m.

As I sat there in Dr. Barocas's office, listening to him talk in plain language about my cancer and what was really going on inside my body, the magnitude of it all hit me. This surgery wasn't an idea anymore. It was happening in less than twenty-four hours.

You already heard me talk about the first part of lament and how I learned just how imperative it is for us to face reality. But there's a second part of lament. And it's a doozy. Maybe it's just as hard as the first. And it's this: you have to face the emotions that *result* from that reality. I mean, just truly face them.

> ### HOW TO LAMENT
> ### Part 2
>
> **STEP 2:** You must face the **full force of the emotions** that you're experiencing (whatever they are).

And let me tell you, once you open your eyes and stare at reality, emotions *will* come.

As I sat there in Dr. Barocas's office, it was all so overwhelming. Just overwhelming. I felt like my mind was a circuit breaker, and for the entirety of my life, it had been accustomed to a certain voltage of emotions. But now it was suddenly flooded with ten times that. And I don't even want to say this out loud, but I will tell you, the primary emotion that I felt was...fear. Just abject fear.

- I was afraid I might not make it out alive.
- I was afraid that I didn't have enough time to get my house in order.
- I was afraid I didn't have enough time to say goodbye to all the people I needed to say goodbye to.
- I was afraid that I hadn't truly had an impact on the world and the people around me.
- I was afraid that I hadn't done enough.
- I was afraid that I simply didn't have enough time.

I've been told that when we're afraid, our bodies release epinephrine and adrenaline, which cause your heart rate to go up, your blood pressure to elevate, and your eyes to dilate. That's the biological side, right? But I found the worst part wasn't that. The worst part was what was going on in my heart and brain. It just felt like a tsunami of anxiety came crashing in on me, causing this grasping, desperate, almost flailing hopelessness. My body began reacting to my brain, and I almost hyperventilated.

It was too much.

If the second part of lament is to feel the full force of the emotions, this was *not* what I wanted to do. I would sooner stare down a tarantula.[4]

No. My immediate temptation was to just shut all this out. I needed to get away from these emotions. I needed to get away from these feelings. And get away from them now.

Looking back on this moment now, with a bit of experience and distance under my belt, I know that my instinct to stiff-arm these overwhelming feelings wasn't that surprising. A lot of people aren't good in these situations.

But for me, it wasn't just that I wasn't good at it. It was that I had been *taught* not to be good at it.

I'd been trained. And I still remember the first time I learned that strong emotions are to be avoided at all costs.

And to explain this, I need to tell you two stories that involve three dogs.

Trust me, stay with me. It's going to be an Incredible Journey.[5]

So first up, two dogs that I first read about in fifth grade that go by the names Little Ann and Big Dan.

RED ROVER, RED ROVER,
SEND TRAUMA RIGHT OVER

First of all, I need to apologize to all of you reading this because I am about to talk to you about a book I first read in fifth grade. This book I'm talking about is so traumatizing that it should come with a trigger warning. And here is what that trigger warning should say:

---

4.   Even writing that sentence, I scared myself.
5.   See what I did there?

Trigger Warning: You're about to read a book that will scar you emotionally and psychologically for the rest of your little fifth-grade life, and there's not a damn thing you can do about it. You think you're a tough guy, little man? You think you can handle this? You think it's just a book? You ain't ready. You will never be ready. This book will *end* you. This book will mess you up so bad. How bad will this book mess you up? I will tell you. Years from now, when you are squarely middle-aged, you will write a book. And in that book, you will write about *this book* and how bad it jacked you up. So don't even think about writing your name in this book, because you don't own this book. This book owns you.

And that book, my friends, is called *Where the Red Fern Grows*.

Now, if you've read *Where the Red Fern Grows*, then you know that trigger warning isn't being dramatic. If you've gone this far without reading it, then, just like with *A Nightmare on Elm Street*, someone has loved you well.

This book is the most traumatizing piece of literature ever created by the hands of men.

It was written in 1961 by a man named Woodrow Wilson Rawls. The story revolves around a ten-year-old boy named Billy who grew up in extreme poverty in the Ozarks in Arkansas. After seeing an advertisement in a magazine for Redbone Coonhound puppies, Billy works odd jobs for two years to save up to buy two dogs, one boy and one girl. Billy names them Little Ann and Big Dan. Throughout the next 300 pages, we follow along as these two perfect puppies grow up to become the best, smartest, bravest hounds in the entire region. Every kid who reads this book realizes three things:

1. The best characters in this novel are the two dogs.
2. It's not even close.
3. These might be the best fictional dogs in history.[6]

But here's the thing. And this is a big spoiler, but I don't want you to read this book and go through that level of emotional trauma, so I'm going to ruin it for you:

SPOILER:
BOTH DOGS DIE AT THE END OF THE BOOK.

That's right. The dogs *both* die. They die. Wilson Rawls makes you fall in love with these two dogs and then kills them off, like a psychopath, leaving fifth-grade teachers to pick up the emotional wreckage.

God.

This book is just the worst.

I'm aware that not everybody has read this book. So I'm going to get into the ending because that's the worst part of the book. And even though it meant that I had to call my therapist after writing this next part, I did it for you. Because I care about you *so much*, Reader I've Never Met.

So let's get into it. At the end of the book, during a routine raccoon hunt (reminder! We're in the Ozarks, where phrases like "routine raccoon hunt" make sense) a giant mountain lion attacks Billy. The dogs were not about that mountain lion life, so Thug Dan and

---

6. Turn to the back of this book to the Appendix for a top-ten list complete with rankings and commentary. Is this kind of list necessary? No? But is it interesting? Again, no. But is it fun? Maybe. Check it out.

Thug Ann move to protect their boy Billy! And for seven pages— seven breathless pages—they fight. And eventually, they win, and Billy kills the lion with his axe.

I remember reading this part of the book. I sat there, sweating, almost crying from relief that Billy was able to kill the devil cat without Little Ann or Big Dan getting hurt. There's blood everywhere, and Billy is carefully checking his dogs. Big Dan refuses to let go of the mountain lion, his powerful jaws locked on the cat's throat. A death hold.

But then...

Just when you thought it was all fine...

We find out that the lion had torn into Big Dan's vulnerable belly, and disemboweled him. And my little fifth-grade self had to watch as this strong, brave dog whimpered as its entrails spilled out onto a huckleberry bush.

I just sat there in shock and disbelief along with Billy, as he attempted to put his brave dog back together.

But it was too late.

The wound was too deep.

Billy carried his wounded dog back to his home, and his mom and dad tried to do everything they could to help Old Dan. But it was too late.

And then.

On page 199. This line.

I knelt down and laid his head in my lap. Old Dan must have known he was dying. Just before he drew one last sigh, and a feeble thump of his tail, his friendly gray eyes closed forever.[7]

---

7. Wilson Rawls, *Where the Red Fern Grows*. Random House Children's Books. Kindle Edition, p. 199.

What.

What?

No.

No no no no no no no no no no.

Dan can't die.

He just can't! He can't!

"Don't leave me, Dan. Don't leave. Don't leave," I pleaded.

And then, a couple of pages later, Little Ann crawls to Big Dan's grave and, refusing all food and water, simply gives up. And then *she* dies. Little Ann dies of a broken heart.

What the hell did I just read?

I fell on my knees, like Billy, cradling the tattered paperback like the stilled, bloody body of a coonhound I'd loved more than anything else on God's green Earth.

And then?

Then it happened.

EVERYBODY HURTS. SOMETIMES.

At this point, you probably *think* you know what happened. You think I started crying uncontrollably. That's a good guess. It certainly is what I'm doing with my therapist after rereading that ending.

Because, my goodness, that book packs an emotional punch. It's one of the reasons elementary school teachers have adored this book for decades.

Where the Red Fern Grows is a beautiful and terrible journey into grief and loss and sadness, and that's the whole point. For decades now, this book has been an incredibly helpful tool for adults to help maturing kids begin to understand the world around them.

It helps kids process the idea of lament. It's a story about the painful, searing truth that life will inevitably bring loss. *But* that loss is also commingled with the joy of having loved really well (and the joy of having been loved). Through the years, *Where the Red Fern Grows* has allowed caring adults and educators to introduce the important topics of mourning and grief and loss.

That is a helluva lesson for a fifth grader.

And in my case, it was too much.

I didn't cry. I didn't sob. I simply closed the book, put it on the ground, and kicked it back under my bed. I heard it slide along the carpet and thud against the baseboard back in the darkness.

I was not going to talk about what that book did to me emotionally.

*STEP 2: You must face the full force of the **emotions** that you're experiencing (whatever they are).*

Yeah, I wasn't about to do that. In fact, I wasn't going to tell anyone about it.

"Well," my fifth-grade brain said to my fifth-grade self, "looks like we're going to be carrying *that* around in our emotional backpack for the rest of our life."

And with that, I zipped up the metaphorical backpack of my metaphorical emotions and I went on with my day. Because I knew how to deal with really powerful, really strong emotions. In fact, I even knew how to deal with this specific emotion of grieving the loss of a dog.

In that moment, I thought I was just reacting, but really, it was a learned response. I had been trained how to push emotions aside. I'd been learning it all my life.

From my dad.

Two dogs down. One to go.

A DRIVE-BY IN A 1976
MAROON MONTE CARLO

When I was in first grade, my father moved our family to Las Vegas. My dad was a world-renowned marine biologist who was the primary shark consultant for Caesars Palace, who wanted to build a 150,000-gallon-aquarium-themed underwater restaurant.

People, even my fingers wanted to stop typing because they didn't believe what I was just saying. Black people ain't out there trying to mess around with no sharks.

Real talk, my dad was a military man who was transferred to Nellis Air Force Base just outside of Las Vegas in June of 1982. He was assigned to be part of a top-secret classified team that worked on the F-117A, otherwise known as the Stealth Fighter. This is actually true. Actually, my dad's real story sounds like I made that up, too. But I didn't.

A few years later, when I was in third or fourth grade, my parents decided that they wanted to get me a puppy. My mother worked long hours at the bank, and my father was literally gone five days a week working, so to them it just made sense. They got me a midnight-black cocker spaniel. Just a beautiful dog. My dad named him Nighthawk, which was the name of his Air Force squadron. I could not have been happier.

One day, before my dad left for the week, he reminded my mother to make sure to take the dog in to get its shots. But my mom was busy and just kept putting off the vet appointment. There's a particularly nasty, highly contagious virus called parvo that kills a lot of young dogs, which is why they need the vaccination shot. At some point, Nighthawk came in contact with the parvo virus (which is easy to do for puppies). And my sweet boy got very sick.

One day, I was walking home from school, and I saw my dad pull up. He was driving his 1976 Chevy Monte Carlo. It was burgundy, with iridescent flakes in the paint that made it shimmer. Its vinyl top was a rich cream color. Prince would have willingly driven this car, and would have liked it.

I was surprised to see him home. My dad pulled up next to me on the sidewalk.

"Boy," he said to me out of the window. "Your dog is dead. He got sick and died."

He didn't get out of the car. He didn't say anything else. Just that one sentence, very matter-of-factly.

"Boy. Your dog is dead."

Now, in any regular world, a young boy's puppy dying is an emotional thing. It's the role of the emotionally mature parent to help support a kid through that.

But my dad did not help me.

He just drove away in his 1976 maroon Monte Carlo with the cream-colored vinyl top.

Why? Because my dad, like most Black men, like most Black people, like most modern Americans, does not know how to lament.

And if you don't know something, you can't teach it to your son.

YOU GOT ME FEELIN' EMOTIONS. DEEPER THAN I EVER DREAMED OF.

Back to lament. The first part is having the courage to actually be honest about the reality of the situation. But part two also demands courage—the courage to face and feel the whole gamut of emotions that will inevitably rush in.

And remember, this is *exactly why* educators and adults loved *Where the Red Fern Grows*—because it helped preteens and young teens learn how to lament and process the strong emotions that come with grief. Recently, I was rereading *Where the Red Fern Grows*, and it's clear this is what Rawls is doing. He knew this book was about lamenting, which is why, in the book, he does something brilliant. He uses Billy's mom and dad to put forth *absolutely terrible ideas* about how to deal with suffering, and almost all of them involve *avoiding* or *minimizing* strong emotions. Even a fifth grader will read these and say, "Aw, hell nah." Kids are smarter than we give them credit for. Look how smart Rawls was. Here are three terrible, terrible examples of how *not* to grieve from Billy's well-meaning, but very emotionally stunted parents:

EXHIBIT 1: Papa tried. "Billy," he said, "I wouldn't think too much about this if I were you. It's not good to hurt like that. I believe I'd just try to forget it. Besides, you still have Little Ann."[8]

This is textbook denial. Try to forget it. "It's not good to hurt like that." This is terrible, terrible advice.

EXHIBIT 2: "Billy, you haven't lost your dogs altogether," Mama said. "You'll always have their memory. Besides, you can have some more dogs."[9]

---

8. Rawls, *Where the Red Fern Grows*, p. 200.
9. Rawls, *Where the Red Fern Grows*, p. 203.

This is classic minimizing. Billy *has* lost his dogs. He must face that reality and grieve.

EXHIBIT 3: Mama came in. "Why don't you go to bed," she said, "and get a good night's sleep. You'll feel better tomorrow." [10]

This is empty positivity and, frankly, emotional avoidance. Billy will not feel better tomorrow. This is not how grief works. These emotions will not magically go away.

Or, like my dad. Just lock all those emotions away. Like I said in the previous chapter when I discussed the state of Black mental health, Black people don't lament very well.

And if that's true, then it's doubly true that *Black men* don't lament well.

I KNOW A MAN AIN'T SUPPOSED TO CRY...

I have no memories of my father crying. None. There were moments, historically, when my father absolutely should have cried. He did not. I remember when his mother (my grandmother) passed away. I was almost thirty at this point, and we flew down to Eutaw, Alabama, where my mom and dad were from. Her name was Mary Ethel Walker, because of course it was. That is a proper name for an older Black woman in the South. I remember looking over at my father, during the funeral, to see if he was crying.

He was not.

I called him a few weeks ago, and I asked him about it. I thought maybe I missed something or remembered incorrectly.

---

10. Rawls, *Where the Red Fern Grows*, p. 206.

"Hey, Dad, did you cry at Grandma Walker's funeral?" I asked.

Without hesitation, he said, "No, I didn't cry."

Now, part of this is that my father was a military man. In the fall of 1968, my father and his twin brother both received a letter drafting them to serve in the Vietnam War that started out: *Greeting: You are hereby ordered for induction in the Armed Forces of the United States.*

My father was seventeen. Seventeen! He hadn't even graduated high school yet. The military makes men hard, and actively discourages any signs of emotion. You can't have soldiers crying, after all. You have to tamp down all emotion and get on to the death and killing. So I get it.

But there were other forces at work, too. As we talked about before, 63 percent of Black people believe that a mental health condition is a sign of personal weakness, and 26 percent think it's not even appropriate for family members to talk about difficult topics like mental illness. That's a problem.

This.

This right here is exactly what I mean when I talk about not being able to lament.

Avoiding pain and deep emotion, pushing it down, repressing it, numbing out through activity, or avoidance—these are all survival techniques that my father, because of his rough and incredibly difficult life, had learned.

Emotion was too dangerous to feel, so it got locked away, behind several layers of thick blast shield walls. I remember when I used to get spankings. When my dad would grab his belt, I knew the whooping was on. Now, with my mother, if I cried hard enough, demonstrably enough, sometimes my mother would relent. But my father?

No.

Crying was not an effective deterrent.

"Boy, what are you crying for?" he'd say.

The lesson was "crying didn't belong in any of this."

Except that...it did.

It's amazing where your mind goes when you're full of fear.

DATE: DECEMBER 22, 2020

So there I was, in Dr. Barocas's office. And I knew that I couldn't run away from these strong emotions of fear, nor could I pretend that the fear didn't exist. I needed to feel it. I was still overwhelmed, but:

I wasn't going to drive away in my maroon-and-cream Monte Carlo.

I wasn't going to pretend like nothing happened.

I wasn't going to kick the book under my bed.

I wasn't going to be stoic at my own mother's funeral.

I wasn't.

And although it scared the hell out of me, I did my very best to feel and face my fears. Face those emotions. My eyes began to well up with tears.

"Dr. Barocas," I said, "I need you to be really Scottie Pippen-y tomorrow, sir. Please."

Now I was crying.

"I know you don't know who I am. I mean, why would you?" I said. "But I just finished writing a book that I feel is pretty important.[11]

---

11. NOTE: I'd just turned in the final manuscript for my first book *I Take My Coffee Black: Reflections on Tupac, Musical Theater, Faith, and Being Black in America.*

And I feel like I have a lot more to do, a lot more I want to give to this world. I need you to make sure I make it out of this surgery."

At this point, the fear had taken over me. But. I had admitted out loud to how afraid I was. I had admitted, out loud, to my mother, that this was serious. I'd admitted, out loud, to Dr. Barocas, that I was scared. The fear was still there, but somehow, admitting it out loud, talking about it, and naming it had helped.

Being vulnerable about my feelings also ushered in words of support, care, and encouragement from Dr. Barocas. He assured me he would do his level best.

Before I left, as a preparation for the surgery, I had to drink this awful, black, chalky drink that basically emptied out my entire digestive tract. It tasted like someone had taken a charcoal briquette, rolled it around in crushed aspirin, had fourteen cats pee on it, and then ground the briquette up into lukewarm dirty creek water. Or about as disgusting as a single banana.

The theme of lament jumped out at me again. There was no pretending with this black, milky fluid. I couldn't pretend this was delicious.[12] It also struck me that this fluid was removing all the waste from my body. It was cleaning me out. Removing the toxins.

Lament does the same thing, I think. You have to feel those emotions. You have to let those emotions out. You have to get that grief out, I guess. Just like that black, charcoal sludge.

Literally removing the toxins, I suppose.

The abdominal cramps that happened in the hours after drinking that fluid were about as fun as you'd expect. Again, reality knocking at my door. Dr. Tan said this drink would "evacuate my

---

12. If this were a milkshake, it would bring zero boys to the yard.

bowels." He didn't tell me it would be a fire-alarm stampede. I couldn't eat anything, either. Or really drink anything.

But that night, I faced my fears, named them, and spent a lot of time alone. Lamenting. I was afraid. But at least I was honest about it.

DATE: DECEMBER 23, 2020, 9:30 a.m.

The next morning, my mother and I drove to the hospital. I didn't talk much. I tried to listen to my mother's voice. Like I've said before, just the sound of her voice is like cocoa butter to the skin of my soul.[13]

They started prepping me for surgery. I was breathing deep.

Dr. Barocas walked in.

"Hey, Doc," I said.

"Hey, so, Tyler, last night, I watched some of your Tyler Merritt Project videos," he said. "You weren't kidding. The world needs you, Tyler."

I was floored. This guy was a doctor—a surgeon. He probably had one million things to do. And he was watching my videos.

"I'm gonna be *playoff* Scottie Pippen," he said to me, patting my leg.

I'll never forget that. This man was a big-shot surgeon, who probably sees a thousand patients a year. But he *saw* me. He had watched me deal with my own fear. He saw me break down, in front of my mom. He saw the human in me. He did his homework. And he spoke to me in the most encouraging way possible.

---

13. Tyler Merritt, *I Take My Coffee Black*, Worthy, 2021. Kindle Edition, p. 3. Yeah, baby, I just footnoted *myself.*

Because Scottie Pippen was undefeated and 6–0 in the NBA Finals, baby.[14]

I thought about fear. About how at the end of *A Nightmare on Elm Street*, Freddy is defeated when Nancy realizes that he gains power from fear. He loses all his power if you face him head-on.

I sure wished cancer were like that.

The doctors unlocked the wheels of the hospital bed and began to wheel me down the corridor to the operating room.

I breathed deep.

"Mom, you might wanna take a picture," I said.

"Now, why would I want to do that, Tyler?" she said.

"Because it might be the last one you get of me!" I said. "Haha."

The nurse at my shoulder hit me on the arm.

"Don't you joke with your mom like that," she said.

"I love you, Tyler," my mama said.

"I love you, too," I said, through tears.

My dad might never have cried in front of his mama.

But that didn't mean I couldn't.

---

14. For all my musical theater people, I know all you heard was "*sports sports sports*" but Scottie Pippen is like the Audra McDonald of basketball.

CHAPTER 4

SURVIVOR'S REMORSE

Tick.

Tick.

Tick.

The countdown.

I know over the last few pages, I haven't talked much about it, but it's the only thing I think about.

All. The. Time.

Every six months, I find out what my fate will be. The countdown is always at the forefront of my mind.

Just this morning Dr. Tan's office sent me a reminder that in four months, I will have to go back to the Vanderbilt-Ingram Cancer Center for an appointment. A half a year might not seem like a big deal, and for most of my life, six months was just a chunk of time. Six months until Christmas. Or six months and it's college football season. But now that chunk of half a year is a threat. It's a cutoff point where I might learn that the cancer has grown, and they'll have to sedate me and cut my entire abdomen open to try to cut the cancer out of me.

A cancer that might never go away.

A cancer I might never fully get rid of.

As of this moment, the appointment is seventeen weeks away. That's 119 days. 2,856 hours until I find out what's next for me.

Tick.

Tick.

Tick.

Damn. 119 days.

Not that I'm counting.

PHAT FARM

Did I mention that I have a type of cancer that doesn't respond to chemo? Radiation isn't an effective method to kill it, either. So when Dr. Tan cut out that twenty-seven-pound tumor from my abdomen, he took out *most* of the cancer, but there were still some little itty-bitty cancer cells left. They took the advice of the wise philosopher-poet from the late 1900s, Adam Duritz of the Counting Crows and they were just "hanginaround."

But despite this—and I hesitate to even say this—I am very lucky.

Because the type of cancer that I have is—well, how do I put it—dumb.

It's dumb.

It's really, really dumb.

The cancer I have is called liposarcoma. *Lipo* means fat, which means this cancer is basically just a fatty mass of dumb cancer cells. Yes, it does have a brain of its own, but that brain is very, very dumb.

Frankly, it could have been different. So many types of cancers are wildly deadly. They are not to be trifled with. They take people's lives. And quickly. Those types of cancers are like ninja assassins.

They move fast, they move quietly, and they are on a lethal mission. They huddle in the dark, sharpening their swords.

"Okay, here's the plan. Nobody make any noise. We wait until the last minute to attack, when it will be too late. They will never see us coming. And don't forget the pizza."

Sorry. I forgot to mention that the ninjas in this scenario that I've created are teenage turtles who are also mutants.

Anyway, back to cancer!

We've all heard stories about people who found out they had cancer on one random Thursday and were given weeks to live.

Cancer sucks.

But my cancer? It's just not very ambitious. My type of liposarcoma is sorta like Stoner Cancer.

"I'm just gonna sit here in the basement and eat Doritos."

And like a stoner sitting in your basement, the only way to get rid of it is to have a five-foot-nothing, 100-pound highly educated Asian man from Australia come cut it out.

So these upcoming six-month appointments are to see how much the cancer has grown and when Dr. Tan will have to operate.

And that thought? That thought fills me with anxiety every day. Because the last time Dr. Tan operated, I almost didn't wake up.

MAMA, I DIDN'T MEAN TO MAKE YOU CRY

So I'm about to tell you a story I thought I knew. Ever since the surgery, I would tell people, "The surgery went well, but it was kind of touch-and-go there for a minute." But in preparation for this chapter, I did some research and decided to do something I wished I hadn't. I asked my mom what really happened.

Honestly, I was hoping she'd share with me some funny, quick-witted things I said coming out of the operation, still loopy from the anesthesia. You would chuckle and say to yourself, "Dang! Even while medically sedated, that Tyler is still world-class funny."

I thought I was ready. But I wasn't.

My mom was not in a joking mood.

"Oh, I hated that," she quickly said, when I asked her to recount the operation. "Hated."

Whoa.

I knew that my mom had people in her life who went into the hospital for operations, were put under anesthesia, and never woke back up. I didn't know how difficult my surgery would be for her and just how close *I* came to not waking up.

So let's get into the actual surgery, shall we? Also, be warned that this next section will be written with the medical precision of a third grader. And not the most gifted third grader. I'm talking about that third grader who was still eating paste and putting his Superman Underoos on backward. You know the one.

So after all the presurgery prep was done, the nurses wheeled my bed into the operating room in the early afternoon, where Dr. Tan and his sidekick Dr. Barocas would operate on me.

For eight hours.

Eight hours.

And while Dr. Tan was leaning over my insides, trying to wrangle this twenty-seven-pound behemoth of a tumor, my mom was sitting in the hospital waiting room.

She was willing to wait for it.[1]

After a few hours, it became clear that the tumor was entirely wrapped around my left kidney.[2]

At any rate, Dr. Tan made the call to cut out my kidney. But doing that also meant he had to cut through a nearby artery. As you and I clearly learned from the episode "There's No I in Team" (season five, episode five) of *Grey's Anatomy* where Dr. Miranda Bailey had to orchestrate a massive twelve-person simultaneous "domino" surgery with six separate kidney transplants, there are two renal arteries, a left and a right one, that go into each kidney. We also learned that Alex and Izzie were really into each other, but at this moment, that's less important.

These renal arteries are pretty big. And apparently, the bleeding was so intense, they had to pause the surgery to make sure that I didn't bleed out and die. Yup. You can go back and read that again, if you'd like. "Bleed out and die." After they stabilized me, Dr. Tan and Dr. Barocas finished the eight-hour surgery, sewed me up, and I was wheeled to a recovery room, where the anesthesia would wear off gradually and I'd slowly "come to."

Here's my mom, to the best of her memory, retelling how this went down:

---

1. Yes, that was an unnecessary *Hamilton* reference, put there only to see if you and I can be friends or not. And if you're reading this and got the reference, then congrats, we're now besties. I'll give you your half of our friendship necklace next time I see you.

2. Just like the careers of Tom Brady and Bill Belichick, there was no disentangling them from each other. Just like the sweet, decades-long musical collaboration between Daryl Hall and John Oates, you could not tell where one ended and the other began. Was that the first time Tom Brady and Hall & Oates have been compared to a tumor? Damn straight it was. I'm a literary trailblazer, people. A trailblazer!

IN HER OWN WORDS
QUEEN JERRIE MERRITT

Finally the doctor [Dr. Tan] came down and pulled me aside. He said that the surgery went well, and was successful. Well, I was immediately relieved. Because the people I knew who had passed away hadn't even made it through the surgery. They'd died on the table, see? So I was immediately relieved.

But then Dr. Tan said that for a while there, it was a little touch-and-go. And I said, "Now, what do you mean it was a little touch-and-go?" And he told me they had to cut an artery, and because of that, you started to lose a lot of blood. I guess it wasn't planned, but the artery got cut because the tumor was so big. You almost bled out, so they had to stabilize you.

I asked if I could see you, and he told me you were in a recovery room, and they were waiting for you to wake up, and the nurses would come and get me. And then, like most doctors tend to do, he quickly left. He just took off.

And I was grateful, but I remember thinking, "I could have done without him telling me about almost losing my only child in surgery." Yeah, I could have done without that.

She told me she waited patiently for another two hours, waiting for the nurses to take her to my recovery room. Keep in mind, we're now about ten hours in.

Eventually, my mom went to the nurses' station and asked if she could go see me in my recovery room. The nurses checked their computers and one of them said, "Oh, he's not in a recovery room." What the nurse didn't tell my mom was that I wasn't in a recovery room *because I wasn't recovering.* I was in an intensive care room.

Now I need to explain some hospital stuff to you. Recovery rooms in a hospital are like flying coach in an airplane. You're just there, and once every couple of hours, someone comes by to check on you.

But ICU rooms are like private jets, where there is a *dedicated waitstaff* who checks on you every seven minutes to make sure you, Barack, and Jay-Z don't want some fuzzy socks or a chilled glass of strawberry-infused champagne. Yes, in this scenario, I'm flying in a private jet with Jay-Z and Barack Obama, probably to Prague.[3]

Back to the hospital and my mom. Two more hours go by. We are now *four* hours post-surgery, and twelve hours total.

Now, my mom is a patient woman. But she's also proactive. She found out what floor I was on, and approached the nursing station up there. "Yes, Mrs. Merritt," the nurse explained. "We haven't come down to get you because Tyler's body went through a lot of trauma, and he isn't waking up, so they moved him to intensive care."

Oh, man. My mom's worst nightmare. Once again, the story as told by my mom.

IN HER OWN WORDS: PART 2
THE OPRAH WINFREY OF LAS VEGAS,
MRS. JERRIE MERRITT

I said, "I need to see him," so they took me back to see you. And you were in total intensive care. Just lying in a bed, and there were tubes everywhere. I took a picture because I could not believe how many machines and tubes there were.

---

3. Hey, people, it's my made-up daydream, I can do what I want. Now, Barack, could you please pass me another one of those pudding cups? Do they serve pudding on private jets? Don't look at me. It's not like I know. Hell, I had to google how to spell "Prague." Did you know the chief export of Prague is motor vehicle parts? I do.

There was even a tube down your throat, and I pointed to it, and one of the doctors said, "Oh, don't worry. He's breathing on his own," and I remember thinking, "Well, he better be!"

There was a flurry of nurses and such, and they never left your side. And I will have you know I did not, either. Well, then at one point, the doctor on call came in and said, "We need to do a test." They wanted to put this big thing on your head, like a helmet.

And the doctor told me this was going to measure brain waves, and that he wanted to make sure there was no brain damage. That he needed to check to see if there was brain activity.

Well, I don't need to tell you, that was a very scary moment. Just a very scary moment. But they did the test, and the doctor showed me that your brain waves were normal. Which was a big relief. But you were still not waking up. And they didn't know why.

Now, when I first heard this from my mom, my jaw dropped to the floor. I had no idea this had happened. I kept stopping my mom, saying, "Are you serious right now? They wanted to check to see if my brain had ACTIVITY?"

Mom. Seriously?

At any rate, Mom was told my lungs, heart, and brain were working fine. But I was still not waking up. My mom told me that the nurses started doing all these things to try to wake me. They would rub my arm and say my name. They would shake my shoulder gently. When that didn't work, they escalated the situation. They squeezed my hand and shouted, "Tyler!" Then they poked me on the bottom of my foot with a needle. They said outlandish things, to get my brain's attention.

- *"We're going to feed you some mushed-up bananas right now, okay, Tyler?"*
- *"Ooooh, Tyler, what do you say we put this tarantula right here on your chest…"*
- *"Hey, Tyler. Jay-Z is not even that skilled as a rapper. And he would never share a private jet with you and Barack Obama, or go to Prague, whose chief export is motor vehicle parts."*

Okay, maybe that's not *exactly* what they said to me, but it should have been.

My mom told me that despite all this, the doctors and the nurses didn't seem too worried. "We just need to give his body more time to recover," they told my mother. "He'll wake up when he's ready."

Which was true. But still, if it is your loved one you're staring at, and they're not waking up, it's frightening. Five hours passed. It was now the dead of night. Final recollection, as told by my mom.

IN HER OWN WORDS: PART 3
NEVADA'S FEMALE EXECUTIVE OF
THE YEAR IN 2021, MRS. JERRIE MERRITT

Well, finally, your hand moved. So I took your hand in my hand, and I said, "Tyler, if you can hear me, squeeze my hand." And your hand moved. And finally, you were showing some signs of waking up. I could see some movement. And you were stirring. But you weren't awake. In fact, that whole night, you never became fully conscious. But at some point, I guess it was early dawn now, at this point, you did finally wake up. And all you wanted to do was take everything out. You couldn't talk, what with all the tubes that were up your nose and in your mouth. And you had something on your head, and you wanted that off, too. But they'd strapped you down, so you wouldn't pull anything out.

And that's when I began to wake up from the long nightmare surgery.

WHY, GOD? SHOW YOUR HAND. WHY CAN'T ONE GUY UNDERSTAND?

For years, one of my favorite songs to sing for theater auditions was the song "Why God Why?" from my favorite musical, *Miss Saigon*. In that song, Chris, the main male protagonist, a soldier in the Vietnam War, was struggling to make sense of why he survived combat when so many other people had not.

It is an important moment because we discover that Chris is suffering from a form of deep PTSD and what many psychologists now might call "survivor's remorse." Now, at the risk of getting all Wikipedia-y, I wanted to give you a formal definition.

SURVIVOR'S REMORSE

(often termed "survivor syndrome")
A mental condition that occurs when a person believes they have done something wrong by surviving a traumatic or tragic event when others did not.[4]

---

4. Hannah Murray et al., "Survivor Guilt: A Cognitive Approach," *The Cognitive Behaviour Therapist* 14 (2021): e28. https://www.ncbi.nlm.nih.gov/pmc/articles/PMC7611691/.

As a cancer survivor, I feel this in my soul. The descriptions of the internal struggles of people—from combat veterans to survivors of school shootings—who felt this. I want to be clear with you: I'm in no way attempting to compare the traumas. Our situations are very different. But that sense of survivor's remorse? That's the same.

Why me? Why do I get to live, when some others don't?

From what I've learned from other cancer survivors, this is actually pretty common. But there's another layer on it for me.

And it's because I'm Black.

SIDE NOTE: I do want to pause for a moment. You'd be amazed how often I get criticized for bringing up my skin color and my race. First, every single day I walk out my front door as a Black man. This will never change.

Second of all, I bring up my race because *how could I not?* My skin color is part—not all, but certainly a big part—of how I experience the world. It's part of my lens about how I see and experience reality. And I acutely feel my Blackness every day, in my interactions, in the way people treat me or don't treat me.

And until there's a world where my being Black isn't seen as a negative thing, or until my being Black doesn't cause others to mistreat me (and people like me), I'm going to keep bringing it up.

ONLY THE ~~GOOD~~ BLACK DIE YOUNG

Fact: Black people do not live as long as white people and other races in the US. Black Americans have historically had a lower life expectancy than white Americans. I'm not trying to be hyperbolic here. I'm just telling you facts. In fact, it used to be a *lot* lower. At the beginning of the 1900s, white people's life expectancy was, on average, fourteen years longer than that of Black people.[5] Fourteen years!

But there's another layer on top of this. I'm not just Black. I'm a Black *man*.

And if being Black is bad for your health,[6] then being a Black man is the worst combo.[7]

THE TOP SIX WAYS THAT BLACK MEN DIE

In 2021, the University of Michigan, Rutgers University, and the University of Washington worked together to research the leading causes of death for young Black men.[8] They are:

1. Accident
2. Suicide
3. Homicide
4. Heart disease
5. Cancer
6. Police officer (deadly force)

---

5. This is from Elizabeth Arias, a health scientist for the center who analyzes national death data and works for the Centers for Disease Control and Prevention's National Center for Health Statistics. Read the whole article from 2022 here: https://www.nbcnews.com/health/health-news/life-expectancy-black-americans -continues-lag-whites-study-finds-rcna35410.
6. Catherine O. Johnson et al., "Life Expectancy for White, Black, and Hispanic Race/Ethnicity in U.S. States: Trends and Disparities, 1990 to 2019," *Annals of Internal Medicine* 175, no. 8 (2022), https://www.acpjournals.org/doi/10.7326 /M21-3956.
7. M. Jermane Bond and Allen A. Herman, "Lagging Life Expectancy for Black Men: A Public Health Imperative," *American Journal of Public Health* 106, no. 7 (2016): 1167–1169. https://www.ncbi.nlm.nih.gov/pmc/articles/PMC4984780/.
8. Frank Edwards et al., "Risk of Being Killed by Police Use of Force in the United States by Age, Race-Ethnicity, and Sex," *PNAS* 116, no. 34 (2019): 16793–16798. https://www.pnas.org/doi/pdf/10.1073/pnas.1821204116.

This list is insane to me. As I read it, and thought about each one, I felt a strong pang of survivor's remorse again. Let's go through this list together.

1. **Accidents.** I guess every man who is over the age of twenty should fall on the ground and thank the Good Lord Above that they didn't accidentally die doing something stupid when they were younger. Fellas...turn to your neighbor and tell them about that stupid thing you did that one time that almost got your dumb ass killed. I'll wait. Also, even though I realize intellectually that I can't do anything to prevent accidents, I still don't drive behind lumber trucks carrying big logs. I'm no fool. I've seen *Final Destination 4*.

2. **Suicide.** The fact that this is second on the list is so deeply tragic to me. It hurts my heart. I want to take a moment here to recognize that suicide doesn't just affect Black men. I'm not naive to think that even you, while you're holding this book in your hand, might be struggling with this. I need you to hear me in this moment. Keep going, my friend. Suicide is a permanent solution to a temporary problem, and tomorrow has the potential to be the very best day of your life. Help is available. If you need to speak with someone, you can call today simply by dialing 988.

3. **Homicide.** I've talked about this before. This could have and statistically should have been my story. Growing up in Las Vegas, I watched as Black kids were immediately targeted, pressured, recruited, and threatened to join gangs. The film *Straight Outta Compton* wasn't a movie for me—it was a documentary. I was left alone by the

older gang recruits (because talent is valued in the hood), but so many of the folks I grew up with weren't. I don't want to preach a sermon here on how violence permeates our communities, but just know, this is number three for a reason.

4. **Heart disease.** I don't know much about this, but just in case, I'm going to keep exercising every day. And I should probably lay off the biscuits. The operative word here being "should." But have you ever *had* a biscuit?

5. **Cancer.** Including twenty-seven-pound tumors.

6. **Police officer (deadly force).** Police, whose motto is "serve and protect." Who are called, in nearly every municipality, "officers of the peace." This is number six on the list. This should not be number six for Black men. This should not be number six for *anyone*.

The point is, if I'm keeping it real with you, sometimes I feel survivor's remorse just for being a Black man. So many sliding door moments that allowed me to avoid the streets, avoid jail, or worse. Even the fact that I was born when I was born. If I were born fifty years earlier, with my skin color, in Alabama (where my parents were both from)...I don't know, man. I don't know.

Black people in general and Black men, in particular, have had to deal with life cut short because of the long history of violence against them. From slavery to the post–Civil War Jim Crow Reconstruction Era filled with lynchings and involuntary incarceration, to the Civil Rights Movement, dealing with violence because of the color of your skin was part of what it meant to be Black in America. Death was always looming. Strange fruit and all, y'all.

What I'm trying to say here is if I as a Black man get to live a long life, sadly I should consider myself lucky. And that's something I am reminded of every day.

HOW AM I SUPPOSED TO BREATHE WITH NO AIR?

My first memory post-surgery as I slowly regained consciousness was the same one that my mother reported. I woke up to find my arms and legs strapped down to the bed. The nurses had done this because I'd been intubated, meaning the doctors had placed a tube down my throat to help me breathe.

But—ironically—the tube actually made it far more difficult for me to breathe. It felt like my lungs were compressed. As though I couldn't take a deep enough breath to get enough air. I was taking frantic, shallow breaths. It felt like I was choking. And honestly, I thought I was going to die.

And your natural instinct, when you're choking, is to go into survival mode. My brain was basically like, "I gotta get this thing out of my throat! And now!"

This. This is why I was tied down. Because in my agitated state, I grew increasingly upset and panicked. I fought against the restraints. I felt as though I simply couldn't get a deep breath—like I was breathing through one of those coffee stirrer straws.

A nurse saw I was agitated and came over. I remember trying to write something on her hand, hoping she'd understand. I wrote:

"I can't breathe."

She didn't understand what I was saying. Nobody could. I felt helpless and trapped. And then, in my panicked state, I could see my mother across the room. I began internally crying out for my mom. But she couldn't hear me. And she couldn't help.

Here I was, internally screaming out into the void that I couldn't breathe. I remember thinking, "Aren't you all here to help me? Why won't somebody help me?"

Mom.

Please.

I was so scared.

"I can't breathe."

I realize that phrase is strange to read now. It's become more or less synonymous with a number of high-profile news stories featuring Black people who have died. And if you are wondering if I knew in that moment that I was aware that I was saying the *same phrase* that's become identified with so much activism and news headlines, I gotta be clear.

No.

No, I didn't realize it.

I wasn't thinking about that. I only had one concern.

I just needed to breathe.

When something is preventing you from breathing, that's the only thing you're thinking about.

Eventually, the nurses calmed me down, and the sedatives took over, and I fell back to sleep for a while as my body healed from the trauma of the surgery. Again, you know how this story ends: I got out of the hospital. They took the tumor out. I'm alive.

I'm one of the lucky ones.

My inability to breathe in that moment was traumatic.

But now that I'm on the other side, the primary thing I remember from the entire event is that moment saying "I can't breathe" and feeling like nobody could help me.

Now, it's almost impossible for me to hear the words "I can't breathe" and not immediately be transported back to Memorial Day 2020.

A moment that changed all of us.

A moment that became so big that it can almost feel like a news headline, or a historical event, distant in the pages of a textbook. Like it was something that didn't actually happen.

But if you can follow me here, I want to walk through this moment when another Black man said that he couldn't breathe.

Because even though he isn't around to tell his story to you, I am.

May 25, 2020

It's a Monday evening in Minneapolis, Minnesota, around eight p.m. In the pre-summer twilight, people gather outside a little corner store called Cup Foods, a small store that's been around for more than thirty years. The store is owned by thirty-five-year-old Mahmoud Abumayyaleh, or "Mike" as he's known to nearly everyone. His family originally called the store "Chicago Unbeatable Prices" or CUP for short.[9] In this spot, almost everyone knows everyone by name, like a throwback to an easier, simpler time when folks felt like they were known in their community.

Cup Foods has a deli, with fresh meats and vegetables, and long rows of shelves with food. It's also got a MetroPCS counter that sells cellphone credits.

---

9.   Aymann Ismail, "The Store That Called the Cops on George Floyd," Slate, October 6, 2020. https://slate.com/human-interest/2020/10/cup-foods-george-floyd-store-911-history.html.

That's why Slim would go there. Slim was a tall, slender middle-aged Black man who lived in a nearby neighborhood. When he had problems with his phone, Slim would go to the counter, and they'd help him out. Folks in Cup Foods knew Slim, and he knew almost everyone by name.

Now, on this day, Mike wasn't there. Just a few hours earlier, Mike had left to go home, leaving the store in the hands of his employees.

Before Slim ever came into the store, another man had attempted to buy some cigarettes with a twenty-dollar bill. One of Mike's employees, a manager who had worked there for some years, used a special marker on the bill. The marker indicated the bill was counterfeit, so the manager refused the sale and handed the bill back to the man, who then left.

A little while later, Slim entered the store and attempted to buy cigarettes. He handed the same twenty-dollar counterfeit bill to a young, nineteen-year-old clerk named Chris Martin. Martin didn't test the bill, put it in the drawer, and handed Slim the cigarettes. But a few minutes later, Chris realized the twenty-dollar bill that Slim had given him was counterfeit.

7:57 p.m.

Chris and another employee from Cup Foods walked across the street to where Slim was parked in his blue SUV. Chris told Slim that the money he'd given him was fake. He asked him to give back the cigarettes. Did Slim know the bill was fake? It's not clear at all. Chris (the clerk) later said that, unlike the first man, Slim didn't seem to realize the bill was fake. But Slim was already smoking the cigarettes. Chris asked Slim to come back into the store. Slim refused.

Chris, afraid he'd get in trouble, told his manager about the fake twenty, even telling him he'd pay for the cigarettes since it was his mistake.

But it wasn't as easy as all that. There's a state policy in Minnesota that requires store owners to call the police if someone attempts to use fake currency.

"As a check cashing business, this is routine practice for us," the owner of the store, Mike, wrote later. "We report forged money, then the police come and ask patrons about the bill to trace its origin." The assumption that police make is that folks don't know they're dealing with forgeries, so they try to trace its origin. At least, that's what they're supposed to do.

8:08 p.m.

The police responded to Cup Foods, investigating a report of forgery called in by the store. Officers Thomas Lane and J. Alexander Kueng got out of their car and went into Cup Foods.

8:09 p.m.

Both officers crossed the street and approached Slim's blue SUV, where he was sitting in the driver's seat. According to bodycam footage, Officer Lane tapped his flashlight on the window and asked Slim to show his hands. After being asked several times, Slim eventually opened the car door while apologizing.

Six seconds after the door opens, Officer Lane drew his gun, pointed it at Slim and said, "Put your fucking hands up right now." He didn't explain the reason for the stop. Then Officer Lane pulled Slim out of the car.

8:11 p.m.–8:12 p.m.
The officers cuffed Slim's hands behind his back. Although the 911 transcripts reveal that the officers had been told that Slim was drunk and out-of-control violent, we can see from body cam footage and security footage that nothing Slim did was violent.

8:12 p.m.
Officer Keung took a handcuffed Slim and told him to sit alongside a nearby wall. Slim was already distressed. He was already sobbing.

8:14 p.m.
The officers moved Slim across the street to their police vehicle. Slim fell to the ground. He complained to the officers that he's scared, he's claustrophobic, and doesn't want to get into the back of the police car. The two officers struggled to get Slim into the back seat.

8:17 p.m.
Two more officers arrived on the scene. They were Officers Derek Chauvin and Tou Thao.

These men had a history with the department. Officer Thao had seven formal complaints lodged against him, and he was sued for brutality in a formal lawsuit in 2017 for throwing a man to the ground and hitting him. Chauvin had seventeen formal complaints lodged against him. He was also involved in three shootings, one of which was fatal.

Seventeen formal complaints, three shootings, one fatal.

8:18 p.m.
Chauvin entered the struggle. He attempted to push Slim into the car. He then pulled Slim all the way through the car, dropping him onto the pavement.

8:20 p.m.

A passerby began recording the encounter with police. Slim was now face down on the pavement, with all four officers (Lane, Kueng, Chauvin, and Thao) around him. Three officers applied pressure to Slim's neck, torso, and legs. Another passerby, seventeen-year-old Darnella Frazier, took out her phone and began recording the encounter. From her video's vantage point, you can see Slim pinned face down by the knee of Officer Chauvin. Also, from her video footage, we hear Slim crying out, pleading with the officers, saying,

"I can't breathe, man. Please."

And there it is.

8:22 p.m.

The officers called police dispatch, requesting a Code 2—a call for non-emergency medical assistance.

8:23 p.m.

The call was then quickly upgraded to a Code 3—a code for emergency medical assistance.

For the next eight minutes, Officer Chauvin put his knee on Slim's head and neck.

During that time, in Darnella's video, you can hear Slim calling out for his mother.

"I can't breathe." Slim says this phrase to Officer Chauvin sixteen times in the next five minutes.

As I write this, I think about being back in that hospital room, lying there. Pleading for your mother because you can't breathe. That's supposed to work.

Fuck.

8:25 p.m.

Slim appeared to go unconscious. Now, a crowd of passersby began calling to the officer to get off Slim. A young white woman, her hair pulled back with a gray headband, approached the officers. She identified herself as a Minneapolis firefighter, trained in medical resuscitation, and asked if the officers needed help. She asked them if the man has a pulse. She began yelling at them, concerned that there was no pulse. Officer Thao told her to get on the curb with the others. He then stands guard.

8:26 p.m.

Bodycam footage from Officer Thao reveals a group of concerned onlookers begging the officers to check Slim's pulse after seeing him lying on the pavement unresponsive. Chauvin pulled out a can of police-issued Mace to keep the crowd at bay. The crowd begged and shouted at the officers to provide medical assistance to Slim. They did not. Finally, Officer Keung relented and checked for a pulse on Slim. He could not find one. Official police protocol for officers who encounter a person without a pulse is to roll them onto their back and begin performing CPR.

The officers did not do this.

8:27 p.m.

An ambulance arrived. Chauvin still did not remove his knee from Slim.

8:28 p.m.

Officer Chauvin lifted his knee off Slim's neck after nine minutes and twenty-nine seconds. Slim was loaded into an ambulance.

8:31 p.m.
En route to the hospital, the ambulance requested assistance from the Minneapolis Fire Department, saying they had a male entering cardiac arrest.

8:36 p.m.
The fire engine reached the ambulance. Two fire department medics boarded the ambulance and found Slim unresponsive and pulseless.

9:25 p.m.
Slim was pronounced dead at the Hennepin County Medical Center emergency room. On the death certificate, they recorded Slim's real name.

George Floyd.

Nine minutes and twenty-nine seconds.

The murder of George Floyd was a profoundly painful moment in American history. In essence, a police officer—an officer of the *peace*—charged by the city and state with the sacred duty of serving his community and protecting it—used his authority to kill an unarmed Black man, despite the frantic and terrified pleas of the citizens gathered around him, slowly murdering an unarmed, non-dangerous man by choking him to death in the street.

According to later courtroom testimony by both medical and police experts, Officer Chauvin prevented Slim from breathing, with the full brunt of his knee on Slim's neck and chest.

Eventually, Slim simply couldn't get enough air. He died of asphyxiation.[10]

When I was lying in that hospital bed at the Vanderbilt University Medical Center, I fought for air for what was probably sixty seconds before I was sedated. That sixty seconds seemed like a lifetime. It was also completely unbearable. But nine minutes and twenty-nine seconds?

"I can't breathe."

My God.

The county medical examiner concluded that the manner of Mr. Floyd's death was homicide. A few months later, a jury confirmed that, finding Derek Chauvin guilty of murder.

Listen. I want to be as clear as I possibly can. In no way am I trying to compare my cancer to the violent assault and murder of my brother George Floyd. They are not the same. I'm simply saying that when we look back on the Top 6 Reasons Why Black Men Die, I was about to be reason number five, and George Floyd was reason number six. And we both said, "I can't breathe."

But here's the thing. George Floyd was six-foot-four, so he's tall, just like me. He weighed 223 pounds, which is pretty close to what I weigh. He was forty-six years old, which is pretty close to how old I

---

10. Dr. Andrew Baker, the county medical examiner, who conducted George Floyd's autopsy, determined ultimately that his "heart and lungs stopped functioning while he was being subdued, restrained and compressed by police officers." It's interesting that the official autopsy doesn't say the word "asphyxiation." Medically speaking, Floyd died because his heart stopped pumping blood (after not getting enough oxygen). Sherry Fink, "George Floyd's Cause of Death Is Crucial in Trial. Forensic Pathologists Explain," *New York Times*, April 8, 2021. https://www.nytimes.com/2021/04/08/us/george-floyd-cause-of-death.html.

am. He had dark skin, just like me. Folks who knew him said he had a big smile that brightened up the room, just like me.

But he's gone.

And I'm still here.

Yeah.

Survivor's remorse.

CHAPTER 5

THE SMELL OF HOSPITALS IN WINTER

Dear Reader,

I think I owe you an apology. I think I underestimated how hard reading that last chapter would be for you. And for me to write it. And to recall those moments with my mother. My God, I almost died.

I left the room heavy.

In times like this, I've found there's an easy solution when the world feels difficult. When things feel hard. And you feel like you can barely make it. When you feel lost, even.

There's a saying I heard once that helps center me, ground me, root me, anchor me. So, if you will, Dear Reader, take a deep breath and say this heartfelt phrase with me:

Vaginal.
Steaming.

But I digress.

(If I lost you here, which is quite likely, I'd recommend going and reading this particular footnote).[1]

LEARNING TO WALK AGAIN

So there I am in the hospital recovery room after doctors spent eight hours wrangling this twenty-seven-pound demented cancer octopus from my abdomen. I can finally breathe. And I'm recovering, but boy howdy, I am:

1. In pain
2. Messed up internally

I feel like I have been hit by a truck. And I don't mean that figuratively. I mean I think if I were actually to get hit by a truck, I might have had less internal trauma than I currently was dealing with.

First of all, I had small wires that went into my nose and down into my lungs. My chest felt heavy and wounded like an elephant had sat on me (Roll Tide). I was often aware of the depth and frequency of my breaths. I was relearning how to breathe.

Secondly, I'd lost my kidney. So my body was dealing with that. Now, I know the question most of you are asking yourself right now. Most of you are wondering:

---

1. Okay, so inside jokes are only fun if you're in on the joke. In my last book, I wrote an intense chapter, and so as a humorous palate cleanser, in the opening lines of the chapter that immediately followed, I made some jokes about Gwyneth Paltrow's lifestyle magazine, *Goop*. This was fun because that magazine contained some very super-rich-white-people nonsense like getting stung by bees on purpose (bee venom therapy) and vaginal steaming. Yes. You read that correctly.

"Tyler, with your background in musical theater, did you hap-
pen to sit down and pen a Tony Award–worthy one-act play in
which you imagine the parts of your body post-surgery as crew
members on a spaceship under attack, and did you include this
one-act play in the back of this book in the Appendix?"

The answer to that question is "Yes."[2]

That's exactly what I did.

But back to the hospital.

Finally, I was very hungry, but I was not allowed to eat. For the
first five days or so after the surgery, the only thing I was allowed to
eat was ice chips, which if you were wondering, are *not* made by Frito
Lay. They're made by a freezer. And yes, they had an IV that delivered glucose to my bloodstream, but, to quote Winnie the Pooh,
there was a "rumbly in my tumbly."

Speaking of Pooh, the reason I was not yet allowed to eat is
because my entire digestive system was completely offline. Just shut
down. Non-operational at every level. Again, forgive my non-precise,
non-scientific explanation, but as I understand it, during abdominal
surgeries if the large or small intestines are jostled, touched, or moved
around, this prompts the body to—and I think this is the proper
medical term—"freak the hell out" and just shut down. They literally
just go dead, like those fainting goats, or a toddler when you're trying
to put a winter coat on them, or my Uncle Junebug when he sips too
much of his "night-night" juice in the middle of the day.

---

2.   And if I know you, dear reader—and I think I do—you have a second follow-up
     question, which is: "Tyler, should I pause reading this book and immediately flip to
     the Appendix and also, in your Tony Award–worthy one-act play, are you hoping
     that the part of "Captain Brain" will be played by Sir Samuel L. Jackson and that the
     role of "Left Leg" will be played by Brad Pitt?" Again, yes and yes.

And as with my Uncle Junebug, nobody knew when my intestines were going to get back to work.

And here's the thing: we don't know exactly *why* the intestines do this, and we don't know *when* they will decide to "turn back on." It's incredibly important for your bowels to start to function again. It's a key marker for health and recovery. But there is literally no way to know that timetable. It could be a few hours. Or a day. Or four days.

But.

There is a way to know *if* your digestive system has come back online.

Now I know what you're thinking. You're thinking, "Tyler, what is that surefire key indicator that all the medical staff are looking for to see if your digestive system is back to functioning?"

And I will answer you.

But know that it gives me zero joy to have to walk you through this.

POOP JOKES AREN'T MY FAVORITE. BUT THEY'RE A SOLID NUMBER TWO.

At this point in the story, I'm afraid the contents of this book will become more scatological and less mature.

Now, my memories are a little foggy on those first days of recovery, but there is one thing I remember clearly. As you remember, Vanderbilt Hospital is one of the premier medical facilities in the nation, and because it is attached to a university, it is a teaching hospital. So every morning, a supervising doctor would take a gaggle of up-and-coming medical students on rounds, quizzing them, teaching them, and explaining how to be all doctor-y.

By the way, this is *exactly* what Dr. Miranda Bailey did when she oversaw the professional development of the surgical residents Meredith Grey, Christina Yang, Izzie Stevens, Alex Karev, and George O'Malley at Seattle Grace Hospital during their internships, as they struggled to balance their personal lives with hectic schedules and stressful residency requirements during the first several seasons of ABC's *Grey's Anatomy*. Is that our third reference to *Grey's Anatomy*? I'll stop referencing *Grey's Anatomy* when the show stops making new episodes. Which is never, people. Never.

In the morning, when the doctors and their interns would do rounds, they would come into my room. And some of these interns (not unlike *Grey's Anatomy*) were very attractive men and women. Why did they look like models? I legit called one of them Dr. McSteamy. So naturally, I wanted to impress the Hot Doctors, but I was all drugged up and drooling while wearing a crinkly hospital gown. But still, I tried to sit up and be professional.

I figured, even in my deeply diminished position, I could still crack some hilarious jokes. Jokes so funny that years from now these attractive doctors would be sitting around in their third houses in the Bahamas with their sun-kissed Patrick Dempsey hair, clinking their drink glasses together and saying things like, "I know we just invented sentient nanobots who can surgically repair any part of the body, but do you remember that one Black guy who was our patient back when we were interns at Vanderbilt? That guy was *hysterical*!"

So that was my state of mind.

The lead doctor came in, with his white doctor coat and his official doctor notebook and his fancy doctor pen, with his entourage of fresh-faced interns behind him. I straightened up in my bed, preparing to unleash a level of hilarity heretofore unseen in this—or any!—teaching hospital in the United States.

"Good morning, Mr. Merritt," the doctor said.

"Good morning," I said cheerily, flashing my thousand-megawatt smile to the Hot Doctors.

"Mr. Merritt," the doctor said. "Have you farted yet this morning?"

***

***

***

Dafuq?

What now?

Did the lead doctor just ask me if I … fff … fff … farted?

First of all, is that even a medical term? What are we? In fourth grade?

- *Hello, Mr. Merritt. Just checking to see if you have cut the cheese yet this morning?*
- *Greetings, Mr. Merritt. My colleagues and I were wondering if you've floated an air biscuit yet this morning.*
- *Hello, Mr. Merritt. Just checking to see if perchance you might have had a small one-cheek squeak, Mr. Merritt? Was it silent but violent, Mr. Merritt?*
- *Good morning, Mr. Merritt. Just checking in with you to see if you knew that beans, beans were a magical fruit and that the more you eat, the more you toot?*

Secondly, I'm not a big "poop joke" guy. My father was in the military, and my mother was a professional banker. They both had very formal personalities and very formal job responsibilities. My father did not come home after working on the classified F-117A Stealth Fighter plane and say:

Hey, son.

Yes, sir.

Go clean your room.

Yes, sir.

But before you go, boy...

Yes, sir.

Pull my finger.

That's just not what happened in my household. We are a proud and professional Black family, descendants of proud Alabama sharecroppers. We don't make immature jokes about flatulence, okay?

Also, it is nearly impossible to seem cool or funny to a bunch of attractive Hot Doctors when the lead doctors ask you that question.

Later on, I would learn that "passing gas" is actually a very important indicator that your digestive system is turning back on. Four days later, when I finally did...you know...pass gas, my nurses were practically over the moon. You'd have thought I'd solved urban poverty, the way they congratulated me.

I understand that, medically, it was good news that things were working, but I have to be honest with you, it's very disorienting for a fully grown medical professional to walk into your hospital recovery room and say:

"I hear you farted, Mr. Merritt!" with the same tone she'd say, "I hear it's your birthday, Mr. Merritt!"

Just all very strange. But pooping turned out to not be my biggest problem.

Number two was problem number two.

My number one issue turned out to be number one.

Ugh. I feel like I'm in a *Potty Time with Elmo* book right now.

A TALE OF TWO NURSES

If you think what you just read was uncomfortable because it was immature, well, this part will make you uncomfortable for a whole new list of reasons.

I didn't mention this before, but to block the pain in my abdomen during the surgery, I was given an epidural. Yep. Just like pregnant women who are giving birth. Epidurals are incredible things: it's a little procedure that effectively blocks all pain signals. So when I first woke up in my hospital bed, I could not feel a thing. Nothing in my belly. Not my legs.

I couldn't feel nothing.

Well, almost nothing.

I could feel something was bothering me in one very specific area.

It was my rather sensitive, private man-parts area—if you get what I mean. I could feel all sorts of weird pressure, and even with the epidural, dare I say a bit of pain. Which is weird, because the tumor *definitely* wasn't in my man-parts area.

After taking a few seconds to gather my composure, I finally figured out what it was. During surgery, I'd been given a catheter.

"I'd been given a catheter."

I make it sound like a present that Santa Claus dropped under my tree on Christmas. *Ho ho ho! Here's your catheter!* Let me put it more directly.

Someone shoved a piece of plastic tubing up my freaking urethra.

And this tube isn't inserted like an inch or two up there. A catheter goes all the way up and through your interior pipes to the bladder. It's there to help slowly drain your urine into a plastic medical bag that conveniently hangs right off the side of your bed.

Because who among us hasn't wanted to lie down in bed next to a bag filled with thirty-four ounces of our own piping-hot urine?

I found out pretty quickly that I had an issue with my catheter. The only thing that hurt, really, was the catheter. And that was after an epidural! A baby should have been able to exit my urethra and I shouldn't have been able to feel it.

On that first day of recovery, I continued to drift in and out of consciousness. But when I woke up, I knew that something was wrong with my nether regions... because it was uncomfortable.

The next day, I was more lucid. And still, the thing that bothered me the most was the catheter. Enter Nurse Nancy.

I *loved* Nurse Nancy.

I loved her with an everlasting love.

Nurse Nancy was a keen caregiver, and she quickly deduced that "the cath" was giving me some problems, mainly because I told Nurse Nancy about my discomfort about one million times during her six-hour shift. I didn't realize it at the time, but I'd developed a new rule for life. It went something like this:

TYLER'S NEW RULE FOR LIFE: NUMBER 1482

When there's something painful going on with my penis, I will pester medical professionals until the pain stops entirely.

I didn't know that was a new rule I had for life. But there it was.

Nurse Nancy knew it was a problem for me, and she told me that the only way she would take out the cath would be if I could guarantee her that I could empty my bladder on my own. I would have to, in her words, relearn how to pee.

I would have learned advanced calculus to get rid of that darn cath. I would sit down and learn the history and intricacies of cricket to get rid of that cath. I would dance to Nickelback, while wearing Crocs, with socks, while eating bananas, as a tarantula watched me nearby to get rid of that cath.

"I will do *anything*," I said.

Nurse Nancy kindly obliged, and she told me she was going to remove it.

I asked her if it was going to hurt.

She said it would "only take two seconds" to get it out and it wouldn't hurt, but there might be some slight discomfort.

Now, I love me some Nurse Nancy, but that b*tch be lying.

It was not "two seconds."

And it was not "some slight discomfort."

You know that weird medieval weapon that has a handle, a long chain, and a spiky metal ball at the end of it? Well, whatever that thing is, it felt like Nurse Nancy was pulling that through my wee-wee. Have you ever heard a teenage girl scream at a Taylor Swift concert? I have. And that's what I sounded like.

And yet, immediately afterward, the pain went away. Before I passed out from the general exhaustion caused by the situation, I stared at Nurse Nancy, and I did my best to express my thanks.

"I love you, Nurse Nancy" was all I could manage to say. Because I did love Nurse Nancy.

Nurse Nancy saved my penis.

Anyhoo.

The next morning, I was doing a little better, so they moved me to an entirely different room. I got an entirely different nurse. Her name was Nurse Kim. After looking at my chart, and assessing her new patient (me!), this new nurse said, "Why don't you have a catheter?"

That's the first thing Nurse Kim said to me.

Mind you, this is before she even introduced herself to me. I explained the situation, and how painful and uncomfortable the cath had been. Nurse Kim was not convinced, nor was she happy.

"Can you empty your bladder on your own?" she asked.

"Yes," I said, not sure I could actually do so. "I can go potty like a *big* boy."

"This isn't funny, Mr. Merritt," Nurse Kim said. "You run the risk of infection or urinary tract problems."

She set a big plastic container lined with milliliter measurement marks on it next to me.

"If you want to be off that catheter," she said, as she slammed the container in front of me, "I need you to fill this jar up."

What was it with hospitals and clear containers of my urine?

Regardless, I didn't like her tone one bit.

"If you can't fill that up, then we're going to have to put the catheter back in," Nurse Kim said. "For your own good."

And then she went to a drawer, pulled out a catheter that was still wrapped in sterile plastic packaging, and she placed it on the tray next to my bed! Gangsta! What a power move. She was like a mobster in a movie sending a warning to a snitch in the hospital under police custody.

Oh, I didn't like this lady one bit.

Not.

One.

Bit.

After she left, I started replaying the conversation in my drugged-out head, and the more I did, the madder I got.

Who did this lady think she was? And why was she so decidedly pro-catheter? Was she on the payroll of Big Catheter? I bet she was. Maybe the Catheter Mafia had taken her family hostage and were threatening to hurt them unless she met a catheter quota. And what about the Constitution? I have rights, dammit. Like Thomas Jefferson once wrote, "We hold these truths to be self-evident" and that all men have the right to "life, liberty, and the right of refusal if someone wants to shove something up your pee-pee hole."

As she walked out of the room, I stuck my tongue out at Nurse Kim. And that's when I thought it. I thought something very unpleasant. I will now tell you what I thought, and I need you to remember, I was drugged up and I had PTSD. Penile Trauma Stress Disorder. I thought:

I hate you, Nurse Kim. I hate you and your stupid catheter-y face.

That's what I said in my mind and in my heart.

I was trippin', man. But it would get worse before it got better.

THE THIRD AND FINAL NURSE

I already confessed to you the bitterness that I held in my heart toward Nurse Kim. But, you guys, that was not the extent of my sickness. I had this other nurse, who was a Latina woman. Listen, I know this is terrible, but I don't remember her name. Just remember, y'all, I was hopped up on a *lot* of drugs at that time in my life.

I don't remember her name, but I do remember that she was not a very good nurse. She didn't check on me enough. She'd forget things, even after being repeatedly asked. I was more than annoyed. I was angry. One night, I got so mad at this nurse that my mom had to tell me to calm down. At any rate, my angry interior monologue went something like this:

Okay, you listen here, Mrs. Latino Nurse Whose Name I Don't Know but Who Vaguely Reminds Me of Julianna

*Margulies but I Don't Want to Say That Because That Seems
a Bit Racisty.*

*I don't like you! I don't care for you one bit. I kinda hate
you right now, actually. And then I said:*

"Do you need me to call someone who can help you do
your job?"

(That was a real thing I actually said to her real face.)

*And then I thought, "I hate you as much as I hate Nurse
Kim, but for different reasons.*

"You have one job. Look. After. Your. Patients."

What I didn't know then, but what I know now, is that I was
not in a good space. Do you remember 2020? Nobody was in a good
space in December of 2020. We were exhausted. We were tired. We
were lonely. We were scared.

And all these things were happening in the world that were
scary and terrible that we needed to lament, and we weren't able to
because we couldn't really come together to mourn or process or discuss these things.

And the internet, which made promises that it would help
with communication, actually made things a lot worse. The ano-
nymity of the medium simply enhanced communicative distance
and made human connection and empathy next to impossible. It
was bad.

In addition, because of the way the internet works with clicks,
the *very worst people* on the internet were gaining way too much
attention. The way to get more clicks is not with empathy, or
thoughtful, nuanced dialogue, but by evoking anger and outrage.
The outrage-makers began trolling the internet, and they were getting rewarded for it.

And during 2020, during that year, unbeknownst to me then (but knownst to me now) I was slowly growing cynical about the world. And that cynicism was making me angry.

I was like a frog, getting slowly simmered in a society of anger and bitterness.

During that time, it became easier and easier for me to slip into looking at the world with antagonism. And like you already heard me talk about, when bad things happen, we need to lament properly and in safe places with safe people. If we don't have that—and during 2020 we did *not* have that—then that grief turns to anger and worse.

It can turn to despair.

Yeah, I had twenty-seven pounds of cancer inside me during 2020, but that wasn't the worst thing I was carrying around in my body.

The worst thing was this hate I'd allowed to metastasize inside my soul. And it kinda felt like something was going to explode.

Little did I know how right I would be.

THE GUY WHO TRIED TO BOMB CHRISTMAS

On the morning of Christmas Day 2020, I was still looped up on drugs and barely conscious. At six a.m., the nurses woke me up to check on me. I don't remember much, but one of the nurses said something like "Merry Christmas" and handed me a fleece Vanderbilt blanket as a Christmas present. She might have been wearing a Santa cap or something cute and festive like that. And I think I remember thinking, "Heck of a way to spend Christmas."

A few blocks away, Nashville police officers Amanda Topping and James Wells approached what appeared to be an abandoned RV.

Some neighbors had heard gunfire and reported a suspicious vehicle parked right on Second Avenue North in Nashville's entertainment district. As the officers approached, they heard an ominous message blaring from the RV. It was a woman's voice.

"Stay clear of this vehicle.
"Evacuate now.
"Do not approach this vehicle!"

At 6:15 a.m., the voice grew more insistent, warning people to evacuate. And then a fifteen-minute countdown started. The officers called for a bomb squad, and soon, more officers arrived and began helping to clear the area, knocking on doors to make sure residents were evacuated.

Then, at 6:30 a.m., the countdown stopped, and the recording switched. In the dead quiet of the abandoned street, the RV's speaker began to eerily play Petula Clark's 1964 hit song "Downtown."

When you're alone
and life is making you lonely,
you can always go
Downtown.

Seconds later, the RV exploded in a giant orange fireball seen and heard from miles away.

The windows in my hospital room, which was not very far away from Second Avenue, rattled and shook as the explosion's shockwaves rippled through downtown Nashville. The lights in the room and hallway flickered. Car alarms and alerts and sirens began blaring down below. Smoke rose in the distance.

I was vaguely aware of a sudden frenzy of activity among the doctors and nurses.

Then I passed out. That's all I remember about the Nashville bombing on Christmas Day 2020.

A SOLITARY MAN

In the hours and days immediately after the explosion, the FBI began searching for clues about who was responsible for the explosion and what their motive was. Thankfully, there was only one fatality from the explosion, and that was the suicide bomber. There was a lot of property damage, though. Even right now, years later, when you drive through that area, they are still rebuilding and reconstructing those buildings.

But in a lot of ways, the Christmas Day Nashville bombing didn't "fit" with some of the more clear definitions of terrorism. Yes, it involved a suicide bomber and a car fitted with a homemade explosive device, but:

- The bomber warned people to evacuate, in order to minimize death.
- There wasn't a manifesto.
- The bomber didn't seem to do this to gain attention to a cause.
- There wasn't a clear political or religious motive.
- The bomb involved his own death, but no one else's.

The bombing turned out to be the work of a sixty-three-year-old man from Nashville named Anthony Q. Warner.

Less than a week before Christmas, Warner's neighbor, Rick Laude, said he saw him standing at his mailbox. Laude said he casually joked, "Is Santa going to bring you anything good for Christmas?" Warner smiled and said, "Oh, yeah, Nashville and the world is never going to forget me," Laude recalled to police.[3]

While opening presents on Christmas morning, another neighbor, Crystal Beck, heard news reports about the bombing and knew immediately it was Warner. A few weeks earlier she had found him fiddling with a prerecorded female voice on his laptop. And he had played her the 1964 Petula Clark hit "Downtown," praising the song's "significant spirit."[4] She called the police immediately.

Pretty soon, the FBI traced the RV back to Anthony Warner and searched his house, and determined he was the culprit. But there was still one big, lingering question. Why? What caused Anthony Warner to do this? The answer was shocking:

Isolation.

Actually, that's not too shocking to me. Being alone can do things to a person. Somehow, I understood that and felt that. Deep in my bones.

For years, Anthony Warner had become more and more isolated from people. And this had been exacerbated by the pandemic. And he became more and more obsessed with conspiracy theories that led him to distrust not only the government but his fellow

3.   "After Naming Nashville Bombing Suspect, Focus Turns to Motive," PBS News-Hour, December 28, 2020. https://www.pbs.org/newshour/nation/after-naming -nashville-bombing-suspect-focus-turns-to-motive.
4.   Steve Cavendish et al., "Behind the Nashville Bombing, a Conspiracy Theorist Stewing about the Government," New York Times, February 24, 2021, updated June 2, 2021. https://www.nytimes.com/2021/02/24/us/anthony-warner-nashville -bombing.html.

citizens. In addition to believing that 9/11 was an "inside job," Warner believed that Queen Elizabeth II and George W. Bush (and his father and brother) were reptilian aliens who could shape-shift and were plotting to control the world. Yep. You read that right.[5]

A little while ago, the FBI released their complete report of their investigation of the bombing, and I was struck by these lines:

> *The FBI assesses Warner's detonation of the improvised explosive device was an intentional act in an effort to end his own life, driven in part by a totality of life stressors—including paranoia, long-held individualized beliefs adopted from several eccentric conspiracy theories, and the loss of stabilizing anchors and deteriorating interpersonal relationships.*[6]

This dude blew up downtown Nashville on Christmas Day because he was *alone*. Damn.

- No "stabilizing" anchors of love and friendship and family
- Deteriorating interpersonal relationships

---

5. It gets better. In one *New York Times* profile I read, they said that Warner liked to go camping at the Montgomery Bell State Park (just west of Nashville) because— and I am not making this up—he considered the park to be prime ground for hunting alien reptilians who he believed had invaded the world. At one point, Warner described struggling to spot them with an infrared device, believing they could adjust their body temperature to the surrounding environment, and warned that bullets would just bounce off. "If you try to hunt one, you will find that you are the one being hunted," he wrote. Cavendish, "Behind the Nashville Bombing." https://www.nytimes.com/2021/02/24/us/anthony-warner-nashville-bombing.html.

6. "FBI Releases Report on Nashville Bombing," FBI Memphis, March 15, 2021. https://www.fbi.gov/contact-us/field-offices/memphis/news/press-releases/fbi-releases-report-on-nashville-bombing.

- Which made him more and more isolated
- And more and more paranoid

I thought about his final message to the world, broadcast from his RV. The final words that Anthony Warner heard:

> When you're alone
> and life is making you lonely,
> you can always go
> Downtown.

As I sat in my hospital bed in the days after the explosion, I realized that Anthony Warner was a cautionary tale. Like a lighthouse, whose beacon warns of the impending dangers of the rocky shoreline, his tragedy and violent end were a warning to everyone in Nashville.

And me especially.

"Distance breeds suspicion.
Proximity breeds empathy."[7]

YOU CAN FIND ME IN DA CLUB

The thing is, because of my cancer, I was learning more than I ever wanted to about feeling isolated. When you're told you have cancer, you're in a special group. It's a fraternity that you don't want to be invited into. And you're not in this group unless you've been in a room and a doctor says those words that you'll never forget.

---

7.   This is a quote from Bryan Loritts, which I used as the opening quote in Chapter 10 of my last book, *I Take My Coffee Black*.

"You have cancer."

It's a lonely, lonely place. And here's why: you can't really *talk* about it. I mean you can, but it's so challenging to explain it to other people.

Here's why: nearly everyone has been affected by cancer in some way, but the spectrum of outcomes is so varied and so wide that you can't get a baseline of understanding with people.

For example, I have a friend, Cathleen, who had colon cancer a bit ago. It was an *ordeal*, people. She went through twelve rounds of intravenous chemotherapy, with each session taking about five hours. She had a surgery called a "resection" where they removed about a third of her colon. And medically, that worked. She's okay now. She's in remission.

I have another friend named Elysha who has a cancer I can't even spell. She has to take these pills called antimetabolites that stop the growth of cancer cells. She takes these pills twice a week, and they keep her cancer at bay. For her, she takes pills, and she's okay. Like my buddy Mike does with Claritin during allergy season.

So when I told them I had cancer, Elysha's frame of reference was "You'll be fine."

But Elysha didn't know if I'd be fine.

She didn't even know what kind of cancer I had.

Think how different my cancer was. It was a surgical cancer. Chemo didn't touch it. Radiation would do nothing.

And Cathleen? She hadn't even been diagnosed with her cancer yet. Think how differently she'd respond now as opposed to back then.

But Cathleen and Elysha were doing what we all do—just operating based on their experience.

For some people, when they hear "cancer," they think of the breast cancer that ravaged their mother and took her life. For others, it reminds them of their uncle who had a weird mole removed. For some, it's like hearing "I'm going to die." For others, it's no different than saying "I have strep throat."

And all that makes living with cancer confusing.

You can't explain to someone what it is you're feeling and what you're going through. It's so isolating.

When Dr. Tan told me that I had cancer, it was like the room went dark, and everybody disappeared from view. Except me.

And I began to withdraw. I didn't want to tell anyone. It felt like too much to explain. I didn't want people's pity.

But I also kinda did.

But I didn't *want* to want their pity.

I was scared. Hell, I still am.

Having cancer affected the way I looked at money. I'm single with no kids. Why should I care about saving up for a big retirement account when there's no guarantee I'm even going to be around? Why not spend the money on experiences with people I love?

Having cancer affected the way I eat. When you have cancer, you should probably try your best to eat well and healthy. But I have cancer. So screw that. I want pizza. And maybe some Reese's peanut butter cups. Or some Nerds. Just dump a container of Nerds in my mouth and I will go back to when I was six and Fun Dip was the best food known to humankind.

All this feels lonely.

It affects me in ways I don't like to share with people.

The point is, I think I understood Anthony Warner better than I'd like to admit.

Look, solitary confinement is the worst punishment that humans can inflict on one another. It literally causes us to lose our minds. That's how social we, as creatures, are. I don't care if you're an anthropologist or a theologian, your conclusions are going to be identical.

We just weren't created to be alone.

Some of you know exactly what I'm talking about. And I want to say something to you. Forgive me for the statement that I'm about to make, because I hate it when people say this phrase, but I have to say it.

"You are not alone."

Now, whenever someone used to say that to me, I would roll my eyes. It made me think, "Whatever, man, you don't understand my life."

But the older I get, the more I realized something important about life. *Feeling* alone is not the same as *being* alone. Most of us, if we look around, we don't have to look that far to find someone who genuinely cares about us. Who loves us.

"Feeling alone" and "being alone" are two very different things.

So hear me. You may feel very alone right now. And that feeling may be so strong, it feels like the truest thing about you. But I would bet my very last dollar that there are people out there who are there for you.

- They care about you.
- They care about the real you.
- They care about your well-being.
- They care about your tomorrow.
- They would drop everything to help you if you needed it.
- They would say, "My life is better, in so many ways, because of you."

I know this to be true because, even though I don't know you at all, I am here, typing this almost in tears, wishing that I could look you in the eye and tell you that it's me who cares about you.

Because I do.

Also, don't you ever say you have no one, because you know for damn sure that you've got a friend in the diamond business at Shane Company.

SHAKEN AWAKE

In the days and hours after the bombing, the doctors and nurses at Vanderbilt Hospital were buzzing from the news of the event, and in my sedated state, I caught bits and pieces of the story from the streets below.

I don't remember when this happened, but I do remember this moment, in my hospital bed. There I was, stewing in my own anger and self-focused ickiness, mentally cussing out Nurse Julianna Margulies. And I heard someone talk about the bombing.

The bombing?

What bombing?

Someone bombed Nashville? My town?

And in that moment, my thoughts and attention were ripped away from myself to the city I loved. I instantly grew deeply afraid for my friends and family in the town. Was anyone hurt? Were my friends safe? Did the police catch the guy?

And for the first time since I'd woken up, I felt like I'd...well... woken up. There was a world outside, that I loved and cared about, that was hurting. And that mattered. At least as much as what was going on with me.

I'd lost sight of that.

Hospitals are very sobering places. They're very black-and-white places. And they cause you to deal with uncomfortable realities, whether you want to or not. In the hospital, you have a lot of time to just think. Having major surgery forces you to take stock.

I not only didn't like what was going on inside of me, but I didn't like what was going on *inside* of me.

LEARNING TO WALK AGAIN.
I BELIEVE I'VE WAITED LONG ENOUGH.

I had work to do.

I thought about my Latino nurse. I found out later that, like so many other people during that time period, the pandemic had put a lot of strain on her family financially. It did for a lot of people. Because of that, she'd signed up for as many overtime holiday-pay shifts as she could. She was working back-to-back-to-back shifts.

Dang.

Do you think she *wanted* to be away from her family on Christmas Eve and Christmas Day? To miss that time with her loved ones? No.

Another moment that shook me awake. As I mentioned, I was in the ICU for a big chunk of my time. There were people on that floor who were really sick. And there were people on that floor not that far from me who would later die. At one point, I heard a woman down the hall wailing because she'd been given the news that the person in the bed next to her was not getting better and was dying. There was nothing the hospital could do. Death was approaching rapidly. I didn't know the whole story. Was that her sister next to her? Her husband? Her mother?

And over the sobs of grief, I heard the Latino nurse comforting her.

Minutes later, the nurse walked by, and I could tell she'd been crying.

This woman was not a bad nurse. And she certainly was not a bad person. In fact, from the deep empathy I had just seen, she was a great person.

I thought about the toll her job had likely taken on her. I wondered if she was scared of getting COVID. I wondered if she worried about her family's safety. About her loved ones. And I bet she was just exhausted, doing her very best to provide for her family during a tough time.

I looked beyond how she had affected me to see a little bit more of her total humanity.

Then I thought about Nurse Kim.

Was Nurse Kim really evil? I mean, really? The woman was just advocating for me to be as safe and healthy as possible. She wasn't trying to be mean. Her reasons for wanting to put the catheter back in were all about helping me, making sure I didn't get an infection, or develop a problem, or whatever it was that would have happened to my penis!

Where was her focus, honestly?

It was on helping me. And yet I was mad at her? Because it might cause me some discomfort? I called her "evil" and harbored bad thoughts about her because she was trying to . . . what? . . . help me?

I shook my head at myself.

I realized I had a long recovery ahead of me.

And not all of it had to do with my cancer.

CHAPTER 6

TELL ME, DID YOU FALL
FOR A SHOOTING STAR?
ONE WITHOUT
A PERMANENT SCAR?

It's the first week of October. A few days ago, I walked into a store and saw they had Christmas decorations up.

Now, this makes some people mad.

Some people think there should be a Constitutional amendment preventing Christmas decor from being purchased or sold across state lines until after Thanksgiving. Those people have dark hearts and need to be added to your grandmama's prayer list.

I say let's just skip the whole Pumpkin Spice Industrial Complex altogether and jump right on into Cinnamon Spice and Brown Paper Packages Tied Up with String.

At any rate, at least I learned that there are eighty-three shopping days until Christmas.[1]

---

1. I think this is a good time to ask you: who was your favorite Spice Girl? Mine was Scary Spice. I just didn't like that they called her "Scary" Spice. Why not go with "Cinnamon Spice"?

Christmas has always been my favorite holiday, but after my surgery, it's been colored with something new: a mixture of sober reflection and gratitude. After all, as we found out from my mother just a bit ago, I almost *freaking* died on Christmas. So the holidays are tempered with the memory and trauma of that operation. Secondly, that "cancer clock" that keeps ticking is a wake-up call. It's a reminder that makes me keenly aware that there's no promise about how many Christmases I am going to have going forward, so each one is a little more precious to me.

Also, if you ever have the chance to spend Christmas in a hospital, I'd advise *not* doing that. 0/10. Do not recommend. I still remember the festive green-and-white-and-red decorations in the hospital rooms at Vanderbilt Medical Center. I know they were trying to add a nice touch, but it's like trying to throw a birthday party in a morgue.

The balloon bouquet is lovely, Janice, and these gifts are wrapped immaculately, but oopsie, I think you left the tag on that one...no... oh...no...that's attached to the toe of a dead guy. Suddenly I don't want cake, Janice.

Okay, now I'm grossed out thinking about serving a Baskin-Robbins ice cream cake on those sterile, stainless steel surgical tables they have in morgues. Yuck. Ick. Blech. But also...I mean...ice cream cake.

Anyway, as you recall, I was admitted to the hospital on December 23. It was now almost a week later, and the doctors were just trying to stabilize me enough so that I could recuperate in a more comfortable environment, namely my home in Nashville. They had me walk around the wing of the hospital using a walker. It hurt to walk. Man, did it hurt to walk. Anything that jostled my insides even a little was miserable. The doctors and nurses continued to monitor my flatulence with a precision that should not be allowed by anyone over the age of ten.

But the pain was getting better. And I didn't need a breathing tube anymore.

Finally, the doctors made a determination that I was well enough to be discharged on December 30. My mother drove me back home that day and stayed with me for the next few weeks. She did her best impersonation of a live-in nurse for the second leg of my long road to recovery.

Have I mentioned recently how amazing my mother is? She really is the best. I want to use this moment to do something. If you are still lucky enough to have your mother around, go ahead and pause this book and go and call your mother. Just put the book down, pick up the phone, and call your mama. Let her know she's a queen.

I'll wait.

Did you tell your mom I said hello? I kind of feel like you could have at least done that. Since I was the reason you even called her in the first place. But whatev.

WE...ARE NEVER, EVER, EVER... GETTING BACK TOGETHER

I had two issues in this stage of my recovery. The first had to do with the fact that I was down one kidney. I was told by my doctors that I would need to "drink more water and cut down on my salt intake."

What my doctors meant was "no added salt in your diet and check the nutritional information." What my mother heard was "no salt in anything that Tyler eats for the rest of his life or he'll die."

My mom cooked for me the next two weeks, and let me tell you, it is the healthiest I have eaten perhaps in my entire life. It was also the absolute worst.

Do y'all know how good salt is? You have no idea how good it is. No, you don't. You take it for granted, and day after day, you don't realize just how good you have it, and you won't know until someone comes along and snatches one of your kidneys. And the very first day that the salt is gone will be the very first day that you realize how much salt did for you, only you never realized it. Have you ever taken time to thank salt? No? No, you haven't. I have. Then, and only then, will you understand the enormity of the role that salt played in making your life what it is: better.

Salt makes life worth living.

Salt is life.

Also, you have no idea how *much salt* is in everything. I don't know about the rest of y'all's races, but us Black folks love us some salt. Come to think of it, there's a lot of salt in a lot of good minority food.

Latino people. Salt is everywhere in Mexican food. On the chips, in the guacamole, around the rim of that margarita.

Asian people. You guys invented MSG. Also, can we keep it real? Soy sauce is just salt in brown, liquidy form.

Hawaiian people. Y'all put *rock salt* on your kalua pork. Giant pebbles of salt. Respect.

Black people. All our best foods are heavy in salt. Collard greens. Fried green tomatoes. Fried chicken. None of this is low-sodium, people. And everything has butter on it, and that butter has salt in it.

White people. Now, some of you might be wondering: what is "white people food"? Is it hot dogs and apple pie? No. White people food is casseroles.[2]

White people, you know y'all love you some casseroles. Think of all the casseroles y'all just invent, for no good reason. You be throwing everything in a casserole. Three examples:

Green beans.

Are they delicious and tasty when prepared on their own?
Yes.
Do you just need to blanch or steam them, and add some butter and salt?
Yes.
Would that be delicious?
Yes.
Do white people do that?
No.
They say, "Okay first of all, let's stay away from fresh green beans. Let's make sure they're from a can. That way, they have a better chance of being rubbery, which is the texture we're going for. And then we'll pour them into a white porcelain Corningware dish,

---

2. And listen, all you white people who aren't from the Midwest, and who know what real cooking is, I'm just playing with you. And I know all you white people from the South know how to cook. As Jen Hatmaker once said, salt is practically a food group for y'all. I'm just making some funny broad generalizations about that group of white people who think Velveeta is a legitimate type of cheese.

preferably with some blue French flower symbols on the side, and then we will cover them—and I mean drown them like those men in the boiler room on the *Titanic*—in some sort of thick soup. It's gotta be from a can, of course, and condensed, and cream-based. Just dump that in there. And then we'll put some onion rings on top. But not real onion rings! No! We're gonna need some fake, processed onion rings. Like from a can. Like Pringles. Think one level up from Funyuns, because that's…well…classy. Boom! Green. Bean. Casserole!"

Sweet Potatoes.

Are these delicious and tasty when prepared on their own?
Yes.
Do you just need to bake them and add some butter and salt?
Yes.
Would they be delicious?
Yes.
Do white people do that?
No?
They say, "Hey, guys, you know how we prepare every single other potato by wrapping it in foil in an oven, or turning them into fries? Well, just a wild idea here. What if we took this potato, and instead of doing that, let's cut them into giant blocks and put them in our largest, say blue-and-white nine-by-thirteen-inch baking dish that sits in our bottom cabinet. Then we'll plop on in some orange juice concentrate and just a little dippy bit of Jack Daniel's. Then we'll cook it until they turn into mush, like literally, wet orange mush. Imagine Ernie from *Sesame Street* in a wood chipper. And then let's

cover the whole thing with marshmallows and chopped nuts, like you would a banana split. Boom! Sweet. Potato. Casserole!"

Jell-O.

Is Jell-O delicious and tasty when prepared on its own?

No. Not really.

Do you just need to prepare it in individual bowls or cups and add some whipped cream?

Sure, still not great, but yes.

Would that be delicious?

Again, questionable.

Do white people do that?

No.

They say, "Okay, guys. How about this? How about instead of following the clear directions on the package, why don't we pour the whole thing in a nine-by-thirteen-inch baking dish that we don't ever remember buying but has somehow always been in our kitchen, buried deep in the bowels of our cabinets. Yes. And then let's dump some fruit in there. But not fresh fruit, like strawberries or raspberries. No, let's go with canned fruit cocktail. Make sure the can says 'heavy syrup,' okay? Because all the *best* fruit comes packed in syrup. And then we'll just mix it around and let it chill for several hours. Because the only thing better than eating Jell-O is eating Jell-O with a processed grape embedded in it. Oh, and if we don't have canned fruit cocktail, don't worry! We can always just dump in some shredded carrots. Because the Jell-O is orange, and carrots are orange, so it works. And then we'll call it a Jell-O *salad*. Are we stretching the semantic range of the word 'salad' to its logical breaking point? Sure we are. But no worries, because it's served in our finest casserole dish, so it's a casserole, dammit. Boom! Jell-O. Fruit. Carrot. Casserole."

Wait. Where were we? Oh, yeah, white people and the general lack of salt in your food. Can the other races maybe help you find some seasoning?

Hmm. Maybe all white people only have one kidney.

Anyhoo, for the next two weeks my mom cooked for me. Vegetables without salt. Grits without salt. Onions and zucchini, without salt. I realized I don't like onions unless they're in ring form, then fried, and then heavily salted. Then dipped in ketchup, which is just red, liquidy salt. Red soy sauce, if you will.

The point is, all the healthy things I was supposed to do, my mom was making sure I was doing.

I had one more medical concern, and that had to do with caring for the giant incision the surgeons had to make to get into my body. I had a huge cut that ran from my sternum straight down my chest about eighteen inches. Just a huge line that looked like someone had Sawzalled me from my nipples down past my belly button.

Also—and this is crazy, people—do you want to know how the surgeons make sure this wound heals properly? I'm sure in the twenty-first century, where we have untold computing power on the phones in our pockets and self-driving cars, you wonder what kind of high-tech solution medical professionals use for incision care. Lasers? Nanobots? AI?

Nope.

They glued my ass together and then finished it off with some staples. Staples!

Like I was a second-grade art project. I'm not joking. They take a special medical superglue that bonds to skin. (I think it's called DermaBond, *derma* from the Latin word for "skin" and *Bond* from the Latin word for "Special Agent who goes rogue and frustrates his superiors, but gets the job done eventually.")

The doctors just stuck the two superglued sides together. Then they stapled the wound together with a staple gun. If what you're picturing is a staple gun used in construction projects, then that's about what it looks like. I am told these staples are different because they're sterilized and bend differently to hold the wound together. Whatever. It looked like Bob the Builder had come in and stapled my tummy.

So, to recap, the doctors and surgeons stapled and glued my giant wound.

And the staples did not feel good. I don't think, as humans, our midsections are meant to be stapled. Maybe the staples themselves were mad.

"Here I was, hoping to be used to hold electrical wire to a two-by-four inside a nice Victorian home and I got stuck holding this Black guy's stomach together."

Did I just write the imaginary interior monologue of a staple? Y'all are six chapters deep by now. You should know this is what I do.

But none of that stuff bothered me that much.

But there *was* one thing that bothered me. I had to clean and dress the wound, to make sure it didn't get infected or anything. I hated looking at the wound.

In fact, I *couldn't* look at it.

I literally could not.

Whenever I got out of the shower, I purposely didn't look at my stomach. It creeped me out something fierce. In fact, it creeped me out *too* much.

FEARLESS (TYLER'S VERSION)

It turns out, there's a psychological diagnosis for what I have. It's called "trypophobia," and it is a fear (a phobia) of the sight of regular patterns, especially clusters of small holes or bumps. It's a real medical diagnosis.[3]

Whenever I tell people this, they always say, "You're making that up." And then they google it. Go ahead. I know you want to. Go google it.

See? I wasn't making it up.

Researchers have studied two main theories about why this phobia exists. A working theory is that some venomous creatures exhibit trypophobic patterns[4]—like the eight eyes of a tarantula or the skin patterns on some snakes. Another theory is that there are several deadly skin diseases, such as smallpox, that create clusters of circular lesions. So these are meant to creep humans out and make them stay away.

All I can tell you, when I look at something with tiny little holes in it, it just freaks me out. From coral reefs to pomegranates to sponges, man, I hate all of it.

Lucky for me, I didn't have to deal with the staples for *that* long. About two weeks later, on January 12, the doctor called me to come in to have them removed.

Whatever you think of when you hear the expression "staple removal," that was pretty much the process. I was expecting some sort of numbing solution, but no. The doctor just started taking this small tool (which looked a little like a butter knife) and started

---

3. Geoff G. Cole and Arnold J. Wilkins, "Fear of Holes," *Psychological Science* 24, no. 10 (2013): 1980–1985. https://pubmed.ncbi.nlm.nih.gov/23982244/.

4. Trisha Pasricha, MD, "Why Do Tiny Holes Freak Me Out?" *Washington Post*, August 28, 2023. https://www.washingtonpost.com/wellness/2023/08/28/trypophobia-tiny-holes-fear/.

ripping the staples in my stomach out, like an angry accountant at tax season. There were about forty total staples, I'd imagine, but it felt like there were about 525,600.

It was interminable.

And it was gross. The line down my stomach was a mess of black skin, and there were still some raw, pink parts where some of the incision was not quite healed. And man, every staple hurt. And the doctor dude just kept going and going. He was reassuring me, "We're almost done."

But he was lying.

He was not almost done.

I think at one point, I started yelping like a wounded dog. Perhaps this was my subconscious way of trying to evoke empathy from the cruel physician, Dr. Staple. Maybe if I made a noise like a wounded puppy, he'd stop, or slow down. This did not work.

Dr. Staple hated me and, apparently, he hated puppies, too.

After he was done, he put a special antibiotic ointment on the incision, and that was that. With the staples gone, I looked down at my nearly healed stomach.

And that's when the ish got real.

With the staples and their tiny holes removed, I was finally able to look at my naked abdomen. It was abundantly clear that the operation would leave me with quite the scar. I was forced to look at it, and I knew I would live with it for the rest of my life. As scary as it was, this would be a sign of BC and AD. Before Cancer and After Diagnosis.[5] This scar was also the thing that made me realize that I had been changed, irrevocably, by this Christmas experience in the hospital.

---

5. Damn. That was actually pretty clever. Proud of me for that.

My body was now different, in some important ways, by the cancer. But it was deeper than that. The scar was an icon; a physical reminder pointing to something else.

My body had been forever changed.

I knew then that I needed to change, too.

OUT OF THE WOODS

Coming out of the hospital was a fitting metaphor for my reentry into the real world. As we learned last chapter, in a little more than a week, I went from:

- Having a heart-to-heart with God, promising that I would never take life for granted ever again and would work every day to make the world a better place if He'd just get me through this operation...to...
- Ripping my care nurse a new one because she didn't get me a sippy cup of juice fast enough.

I remembered back to that moment in the hospital, when I was mentally cussing out the Latino ICU nurse, stewing in my own anger and self-focused ickiness. I not only didn't like what was going on inside of me, I didn't like what was going on *inside* of me. You feel me?

Leaving the hospital was reentry into the world, and I had some decisions to make about how I was going to live and what I was going to change. I felt like one of those guys who made a last-second plea: "God, if you get me out of this, I swear I'll do anything." And then God gets you out of it, and you promptly forget you even made that promise.

I didn't want to be *that* guy. But I didn't know the way forward.

As I looked down at myself, I saw the giant, eighteen-inch-long zippered scar that bisected my stomach, running from my belly button to my sternum.

Listen, I make no apologies for the way I see the world. As a Black man, I tend to pull from particular things to give me strength during difficult moments, and a lot of times those stories come directly from the fertile soil of my culture and my historical legacy as a Black person in America.

In this moment, I could not help but look at my scar and think about one of my personal heroes.

I couldn't help but think about how this man had scars that defined him in a way that he could never have anticipated.

His scars were the way forward for him.

I knew in that moment that my scar had to mean something more.

I KNEW YOU WERE TROUBLE WHEN YOU WALKED IN

Nearly six months before my diagnosis, back in July of 2020, the world lost a legend. John Lewis, the civil rights activist turned congressman from Georgia, died.

John Lewis was a hero of mine, for a number of reasons. In fact, one of my prized possessions is a picture of me and the legend himself.

Lewis was a tireless worker. He was one of the thirteen original Freedom Riders, who rode buses to protest bus segregation.

It's always crazy for me to think how recent this was, but it was just in 1946 that the Supreme Court banned segregated busing for all interstate trips.[6] But the South was gonna South and continued to segregate all bus terminals, restrooms, and other facilities associated with interstate travel. But then, in the winter of 1958, Bruce Boynton, a Black law student from Howard University, was arrested for eating in a "whites only" restaurant at a bus station in Virginia. So he sued for a violation of his constitutional rights, and in *Boynton v. Virginia*, in 1960, the Supreme Court[7] found making bus terminals and stations segregated was *also* unconstitutional. And what do you know, this did not go over well in the South. They didn't like the "Northern intrusion" on their God-given right to remove Black people from white people spaces. So they refused to cooperate. So in May of 1961, a group of seven African Americans and six whites left Washington, DC, on a Freedom Ride[8] in two buses bound for the Deep South (New Orleans, actually). They knew Southern white people would likely violently protest their constitutional right to, say, use the restroom or eat in restaurants marked as "white only," but they hoped to bring attention to the issue and provoke the federal government to enforce the *Boynton* decision.

John Lewis was one of those first thirteen people.

Lewis also helped organize and lead groups of people from the Northern states to help register Black folks in the South. He led the sit-ins right here in Nashville to protest segregated lunch counters and the Jim Crow laws that allowed for such things. He was arrested dozens of times—forty instances in the 1960s alone—and

---

6.   Because these bus trips were between two (or more) states, the Court ruled this fell under federal law and the Interstate Commerce Act.

7.   "*Boynton v. Virginia*," Oyez, n.d. https://www.oyez.org/cases/1960/7.

8.   "Freedom Riders," History.com, February 2, 2010, updated January 20, 2022. https://www.history.com/topics/black-history/freedom-rides.

faced angry and violent opponents as he fought for desegregation and the equal inclusion and dignity of Black people in American civil life.

What a lot of folks don't know (but is one of my favorite things about John Lewis) is that he was one of the primary organizers for the famous 1963 March on Washington.[9] You know Dr. King's famous "I Have a Dream" speech? Well, Lewis stepped up to the microphone right before that. He was the youngest speaker that day.

Just for those reasons alone, he was always a bit like a rock star to me. But that's not all.

John Lewis had a scar.

In fact, he had several of them. Multiple scars. On his head. Near his ear. Above his eyebrow. As he got older, the scars and cuts became somehow less prominent, visually fading as time passed.

And as I looked at *my* scar, I thought about one of Lewis's scars in particular.

There's a bigger one, on his forehead. John Lewis even said once in an interview, "'From time to time, looking in a mirror, I tend to notice it."[10]

And the story about how he got *that* scar? Well, buckle in, because it's a powerful one.

It was March of 1965, and John Lewis was marching with thousands of Black people as they traveled roughly fifty miles from Selma, Alabama, to the state capital of Montgomery for the right to . . .

---

9. https://www.loc.gov/item/2011645462/
10. Susan Page, "Appreciation: For John Lewis, a Lifetime of Making 'Good Trouble' Left Scars and a Legacy," *USA Today*, July 18, 2020, updated July 22, 2020. https://www.usatoday.com/story/news/politics/2020/07/18/john-lewis-and-good-trouble-left-scars-and-legacy-nation/5464195002/.

<pause for dramatic effect>
VOTE.

Some background: at that time, the population of Dallas County, where Selma was located, was 57 percent Black, but of the 15,000 Blacks old enough to vote, only 130 were registered (fewer than 1 percent).[11] White city leaders enacted all sorts of tricks to prevent Black people from voting so they could win all the elections and retain political power. These tricks included:

- Poll taxes (which poor Black folks couldn't pay)
- Literacy tests (Black citizens didn't have the same access to education as white people)
- Impossibly hard civics quizzes (Example: Who was the Secretary of the Interior under John Quincy Adams?)

And you guessed it. All of this was perfectly legal at the time. This was all designed to keep the white leaders in power. It's always about power or money, isn't it? At any rate, Lewis had been trying to register Black people to vote, but the white-powers-that-be really didn't want that.

Lewis went on the march to Birmingham expecting to get arrested. What he didn't expect was to be physically assaulted by the Alabama Highway Patrol.

But that's exactly what happened.

In anticipation of the march, county sheriff Jim Clark had issued an order for all white men over the age of twenty-one to report to the courthouse that morning to be deputized. They were given batons

---

11. "Selma to Montgomery Marches," Wikipedia.com, https://en.wikipedia.org/wiki /Selma_to_Montgomery_marches.

and riot gear and instructed to attack the peaceful protesters if they crossed the Edmund Pettus Bridge leading to Selma. Never mind that many of the people marching were women. Or elderly. The orders were given.

Beat back the Black people.

As the group crossed the bridge, they were told via loudspeaker by Jim Clark to turn back. When they did not, the troopers moved forward and began shoving those marching, knocking many to the ground and beating them with their batons and nightsticks. Another detachment of troopers fired tear gas, and mounted troopers charged the crowd on horseback.

John Lewis was right there on the front line.

That day in Selma was critical in the Civil Rights Movement because it showed the brutality and ugly racism of Alabama. That night, Americans saw on their television the brutal attack *by the police* on the nonviolent marchers, many of whom were left bloodied and injured simply because they wanted to

<checks notes again>

VOTE.

This event roused support for the civil rights campaign. Images from the Edmund Pettus Bridge were on the front page of newspapers around the world.

And a twenty-five-year-old John Lewis was right there.

Right in the front.

In all, seventeen civil rights marchers were hospitalized, and fifty were treated for injuries. And here's the thing I want to focus on: during that day at the Edmund Pettus Bridge, John Lewis suffered a skull fracture. The police literally cracked his skull.

And John Lewis would have scars on his head from that day for the rest of his life.

At one point, Lewis was in the hospital, recovering from the attack, and he looked in a mirror and saw his scar.

And in that moment, John Lewis realized he had a hard choice to make. Was he going to allow anger and hatred to harden him and his heart against his attackers? Or would he listen to the wisdom of his mentors, like Reverend Dr. Martin Luther King Jr., and forgive?

Was he going to get bitter?

Or get better?

That scar was a symbol of his choice.

A scar.

In a book of his essays that was published posthumously, Lewis wrote about this choice, saying, "Having compassion for your attacker means you harbor no malice and seek no retribution for the wrong that has been done. It is an offering of love that asserts the victim's self-worth."[12]

This thought is profound to me.

If you want to seek justice and a better world, you can't go after it with a heart full of anger or hate. If you do, you'll be going after vengeance, not justice. You'll be like John Wick, wanting to exact some measure of punishment from someone because they did something wrong. Granted, it was super messed up that those gangsters killed his puppy, but man, that's a lot of death, Keanu. In retaliation for a dog. I mean, I like puppies, too, but you need to learn to forgive, my man.

One of my favorite quotes about forgiveness is from the master orator himself, the Reverend Dr. Martin Luther King Jr., who in a sermon in Detroit titled simply "Love Your Enemies" put it like this:

---

12. John Lewis, *Across That Bridge*. Grand Central Publishing, Kindle Edition, p. 145.

We will meet your physical force with soul force. Do to us what you will, and we will still love you... And so put us in jail, and we will go in with humble smiles on our faces, still loving you. Bomb our homes and threaten our children, and we will still love you... Send your hooded perpetrators of violence into our communities at the midnight hours, and drag us out on some wayside road and beat us and leave us half dead, and we will still love you. But be assured that we will wear you down by our capacity to suffer. And one day we will win our freedom, but not only will we win freedom for ourselves, we will so appeal to your heart and conscience that we will win you in the process. And our victory will be a double victory.[13]

My God. We live in a time where everybody wants to quote MLK, but the kind of love he was talking about was absolutely radical. That kind of love is hard. That kind of love is difficult. That kind of love will cost you your very life. And that kind of love is world-changing.

True justice isn't just about putting things right, or making people pay, it's using forgiveness and love as a powerful redemptive tool that can actually change *other people* as you seek justice. As author Lewis Smedes once wrote, "You will know that forgiveness has begun when you recall those who hurt you and feel the power to wish them well."[14]

---

13. "Loving Your Enemies," Sermon Delivered at Dexter Avenue Baptist Church, The Martin Luther King, Jr. Research Institute, Stanford University. https://kinginstitute.stanford.edu/king-papers/documents/loving-your-enemies-sermon-delivered-dexter-avenue-baptist-church.
14. Lewis B. Smedes, *Forgive and Forget: Healing the Hurts We Don't Deserve*, Harper-One, 2007.

And that's when I had an epiphany, thanks to the scars of John Lewis.

I realized that, yes, my body was healing. But the most broken part of me wasn't my lungs, or my stomach, or my digestive system, or even my missing kidney. The most broken part of me was my heart.

I needed to relearn to breathe.

I needed to relearn to walk.

But I also needed to relearn how to love and forgive.

BETTER THAN REVENGE

After he died, so many people paid tribute to John Lewis. One of his most retweeted quotes was a beautiful and inspiring message about the power of forgiveness. Lewis said:[15]

> **John Lewis** ✓
> @repjohnlewis
>
> Do not get lost in a sea of despair. Do not become bitter or hostile. Be hopeful, be optimistic. Never, ever be afraid to make some noise and get in good trouble, necessary trouble. We will find a way to make a way out of no way. #goodtrouble
>
> 8:44 AM · Jul 16, 2019

I know I've been going on about John Lewis for a while now, but I can't leave without telling one more story about him that's just *mind-blowing*.

As I mentioned, Lewis was a Freedom Rider. And one night in 1961, the bus stopped at a Greyhound station in Rock Hill, South

---

15. John Lewis (@repjohnlewis), July 16, 2019. https://twitter.com/repjohnlewis /status/1151155571757867011.

Carolina. After Lewis got off the bus, he was attacked and beaten by a group of white men. Keeping with his deeply held religious beliefs about nonviolence, Lewis did not fight back.

Let me say that again.

He was attacked.

But he refused to fight back.

Later in life, one of those men who beat Lewis, a former Klansman whose name was Elwin Wilson, motivated by the election of Barack Obama and his own fear of hell, began examining his beliefs and life.[16] He realized he wanted to try to find the man he'd beaten all those years ago and seek his forgiveness. And that's when he discovered the man he'd beaten was John Lewis.

Wilson traveled all the way to Washington, DC, with his son. He met with Lewis and apologized for his actions.

Lewis recalled that after apologizing, the man said, "Mr. Lewis, will you forgive me? Do you accept my apology?"

Lewis said, "Yes I forgive you, I accept your apology."

Recalling that powerful moment, Lewis said, "The man's son started crying...he started crying and they hugged me and I hugged them both back and I started crying too, they started calling me brother and I called them brother."[17]

Elwin Wilson and his son visited John Lewis numerous times after that first encounter.

When asked if it was tough to accept the man's apology, Lewis didn't hesitate for a minute.

---

16. William Yardley, "Elwin Wilson, Who Apologized for Racist Acts, Dies at 76," *New York Times*, April 1, 2013. https://www.nytimes.com/2013/04/02/us/elwin-wilson-who-apologized-for-racist-acts-dies-at-76.html.

17. Borislava Manojlovic, "John Lewis," Love & Forgiveness in Governance, Seton Hall University, n.d. https://blogs.shu.edu/diplomacyresearch/2014/01/20/john-lewis/.

"It's in keeping with the philosophy of nonviolence," he said. "That's what the movement was always about, to have the capacity to forgive and move toward reconciliation."

This still hits me hard.

As I studied and reflected on John Lewis, his words and his life, I knew this was the right answer. John Lewis was right. I knew that embodying that kind of love was the right thing to do.

But there's a difference between "knowing" something and living it out.

Little did I know, there would be a moment very soon when I'd learn that difference.

A moment when I'd have a choice to live out these ideals (or not).

A simple moment, but a moment that would come to be incredibly defining for me.

And it happened the very next Christmas. A moment where I would become so frustrated with my family that I would go to bed wishing they would disappear, and then, through a series of comic events, my entire family would leave on vacation without me, leaving me alone to defend my house against two bungling burglars...

No, wait.

That is the plot of *Home Alone*.[18]

Macaulay Culkin is the one who learned that lesson.

Dang it. I'm sorry. I often get that movie confused with my normal life.

But, just like Macaulay Culkin,[19] my lesson would happen at Christmastime.

And it did involve my family.

---

18. KEVIN!!!!
19. It's never occurred to me until this moment how *weird* a first name "Macaulay" is. Seriously. Do you know any other Macaulays? I don't. Anyway.

And just like Macaulay, it would be a lesson that would change me.

BACK TO DECEMBER
(LOOK WHAT YOU MADE ME DO)

It was a year after my surgery. It was Christmastime, and I was getting ready to fly out to Las Vegas to spend the holidays with my mom and dad. I'd only missed one Christmas with them my entire life, and I was not about to make it a habit.

As I scurried around Nashville, doing some last-minute shopping and errands, I got out of my car and felt a little…something. Something pulled, back in my leg. Like a strain. To paraphrase the wise Latina philosopher Shakira, "When one's hips speak, one should listen. They tend not to lie." And mine were starting to hurt.

I ignored it, but as I flew to Las Vegas, it started tightening up. Ouch. By the time it came time to deboard, I was barely able to stand. And when my mom picked me up at the airport, I found I could barely get in and out of my parents' car.

Something was wrong.

Now, something you need to know about me. I tend to not be whiny. I'm not a whiny guy. In fact, whining is one of the traits I find the least attractive. Neither of my parents were whiny people, and they didn't tolerate it from me.

And secondly, I'm not easily angered. I'm pretty even-tempered. Chill, even. You could shadow me for an entire year and you might not see me lose my cool or blow my top. I think this might come in direct opposition to my dad, who, when he was younger, was pretty quick to anger. I wasn't a fan of my dad's temper, so at a fairly young age, I vowed to not be like that.

But.

But.

When I am in physical pain, those two values go out the window.

After landing in Vegas, I was turning angrier and whinier and was complaining more than a Karen at a local public pool.[20]

"My hiiiiiiip hurrrrrts," I whined, sitting down in a recliner in my parents' living room.

"Ty, why don't you go to the urgent care to get that looked at," my mother patiently suggested. "Figure out what's wrong."

"Okayyyyyyyyyy," I said.

I went to bed but didn't sleep great because of the pain in my hip. I woke up and went into urgent care first thing in the morning. But it was a holiday week, which means that the clinic was dramatically understaffed and the lines were out the door. It was like a Black Friday shopping event, only nothing was on sale, and instead of TVs, we were all just trying to get some of that sweet health care.

I waited for hours. *Hours and hours.* I got there about nine a.m., and I wasn't seen until almost three p.m. *And*...there was no food in this urgent care.

So I was tired.

In pain.

And hungry.

This was not a good recipe.

The doctor gave me some pain meds and recommended some particular stretches I could do to loosen up my hip flexors. This was helpful, but not *exactly* what I wanted. I wanted him to do some

---

20. I want to make a comment about this. The name "Karen" has taken a wrong turn in this world. It's not your fault you were named "Karen." Not since "Dick" (aka Richard) has a name taken on more unintended, unfortunate meaning. Also, super sorry to anyone out there whose initials are "O. J."

chiropractor voodoo and bend me in a weird position and then—crack-crack!—do something that made my hip instantly feel better.

When I got home, the living room was abuzz with family. My nieces, Bella and Gigi, ages four and six, were running around looking adorable. Family members walked around, grazing on holiday platters of cheese and crackers or nibbling store-bought Christmas cookies.[21]

I hobbled in, exhausted from the day. I quickly made a plate of things to tide me over and excused myself to go up to my room to eat and then fall asleep. It was one of those days you just wanted to be over with.

As I headed up the stairs, my dad came in from the garage and looked at me.

"Where you goin'?" he asked.

"I'm going to lie down," I said.

"You been at the doctor's this whole time."

"Yes, sir," I said. "All day."

I turned to go up the stairs, just wanting to be unconscious.

"Well," my dad said, under his breath, "that's what you get for not getting there early enough."

"Well, I got there at nine a.m., which is pretty much when they opened," I said, "But they were slammed."

"If you'd have woken up and got there earlier, it wouldn't have been a problem," my dad insisted.

I knew what he was doing. His military-ness was trying to make a point. Wake up early. Before dawn bugle call. Early bird gets the worm. Hustle in, hustle out. And all that jazz.

---

21. I've always wished that my mom was the kind of mom who made homemade Christmas cookies. But she didn't. That's why I'm notating, in this book, that the cookies were store-bought. That's on you, Mom, that's on you.

But I was not in the mood. And I felt horrible.

"They were running so far behind because it's the holidays and they're not fully staffed," I said.

As I made it to the first landing, I just wanted to eat this cheese and some of that dip and be done. I didn't have a lot of strength left.

"Harrumph," my dad said, spinning around to go to the kitchen. "Shoulda gotten there earlier, boy," he said, as a final act of passive-aggressiveness.

And that did it.

Pain + Hunger + Tired = Bad Tyler Casserole

It was that *one more comment* that really just got to me. I spun around on the landing. I swiftly descended the stairs and took three paces toward where my dad was. I stepped up to him, face-to-face. I was going to give him a piece of my mind. I was hot.

"You just can't help but say something else," I said, raising my voice. "You can't help but not say anything, can you? You can't leave it alone, can you, Dad? This had nothing to do with me!"

The room got quiet. Everyone stopped. Tears started coming out of my eyes.

Now, at this point, I would have imagined that a rational TV dad like Carl Winslow[22] would probably assess the situation and say to himself, "Hmm. That's weird. My son who typically does not yell at anyone just blew his top. I should probably think about my words, stop antagonizing him, and maybe pull a Ralph Tresvant and lean toward sensitivity."

---

22. Yes, I too wanted to write "Heathcliff Huxtable" in this example, but, well…you know…

But my dad was not rational at that point. Maybe it was his life as a poor sharecropper in Alabama, the subject of degradation day after day. Or maybe it was his military background, where you don't talk back to a superior officer. At any rate, my dad went from zero to sixty in three seconds flat.

Scrap that.

My dad went from zero to a hundred real quick.

My dad went *hard* at me. Like an NFL running back, he moved toward me with a quickness I was not expecting. Then came the volume. Almost barking, he got in my face and let me have it.

Boy.
I'm still your father, don't you ever talk to me like that.
Don't you ever disrespect me like that.
Do you not remember who the hell I am?

I don't remember what happened next, exactly. But I do remember what I thought, and what I saw.

I saw my Gigi and Bella, sitting by the tree in their Christmas dresses, looking up at my dad and me, startled faces beginning to contort into fear.

My nieces were watching all this unfold. I had a vague sense that this could be a traumatically formative moment for them, if I handled this wrong.

And then I heard it.

Tick.

Tick.

Tick.

The clock.

Yes, I was angry. Yes, I was tired. Yes, I was hungry. But I was also keenly aware of time. I did not have time. I did not have time to start a fight with my father on Christmas. I did not have time to dig into my own self-righteousness and storm upstairs and ruin an entire night of the holidays with my own stubbornness.

I did not have two days to waste as my father and I avoided each other in his own house, tiptoeing around each other as we avoided discussing what had happened.

How many days was I here? How many days and hours did I have in Las Vegas until I got on a plane and flew back home? And more than that, how many more Christmases did I have in my parents' home, with both of them here? With me there? Had I learned nothing from the cancer surgery? I had no guarantees.

I didn't have two days to waste like that.

I didn't have *one* day to waste like that.

I didn't have *one hour* to waste like that.

Tick.

Tick.

Tick.

I could almost feel the scar under my t-shirt. And I could almost hear John Lewis, whose words I'd been marinating in that entire year, reminding me.

"Forgive, Tyler. Forgive and ask for forgiveness. This is the Way."

Okay, I made that sound like John Lewis showed up on the landing of the stairs to talk to me, like a Black Yoda or something.

But that's really what went through my mind.

I stopped my father. A switch flipped in me.

"Dad. I'm so sorry. You're right. I should not have talked to you like that. I'm sorry."

Was he wrong to yell at me? Yeah, probably. Had he antagonized me? Yes. But was I wrong to snap at my dad in front of my nieces? Yes. Had I triggered him by attacking him in front of a house full of relatives? Yes. I was wrong. He was wrong. I was flawed. He was flawed.

We both needed grace.

But someone had to move first, and it had to be me. I moved in and I hugged him. My dad is not the warmest person ever, and certainly not the best hugger. In that moment, he didn't hug me back, but he let me hug him.

I looked over at Gigi and Bella by the tree. They sighed and went back to playing. The other family members went back to their conversations. Dad went to the kitchen to get a piece of Mom's store-bought pecan pie.[23] Mom went back to sipping her Christmas punch.

The smooth, dulcet tones of "Silent Night" by The Temptations began playing, magically, in the room. Okay, I don't know if that happened, but it kind of seemed like it did. The room had been calmed. Relationships had been smoothed over. Christmas, which had been on the verge of being ruined, was saved.

I retired to my room to sleep it off.

As I got ready for a nap, I took off my shirt and looked at myself in the mirror. I saw the purpled scar, and I had an honest-to-God moment. I realized that this scar would be a reminder. It would remind me that I don't have the time to get dug into intractable arguments with people I love and who I know. I don't have time to get into a day-long, or a week-long, or a months-long misunderstanding.

---

23. Mom didn't make pies, either. Again, on you, Mom. Do better.

The scar was a reminder that I don't have time to play games, like avoiding people, giving them the silent treatment, or offering up cold shoulders.

I know my dad is flawed. He'd been actively disrespected his whole life. I knew that the way I'd talked to him in his own home was triggering. It had to be.

But whatever his flaws, there was something that mattered far more than being right. I wanted to be connected to my dad. And in that moment, it was either forgive and ask for forgiveness or...what?

A days-long fight?

Fly home in a huff?

I lay down convinced of one thing. The right thing to do was what I had done. I was going to wake up from my nap in a little bit, and I would be able to quickly and easily rejoin my family in a Christmas house of peace and family.

Thank you, John Lewis.

This is the way.

BAD BLOOD

I flew back from my parents' house after that first Christmas.

It was almost the New Year, so I checked the calendar, which told me how many days I'd have until my six months would be up. Then I would have to go back to Vanderbilt University for a CT abdomen pelvis scan with contrast. That means they will have to insert some dye into an IV. You feel it go into you. Your whole body feels warm, and you immediately feel as though you have to pee. It's like hot water being pumped through all your veins. Then, they will slide me into a big, round cylindrical scanner. The machine talks to you, giving you instructions in a soft, female voice. Kind of what you'd imagine Aunt Jemima sounds like, telling you to breathe in and then hold, and then release.

From there, they'll tell me what the cancer is doing. If it has grown. If I have to have surgery or wait. Wait another hellacious six months.

Tick.

Tick.

Tick.

It was a cold, blustery, but clear day in Nashville. Not a bad day to go for a walk, so I got my athletic gear on and tied my shoes. And as a customary part of my pre-walk routine, I grabbed my water bottle and went to the restroom to empty my bladder.

As I went to the bathroom, I suddenly felt a pressure. Like... something was cinched on my insides that was preventing me from going to the bathroom. Then, suddenly, a sharp pain.

I instinctively breathed in a sharp breath through my teeth.

A second later, another pain knifed through me.

I felt like I'd been stabbed. I nearly toppled over and grabbed the countertop.

What was going on?

I looked into the toilet bowl.

It was a dark pink color.

There were bright red spots of blood dotting the white porcelain bowl.

"Oh God" was all I could manage.

CHAPTER 7

STAY ALIVE

So here's the deal. If you know who I am, or know anything about me, then you probably know that I love musical theater.

I love musical theater way more than any six-foot-two, straight Black man should.

But (and prepare for a plot twist here) I am also a huge *sports* fan.

I love sports as much as any six-foot-two, straight Black man should.[1]

The circles in the Venn diagram of "people who *love* musicals" and "people who *love* sports" don't often intersect.

So with that in mind, if you're reading this and know the words to "Bring Him Home," then please know that I am about to go hard in the direction of sports for a few minutes. I know that you don't care about sportsball, my Musical Theater People. I know that you will never care about sportsball, unless—unless!—we are talking about a revival of *Damn Yankees!*

But there are some people out there who do care about sports.

---

1. I know I'm making a wide racial generalization here. Trust me, I literally wrote the book on why we shouldn't do what I *just did*. But you get my point, people.

So even though I know I'm going to lose my musical theater peeps and probably also every white man who has ever seen *Porgy and Bess*, please stay with me.

Now, it is impossible for me to talk about my love of sports without talking about my parents and their origin story. Just follow me for a few minutes.

I promise I'm going somewhere.

My mama, Jerrie Elaine Hicks, and my dad, Milton Merritt, were both born in Eutaw, Alabama. At the time, it was a pretty poor, rural community located near the western edge of the state border with Mississippi. Eutaw is a small town of roughly 3,000 people. For decades, it was home to field after field of cotton plants, irrigated by the hot summer rains and harvested by Black bodies. Slaves, at first, and then, after the Civil War, sharecroppers, which is just a fancy word for "indentured slave."

My grandfather was a sharecropper. And his father before him. And my dad was a sharecropper until he realized that if he was going to have a chance to make it in life, he had to get out of town.

Like I said, my mama was born in Eutaw as well. She worked in a segregated diner off Interstate 20 and Alabama State Route 14. She served the side of the room that was reserved for white people. One day, her family came in to visit her, and she realized that she couldn't even eat in the section where she worked. That's when she decided, "I really got to get up out this piece."[2]

My mom married my father when she was nineteen, right after he joined the Air Force. They left town, and that was that.

The point I'm trying to make here, people, is that my roots go super deep in Alabama soil.

---

2. Translation: "I really need to get out of here."

Deep.

It's like how Dr. Dre mentions Compton all the time.

Or how Snoop Dogg is always repping the LBC.

It's like that.

My mom and dad are the Dr. Dre and Snoop Dogg of Alabama. Does that make me Eminem? Hell, I don't know. Forgive me. I've allowed this analogy to spiral out of control.

The most important thing you need to know for the sake of this story is that Eutaw is only about thirty miles away from Tuscaloosa, the home of the University of Alabama. And their world-famous football team. And in Alabama (similar to Texas), football is not a pastime. It's a state legacy. It's a way of life. It's as ingrained in the culture as grits and sweet tea. And it goes back more than 100 years.

As the story goes, one soggy fall day back in 1907, the University of Alabama's football team traveled upstate to Birmingham to play its archrival Auburn, who came into the game heavily favored. Well, the state's iron-rich soil turned the field of play into a sea of red mud, which stained Alabama's white jerseys. The game ended in a 6–6 tie, and famous sports writer Hugh Roberts wrote that in the wet conditions, the team played like a "Crimson Tide."[3]

And bam! The nickname was born.

Roll Tide.

Also, we have an elephant as a mascot. This is because in East Africa, elephants often make their way to the ocean shore to give birth, and when a baby elephant is born at high tide, the African people would wrap bamboo leaves into an oblong ball called

---

3.　"Traditions," the University of Alabama. https://www.ua.edu/about/traditions.

"kandanda" which is the Swahili word for "hope," and also I am just making all of this up, people. None of that is true.

BECAUSE NOBODY KNOWS WHY WE HAVE A DAMN ELEPHANT FOR A MASCOT.[4]

Okay, back to sportsball. Alabama grew to national fame in the late sixties and early seventies under Paul "Bear" Bryant, who won six national titles.[5] More recently, Alabama has destroyed everyone in college football, winning six more national titles under Nick Saban (2009, 2011, 2012, 2015, 2017, 2020).

So yeah, Roll Tide!

But during that nearly decade and a half of utter dominance and Heismans and national titles, the most famous moment wasn't something Alabama did. It was something that someone else did to Alabama.

Let me set the stage. It was late November in 2013, and it was the final game of the season against our archrival, the evil Auburn University. Alabama and Auburn first played each other in 1893, and have played each other in the last game of the season every year since 1948.[6] This rivalry—nicknamed the Iron Bowl—is one of the oldest and fiercest in all of sports.[7]

Alabama was undefeated and was only a few victories away from its third-straight national title. That's right: back-to-back-to-back

---

4. There are some theories and legends surrounding Big Al, the elephant mascot at Bama, but none of those are as funny as what I just wrote. "Traditions," the University of Alabama. https://www.ua.edu/about/traditions.
5. A national title is the equivalent of a Tony Award, for those of you who need to know that.
6. Alabama Crimson Tide, Winsipedia. https://www.winsipedia.com/alabama/vs /auburn.
7. Only Ohio State vs. Michigan is more storied, and therefore better. My co-writer, David, is from Ohio, and his wife is an alumna of the University of Michigan, so he made me include this footnote.

national champions. Alabama was not only the number one ranked team in the nation, but they were clearly the best team, period. And it really wasn't close. Auburn had a good year, and was ranked fourth, but were still listed as ten-point underdogs at home(!).

This in-state rivalry was rich, but let's be honest, the game was just a formality, and Auburn was definitely going to lose.

The problem here was that nobody told Auburn.

Auburn rallied to tie the game at 28–28 with thirty-two seconds remaining.

Thirty-two seconds, I will remind you, is not a lot of time.

But Alabama had a championship pedigree.

After returning the ensuing squib kickoff to the thirty-five-yard line, Alabama ran for nine yards, then ran for twenty-one more to the Auburn forty-yard line. The referee said time had expired, which put the game into overtime, but Alabama coach Nick Saban threw his red challenge flag. After a review, the officials put one second back on the clock.

Alabama lined up for a potential game-winning fifty-seven-yard field goal. Never mind that their redshirt freshman kicker Cade Foster was hot garbage and had already missed three field goals from forty-four, thirty-four, and forty-four yards.

And yet, as I was watching the game, I agreed with Coach Saban.

After all, there was only one second left. One second. What could happen in one second?

As I was watching the game with my adopted family, Bridget and Scott, I said out loud,

"What's the worst thing that can happen?"

So there we were. Auburn lined up. They didn't even try too hard to block the kick, because a fifty-seven-yard field goal is very difficult. Usually, college kickers don't even try a kick this long.

Just as a precaution, Auburn's head coach put his fastest player, cornerback Chris Davis, in the end zone to field the kick in case it was short. The kick was valiant, but it was short, by about three yards, and wide right. Chris Davis caught the ball nine yards deep in the end zone. He could have taken a knee, and the game would have been over and gone to overtime.

A tie.

"The worst thing that could happen," I thought.

But Chris Davis did not take a knee.

Oh, no.

Chris Davis decided to return the missed kick.

He returned the missed kick for 109 *f—ing yards*, in fact.

For a touchdown.

Auburn won the game on a 109-yard return after time had expired.

Defeating my beloved undefeated Alabama.

And not only did they ruin the Tide's run for a third-straight national title, but they put themselves in the national title game.

Ladies and gentlemen, the Auburn crowd reaction during this final play was SO LOUD that it registered on seismographs across the state of Alabama.[8]

Many sportswriters and sports historians say this was the "greatest moment in college football history."[9]

---

8. Jeremy Henderson, "Iron Bowl Earthquake?," *War Eagle Reader*, December 4, 2013. https://www.thewareaglereader.com/2013/12/iron-bowl-earthquake-suspicious -seismic-activity-registered-saturday-as-far-away-as-huntsville-correlates-to -auburns-last-second-touchdown-to-beat-alabama/.

9. https://nypost.com/2013/11/30/an-ending-well-never-forget/ and https://web.archive .org/web/20201025093605/https://www.huffpost.com/entry/is-the-2013 -iron-bowl-ala_b_4372765 and https://www.wsj.com/articles/SB1000142405270 2303345104579286622672546590.

Those sportswriters weren't there at Bridget and Scott's house with me when that game happened.

Also, those biased sportswriters are obviously on the payroll of Big Auburn.[10]

So to answer my question, "What's the worst that can happen?"

That.

That was the worst thing that could have happened.

The single most deflating moment in sports history.

This is the part where I'm going to encourage you to put the book down, go to YouTube and type in "Chris Davis 109-yard return." For as crappy as it made me feel that day, it really was an iconic moment in sports.

Damn you, Auburn.

IN EVERY LIFE WE HAVE SOME TROUBLE

I think about that Alabama-Auburn game a lot. It's a helpful metaphor. Because sometimes, in life, things aren't going well. So you line up to kick a field goal and think, "What's the worst thing that can happen?"

And if you have an imagination, and if you have any experience in this life, you might even have some worst-case scenarios in mind. But then suddenly, life goes from bad to worse, and some cornerback named Chris is racing untouched 109 yards toward your own end zone. And you realize, "Oh, wow, didn't expect that. In fact, I've never even seen something like that. And yet, here it is, happening to me live."

---

10. Full disclosure: Big Auburn and Big Catheter are owned by the same parent company.

Maybe it's best not to ask, "What's the worst thing that can happen?"

Life has a way of sucker-punching you with the answer.

So there I was, still with cancer in my belly after a major surgery that took out one of my kidneys. But now, I am standing over my toilet, looking at the blood trailing away in the water, realizing things just went from bad to worse.

Like I said, don't ask the question "What's the worst thing that can happen?"

From the conversations I've had with people who have cancer, many of them eventually discover that the cancer brings with it unforeseen and unanticipated complications.

When you have a giant tumor, like I had, you might be tempted to think, "Oh, that tumor is the worst of it."

The problem is that cancer is often like a biological hand grenade. Yes, typically there is a blast radius (usually, a tumor) but there's often shrapnel that explodes out randomly throughout the body. This can be literally tiny cancerous cells, running around the body like little cancerous Chris Davises (God, I hate that guy).[11] Or it can just be biological complications caused by extremely delicate, complex surgeries. Regardless, this "shrapnel" rips through whatever it rips through. Sometimes, it misses everything. Sometimes, it's the shrapnel that's the most damaging. Even fatal.

I was dealing now with some shrapnel.

And unfortunately for me, this shrapnel was in my penis.

I bet you didn't expect to ever read that sentence in your life, did you? Well, even my editor Beth wanted me to stop using the word "penis" in this book. And believe me, I really didn't want to type a

---

11. Note to Chris Davis. I do *not* actually *hate* you, brother. I just *sports* hate you.

sentence that included the phrase "shrapnel in my penis." But here we are.

Here we all are.

Curse you, Chris Davis, as both a real football player and as an effective metaphor for completely unanticipated negative outcomes!

That being said, if you've been paying attention, you might have anticipated this because of all the problems I'd had with my catheter, back during the surgery. What I didn't tell you is that over the past year since I'd come home from the hospital, it had become more and more difficult to urinate. Then, it became more and more difficult to control the flow of urine. When I peed, it just sort of sprayed everywhere, like I was Rambo and the walls and ceiling were enemy combatants.

This is not normal.

I know there are a lot of women out there who have husbands, brothers, and sons who might disagree, but after a man uses the restroom, the next person to walk in should not say, "Why is there pee on the ceiling?" And the response should definitely *not* be, "Oh, sorry, mate, that was me. I can't really control where I pee. It's like when you put your thumb over the end of a garden hose! Kinda has a mind of its own!"

And yet, even when this started happening to me, I dismissed it, saying, "Oh that's fine."

This is what is called "avoidance."

I had just undergone some real medical trauma, and the idea that there might be something else wrong was too much for me. I was scared. I didn't say this out loud to anyone, but looking back at it, I think in general my line of thinking was:

"I simply cannot handle something else."

Maybe some of you out there reading this know exactly what I'm talking about. You're at the edge, and really have no mental or emotional or physical margin for anything else bad to happen.

But pretending that something bad isn't happening (when it clearly is) is not an effective strategy for life. And things kept getting worse and worse.

A few days after what we'll call "the blood in my toilet morning," I woke up and I literally could not urinate. And that's when the panic set in.

I had Dr. Barocas's contact information. (You remember him. Scottie Pippen.) I sent him an email in the medical portal. I think the subject line was:

"Scottie Pippen: I need your help."

He messaged me back nearly immediately, and by three p.m. that same day, I had an appointment. Which is incredible, and special treatment, and also probably maddening to health care professionals.

I basically waited until it was an emergency to tell anyone I had a problem.

As I sat in the waiting room at the Vanderbilt University Medical Center, I was nervous. I'm not sure if you're aware of this medical reality, but as humans, we need to be able to go pee. It's a proper metabolic function. Were they going to be able to fix me? Was my other kidney malfunctioning? Had the cancer spread to my man-parts? Did I have wee-wee cancer? Penis-sarcoma, if you will?[12]

---

12. You know who won't? Beth. She's tired of me using that word. Is that enough different variations of the word for you, Beth? Don't go googling "synonyms for penis." Trust me on this.

After a few minutes, a nurse came out to the waiting room to get me. Now, this woman is going to play a critical role in this chapter. Let's just say, for the sake of this story, that her name was Nurse Katie. She was a nurse in the urology department who worked with Dr. Barocas. She was a veteran nurse, with loads of experience and short, blond hair. She was probably in her late forties. And she had a super-thick country accent. Like "I'm the special host of the Grand Ol' Opry" accent. Whatever Paula Dean/Dolly Parton kind of Southern white woman kind of accent you might be hearing in your head, multiply that by five.

I followed her back to the medical room.

Listen, people, I don't remember all the exact medical jargon that was said to me by these medical professionals during this appointment. I'm sure it was all very doctor-y. But this is my account of how I remember it as I sat there on the medical exam table, unable to pee.

Nurse Katie said, simply, "Now, let's see this penis that's not working."

!!!!!

Not exactly the sentence any man wants to hear. But there we were.

I explained the irregular urine stream and the increasing difficulty I'd been having.

"Well, Tyler, this is not unusual," Nurse Katie said. "If I had to guess, it's that you have a stricture."

"What's that?" I asked.

"It's when there's some scar tissue inside your urethra that's causing some narrowing," she explained.

I thought about the catheter. It was *that* thing's fault. I knew it.

Nurse Katie explained that first they'd probably have to do a cystoscopy (sis-TOS-kuh-pee).[13]

"What is that?" I asked nervously.

"So we're going to take a tiny camera and we're going to go up your urethra and just take a look around, honey," Nurse Katie said, as if everything in that sentence was a completely normal thing to say.

"A camera?" I said. "Up my penis?"

This, by the way, was yet *another* sentence I had not planned on saying. Not that day. Not ever.

"Oh, don't worry, Tyler," Nurse Katie said. "It's tiny. TYE-NEE."

For the record to everyone reading this, she was referring to the camera.

"Will it hurt?" I asked.

"Oh, now, don't worry now," Nurse Katie said. "We're gonna put on some numbing solution so you won't feel anything. I'm going to numb you so well, you won't be able to feel anything for two weeks."

Again, yet another sentence I had not anticipated hearing that day. And yet here I was. Hearing that sentence.

How did I get here? How was this my life?

Eventually, Dr. Barocas came into the room.

"What up, Scottie," I said.

After a brief examination, he looked at me.

"I have a feeling that it's scar tissue from the catheter," Dr. Barocas said. "But it is a stricture, and your urethra has narrowed."

"Uh . . . ah . . . what does that mean, exactly?" I asked.

And then came the words from Nurse Katie that I will never, ever forget.

---

13. Yes, I recognize the irony that the word "pee" is in this procedure.

"What we're saying, baby, is that you just got a tiny peehole."

Just the sweet, singsong deep country way Nurse Katie said that will forever be lodged in my brain. Even now, sometimes just randomly throughout my day, I will stop and say to myself, in Nurse Katie's thick accent:

"You just got a TIE-knee peeeee-hole."

How is that not a line in a country music song? If I hadn't been so scared, I would have laughed. But as God is my witness, I turned to Nurse Katie and promised her, "I am going to write a book about all of this, and in that book, I am going to include that line." I don't think she believed me. Well, Nurse Katie. Here we are.

"The good news," Dr. Barocas said slowly, "is I think I can fix this pretty easily."

"When?" I said.

"Oh, right now," he said.

Right now?

Right now, right now?[14]

At this point, I was about to faint. Because I was teetering on the edge of consciousness, I don't *exactly* remember what happened. What I recall happening is that Dr. Barocas then pulled over a small tray, upon which were dozens of sharpened surgical instruments which seemed to be stainless-steel medieval instruments of torture. Again, did he actually have a tray of medieval urethra-slaying instruments? I don't know. And I'm gonna be honest with you, I had no interest in seeing what this man was doing, or what he was about to do. I didn't want to know. I didn't want to see it. I didn't want to look.

---

14. I said this in the same cadence that André 3000 says, "Forever. For-ever-ever" in "Ms. Jackson."

Dr. Barocas then chose one particular instrument. I mean, I'm assuming. Again, I wasn't watching. I'm assuming it was some sort of DeWalt drill equipped with a urethra drill bit.

"Take a deep breath," Dr. Barocas said to me.

And I don't want to get too graphic, but then Dr. Barocas quite literally "ripped me a new one" and tore open my "tiny peehole" to scrape out the scar tissue and increase the diameter of my urethra.

I don't know how long this procedure lasted, but I know I was hyperventilating.

Afterward, he said, "There, we're done. We're finished."

But I remember thinking, "Yo. Did they use the camera thingy? They need to use the little camera thingy."

"I don't think we're going to need to do that," Dr. Barocas said.

I told Dr. Barocas that if he changed his mind, under no circumstances was I going to be able to get the nerve to come back into his office.

So in a moment of incredible bravery, in what some people might say is reminiscent of William Wallace leading the Scottish people to freedom, I mustered the words:

"Well, hell, you might as well do it now."

So then, just to be sure, Nurse Katie and Dr. Barocas did a cystoscopy, just to confirm that there were no issues farther up in there. They went all the way upstream, on a grand tour of my bladder.

"Do you want to see some images?" Nurse Katie politely asked me, looking at the images from the minuscule camera that were showing on the screen.

"No," I said, more sharply than I should have.

No, Nurse Katie, I do not want to see these pictures. This is not the kind of tourism I enjoy. I wanted this ride to be over, and no, I did not want to stop to take a selfie with my own bladder. And again, not to be crass, but my urethra is a one-way street, and they were going the wrong way.

"Okay, we're done," Dr. Barocas said.

It was over.

I sat there on the edge of the examination table on the white, crinkly paper.

I sat there...

With all my parts...numb...

Wondering how much the medical bills were going to be.

But more importantly, how much therapy I was going to need to make sure that I forgot this ever happened.

I'M STILL STANDING. BETTER THAN I EVER DID.

Now, I told you that story because I still can't believe that all that happened to me. I just spent multiple pages telling you a medical story, and to be honest, sometimes it sounds like I'm telling a story about somebody else. First of all, it makes me all cringy and makes me want to throw up a little. And I for sure don't want to think about it too much, and I don't even want to associate myself with those experiences.

But the fact is, *I went through that.*

It wasn't a friend of mine. It wasn't a distant relative. It was me.

I went through that.

And now I am on the other side. Things were bad for me, and then they got worse. And then I had more things go wrong. And it was incredibly painful.

If you'd told me beforehand that, in a few days, I would be unable to urinate and would have to go have a scalpel inserted up into my penis to enlarge my peehole, I would have fainted. I would have grabbed your arm and begged you to hide me in Canada, somewhere they would never find me. I would have said, "There is no way I can go through that."

But I did go through that.

Just like I went through my cancer surgery.

That was a storm I went through. And well. I'm still here.

And here's the lesson, I think. If I can go through that, who knows what else I can go through?

I say all this not because I'm a badass who deserves a Presidential Medal of Freedom, but because I'm still surprised.

I say all this because I think most of us dramatically underestimate not only what we could go through, but what we have been through.

And, as a result, I think we cut the cord too quickly. Give up. Throw our hands up in dejection.

But what if that isn't an option? It often isn't for me.

So, a few years ago, here in Nashville, one of my best buddies had his family come into town. They were visiting from another state. Now, my buddy is white, and his family is from an area that is nearly exclusively white.

I was hanging out with him and his family, and it was approaching dinnertime. Now, as you know, my parents are from the South, and the general rule of thumb in the South is that if someone is in your home during a mealtime, they stay to eat. Even if there is not enough food, and everyone gets a little less, or the host has to eat cereal for dinner, we will figure it out.

Figure. 👏

It. 👏

Out. 👏

It's not just Southern hospitality. It's polite. It's sharing. It's what families do. And if you're over at my house, you're invited to dinner.

But as dinnertime approached, my buddy's parents motioned to me and said, "It's almost dinnertime. When is he leaving?"

I was like, "Oh, man. Maybe they don't have enough food." Or maybe they don't like sharing food. Regardless, I felt kinda bad, so I left and didn't eat dinner with them. But it occurred to me later that my buddy's family was uncomfortable with the idea of eating dinner with me around, mostly because I was Black.

My buddy felt terrible and apologized profusely.

"I can't believe how rude they were to you," he said, venting to me. "I just refuse to live in a world where people behave that way."

He started wondering what the best response should be. "Maybe I'll just never have them in my house again," he said. "Or, I don't know, maybe I stop talking to them altogether. Cut them out completely. I cannot deal with their nonsense."

"Look, man," I said. "I know you're mad. And I get it. But it's easy to say, 'I don't want to live in a world where racism exists.' But it does exist. It does. And as a Black man, I don't get to say, 'I just can't deal with that' and walk away from everyone. If I'm a Black man in America, it means choosing to keep going. It means that I have to keep talking with people. Keep trying to break down barriers. Keep trying to change people's minds. We don't get to throw up our hands and quit," I said. "No matter what, we gotta keep moving forward."

Perhaps one of the reasons suffering is so difficult for so many of us is because we don't ever expect it to visit our house.

But why do we think that?

LIFE'S A BEACH. AND THEN YOU DIE.

Let's play a game. An imagination game. So...imagine with me, if you will, for a moment. It's the 1940s and I gather a group of eighteen- and nineteen-year-olds around and say, "Okay, guys, get ready! We're going to the beach."

And this group might cheer something like, "Right on!" or "Hot diggity dog, Ace, this is gonna be killer diller," or whatever they said back then. Whatever. And they donned their high-waisted swim trunks with built-in belts and knit cotton linings. Maybe they grabbed some water bottles...Wait. Plastics weren't a thing yet. So, okay, maybe they threw their canteens into their coolers and...Wait. Dang it, coolers weren't invented yet, either. How did these people hydrate back then? Man, I don't know. But undeterred, perhaps this enthusiastic group grabbed their wooden surfboards and piled them on top of the wood-paneled station wagon, and crammed into the car for the ride. Then, they'd get ready to spill out on the beach, without sunscreen (which hadn't been invented yet, either), just ready to run through the summer sun, careless and carefree of the damage that UV light was about to do to their skin.

Can you imagine it? Do you see this picture in your imagination? This pre–Beach Boys, pre–*Bay Watch* idyllic scene?

Oh, sorry, I forgot to mention one thing.

One tiny thing.

The beach we're going to is in France.

Normandy, France.

On June 6, 1944.

That's a *big* difference, isn't it?

Big difference.

One has an expectation of play and leisure and a holiday.

The other is a war zone.

This is what I'm trying to get at.

I think a lot of us—because of the time period in which we live and because of the unparalleled amount of peace and prosperity we have enjoyed in the United States—think that life is about going to the beach. People expect life to be a fun holiday, filled with laughter and leisure and pleasure.

But in reality, life is more like Omaha Beach. It's filled with far more danger and conflict. It can be deadly. And you best come prepared.

Here's another beach-related example. I'm fascinated by sharks. According to Florida Museum of Natural History's International Shark Attack File,[15] 108 people were bitten by sharks in 2022 alone. The United States led the world with forty-one unprovoked shark

---

15. Yes, this is a real thing. https://www.floridamuseum.ufl.edu/shark-attacks/yearly -worldwide-summary/.

bites, which is defined as "incidents in which a bite on a live human occurs in the shark's natural habitat with no human provocation of the shark."

SIDE NOTE: I do not know or understand what a "provoked" shark bite might be. Is that when you tell a shark a yo mama joke?[16] Wrap your hand in sushi and stick it in the water? Dress up like a seal and go swimming at night?[17]

Anywho, back to Shark Week. In 2022, 108 people were bitten by sharks and five died (only one in the US).[18]

Sometimes, when people hear those statistics, they say, "I can't believe that happened."

That is not my reaction.

My reaction is, "I cannot believe this does not happen *more*." The fact that hundreds of millions of people voluntarily go into the ocean—which is where all the sharks *live*, by the way—and more people are not bitten is *amazing* to me.

If you told me one of every ten people who went into the ocean got bitten by a shark, I would shrug my shoulders and say, "Yeah, that makes sense." Why these fools kickin' it in shark's houses, though?

Calling them shark-infested waters isn't helpful, either. That's like calling my house "human-infested." Yo! I'm not infesting my own house. It's where I live! Put it this way. Imagine if each year

---

16. Hey, Shark! Yo mama's so fat, when the fisherman caught her and put her on the scale, the reading was "to be continued." Hahaha, oh no, the shark jumped in the boat and is biting me!

17. Also, just to be clear, with that last joke, I'm referring to seals, the aquatic mammal, not Seal, the British musician, singer, and songwriter who has sold more than 20 million records worldwide, including his most celebrated song "Kiss from a Rose." And was briefly married to Heidi Klum. I wish that man no harm. He is a national treasure.

18. Are you reading this thinking, "How many of the 108 people bitten were Black?" Because that's what I'm thinking about.

hundreds upon hundreds of chicken nuggets just decided to go into my home, just to hang out and relax. Get away from the heat. Just dozens of chicken nuggets, swimming all around my house every single damn day. And over the course of the entire year, I only ate *one*?

I'm just saying that's some restraint. And the chicken nugget community should look at that as though it were almost a certified miracle.

Look, people, what I'm trying to say with this absolutely inspired long-form shark/chicken nuggie analogy is that if you swim in dangerous waters, don't be surprised when dangerous things happen.

And this is where I think the broader American culture can learn a few things from Black folk.

Because Black folk do not walk around this world thinking that life is going to be a beach vacation.

This is largely because of the lived history of our people. There's an unspoken understanding that life is more like Omaha Beach. That life will have suffering. And pain. And unfairness. There is an expectation that this life isn't always going to be an easy ride.

I'm not saying there's a Black seminar that every Black kid attends outlining this.[19] It's just something you learn from being around your family and community. It's just something you feel and know.

Most folks feel like suffering is something to be avoided at all costs. But that's not true. Not only is suffering to be expected but—and this is the crucial thing—suffering can actually be turned around to be a *good* thing.

---

19. Or maybe there is a super-secret Black seminar. But if you're not Black, then I guess you'll never know, will you, will you, Chad?

WORK IT. MAKE IT. DO IT. MAKES US:
HARDER. BETTER. FASTER. STRONGER.

Y'all still with me? Let's look back, for a minute, at the idea of suffering. All the way back in 1889, the German philosopher Friedrich Nietzsche wrote in his book *Twilight of the Idols* the famous line "Now now now that that don't kill me, can only make me stronger."

Okay that might have been Kanye. Or maybe Kelly Clarkson. All three? I don't remember. Pretty sure the German guy said it first, though.

Although it might seem strange to quote a nihilist like Nietzsche in a book like this, I actually think this quote has the reverse effect. Nietzsche is saying that although life might have difficult seasons, those seasons are not meaningless, because they form something important in us.

Suffering...
> **Survived...**
>> **Leads to Resilience...**
>>> **Which is the seedling of hope.**

This means that the more suffering you survive, the more chances you have to practice surviving. And the more you survive, the more resilient you are. Hardened and strong like steel. And that leads to hope.

Again, I think this is where the lives and lessons of folks who look like me have something important to say.

Ooooh! Wait! I have a good story about World War II, people. Trust me on this. Y'all ain't ready!

The South in the 1940s was not an easy time to be an American. Pearl Harbor brought the nation into World War II. But if it was tough for all Americans, it was doubly tough for Black Americans. And in fact, more than one million Black men and women served in the war. And World War II would go on to have an enormous impact on the psyche of Black folks—particularly Black men.

At the time, Black people were viewed as not only intellectually inferior, but morally inferior to white people, so the Army, Navy, and the Marine Corps all segregated African Americans into separate units because they weren't viewed as being as capable as white service members. The prevailing attitude was that we weren't fit for combat or leadership, so most of the time, we were assigned jobs as cooks, mechanics, or supply-chain laborers. And for the few who did make officer rank, they could only lead other Black men. Because, you know, racism.

But then something happened. As the war crept on, massive casualties mounted, and the military had to utilize Black people as soldiers, officers, tank drivers, and even...pilots.

And in the spring of 1942, the US Army formed the 761st Tank Battalion, which had thirty Black officers, six white officers, and 676 Black enlisted men.[20] As this unit went through training, the officer in charge was Lieutenant Colonel Paul Bates (remember that name). Bates, a white officer, was astonished by the teamwork, leadership, ingenuity, courage, and stamina of this unit, saying this was one of the best units he'd ever seen in the entire Army. He asked to be promoted to colonel and lead the battalion into combat in the European theater.[21] His request was granted. The group was given a patch, featuring their logo, with the motto "Come out fighting."

---

20. Hank Heusinkveld, "The 761st Tank Battalion: Fighting the Enemy, Beating Stereotypes," US Army, February 9, 2007. https://www.army.mil/article/1792/the_761st_tank_battalion_fighting_the_enemy_beating_stereotypes.
21. "Paul L. Bates," Wikipedia. https://en.wikipedia.org/wiki/Paul_L._Bates.

In 1944, the 761st was assigned to General George S. Patton's Third Army in France. And you better believe that these brothers became Patton's most effective and decorated tank unit, serving nonstop for the next 183 days and winning battle after battle after crucial battle, including defeating the fearsome Nazi Panzer tanks in the Battle of the Bulge, which is viewed by military historians as the turning point in the European theater.[22] The 761st also liberated the Gunskirchen concentration camp. The men of the 761st received a total of eleven Silver Stars, sixty-nine Bronze Stars, and about three hundred Purple Hearts.

As stories of their heroism and bravery spread, they became known by the insignia they wore on their uniforms. This unit came to be known as (I'm telling y'all, you ain't ready!) . . .

"The Black Panthers."[23]

Now, typically, the idea of "being sent off to war" might seem like the very worst thing possible that could happen to a person.

22. Ryan Mattimore, "The Original Black Panthers Fought in the 761st Tank Battalion in WWII," History.com, April 11, 2018, updated August 15, 2023. https://www.history.com/news/761st-tank-battalion-black-panthers-liberators-battle-of-the-bulge.
23. Yes, that's where the name comes from. No, it has nothing to do with Marvel. Yes, Chadwick Boseman is smiling down on us from Heaven.

After all, as William Tecumseh Sherman, the famed Union general in the Civil War, once said, "War is hell." And beating back the Nazis was its own crucible.

But.

But.

Hear me out. Suffering also produces and forges things in humans.

For example, serving at such a high level in the European theater showed Black men a different world. One where they had equality and equal dignity. One where their gifts could be used and looked at as exceptional. They saw a world where the racial caste system of America, especially the American South, was not the *only* option. And this made them more resilient.

And more hopeful.

And *that* combo made these men far more resistant to the socially embedded injustice they came back to at home.

Fun story: after the 761st completed their training at the segregated army base Fort Hood in Texas, all the men boarded the buses to be shipped off to war. A Black officer from the 761st was approached by a white officer and told to move to the back of the bus.

The Black officer looked around.

No way.

This racist segregation thing might work in the South, but here in the Army, all soldiers were equal. After all, they were all risking their lives to fight in World War II. This jacked-up way of looking at race had to go. The Black officer refused and was eventually brought before the Army for a court-martial. But his officer, Colonel Paul Bates (told you to remember his name!), refused to court-martial him. He sided with his officer, even calling out the prejudicial and racist system.

Oh, yeah, that Black officer who refused to move to the back of the bus?

I told y'all that

Y'all 👏

ain't 👏

ready 👏

That officer was future baseball Hall of Famer Jackie Robinson.[24]

<crack!>

Do you hear that, people? That's what we call a literary, storytelling home run.

You see, once Black people came back from World War II, they had wildly different views about themselves and their place in the world. About their dignity. About their worth. It built in them perseverance in the face of opposition.

The crucible of suffering created by combat in the European theater forged men who wouldn't have a problem fighting another battle, this time on US soil against an implicitly unjust social order. World War II called out courage and determination in Black men— men like Jackie Robinson and so many others. A few years after that incident on the army bus, Jackie was told by a whole lot of white men that he didn't belong on a baseball field because he was inferior. But Jackie had learned from the 761st that that line of racist propaganda was garbage. He refused to quit, and played baseball, winning Rookie of the Year and leading the Brooklyn Dodgers to the World

---

24. I read about this account in the book *Brothers in Arms: The Epic Story of the 761st Tank Battalion, WWII's Forgotten Heroes* written by Kareem Abdul-Jabbar. Yes, that Kareem Abdul-Jabbar. It's a great read.

Series. Two years later, in 1949, he won the award for Most Valuable Player[25] in the entire National League.[26]

World War II set the stage for the Civil Rights Movement. Where was the courage needed for the many battles of the Civil Rights Movement battle-tested? During World War II. Where were the leadership and vision of Black men needed for the Civil Rights Movement developed and deployed in the field? During World War II. Where were the lessons about the inherent worth and dignity of Black people (that the Civil Rights Movement was based upon) played out? During World War II.

Suffering...

　　Survived...

　　　　Leads to Resilience...

　　　　　　Which is the seedling of hope.

THEY ARE GOING THROUGH
THE UNIMAGINABLE

After my experience with cancer, I think I've been awakened to an inspiring reality. Having cancer changes your perspective. Once you have it, you begin to realize how common suffering is. You see how many people have cancer, or have had cancer. It touches so many people. And then you begin to see how much pain there is in the

---

25. Hey, baseball stat-heads. Check this out. In that MVP season in 1949, Jackie Robinson batted .342 with 124 RBIs and 122 runs. !!!

26. Okay. I promise that is the very last sportsball reference of this chapter. And for your patience, I'll reward you with a little-known theater fact. Billy Porter once played the role of Teen Angel in the 1994 Broadway revival of *Grease*, and you need to go to your favorite music streaming service right now and listen to his version of "Beauty School Drop-Out." Prepare to have your mind *blown*. You're welcome.

world. How much unexpected and unplanned suffering, and how much so many people have gone through.

I'm surprised how much humans can take. How much humans can adapt to tragedy. I am continually shocked at the resilience of people.

I think about all the single moms I know. It would be understandable if they just threw their hands up in the air and said, "This is completely unfair for me to have to raise these children alone, without any help whatsoever emotionally, physically, or economically from their father. This is a raw deal, and it's unfair and unjust." Which it is. But these moms don't quit. They don't walk away. They keep fighting. They keep caring, and holding several worlds together with the sheer energy of their love for their kids. They choose to keep going, to keep serving in love. To keep at it.

They have to.

I think about the families I know who have dealt with the tragedy of losing a child. No parent should ever have to bury their own child. It's outside the natural order of things. And I know there were moments when the pain truly felt like it was going to kill them. But they are here. And grief may be a constant companion for them every day of their life, but they keep going.

They have to.

If you're breathing air and reading this, there's a good chance you're familiar with suffering. It's baked into life. It's even written in the Bible that "In this world, you will have trouble..." It didn't say, "In this world, *some* of you *might* have trouble."

It's a universal declaration.

Some of you know that. Suffering comes to every house.

And yet.

And yet.

You made it through that thing. You are standing. You might have thought, "I will never make it through this." But you did. You're alive. It didn't kill you.

So keep going, my friend.

Look back and see what you survived.

Be in awe of what you survived.

Because there will be a time period where you'll face something else. And when that time comes (and I hope to God that it doesn't, but in all likelihood, you and I both know it will), you will be able to gather the strength to face it because of what you've already been through.

You will be able to look back on all that you've been through and say, "Well, I made it through that and I'm still here."

Those past experiences have developed your resilience and ability to move through the world with its land mines of suffering.

You made it through those.

And you'll make it through this.

And that feeling? That feeling of realizing that "what's the worst thing that can happen" might be bad, but you've already seen bad. You've made it through bad. And you're still here?

That's hope.

And no matter what is happening to you, know that you can say: "At least I didn't have my tiny peehole ripped open today."

CHAPTER 8

DYING IS EASY, YOUNG MAN. LIVING IS HARDER.

Y'all.

Entertain me for a second, because I'm about to talk about something controversial. Pets. But walk with me, because I promise, I'm going somewhere with this.

Now look, I don't have any pets. At all. I have no interest in getting any pets.

But ironically, I am known as a Cat Dad.

This is because my ride-or-die bestie Shannon has a cat. His name is Dexter. I don't remember exactly why she named her cat Dexter. I like to think it's after the main character in that TV show about the serial killer. That makes sense to me, because, honestly, I always get the feeling with cats that they're sizing you up and trying to figure out if they could kill you.

When Shannon is out of town, I watch Dexter. When I come over, Dexter comes to check out who is in his house.[1] When Dexter

---

1.   If you have a cat, then you know, even if you pay the mortgage, it's the cat's house and you should feel honored you get to live there.

sees me, sometimes I like to imagine that he's looking at me as if he loves me, as if I am one of his favorite humans. And then I realize what I think is a look of love is actually a look of angry disapproval. Because he's a cat. And that's what cats do. Dexter then slinks away, disgusted that I even exist. Also, I am allergic to cats, so even if he were to want to be near me, Dexter probably subconsciously knows that, unlike Johnny Gill, I'm not going to rub him the right way.

But I don't mind. At least Shannon doesn't have a dog. Man. Dogs are needy as all get-out. You have to take them out to go pee. You have to go for long walks. Sometimes, multiple walks a day, depending on the dog. My buddy has a dog that is this special breed of hunting dog, I guess, and this thing has so much energy that it has to run three miles a day. So this dude takes his dog for a three-mile run. Every. Single. Day. At that point, it's like you might as well just go ahead and get a kid if you're going to have to do that much. Listen, I know grown-ass people who will be at a party, and they will look at their watch and say, "Oh! I have to go. I have to get home to let my dog out."

They will leave a *human* party, with *people*, to tend to their *dog*.

The hell?

This is not the case with cats.

Cats don't need you.

Cats are like, "Need you? I don't even *like* you."

When you come home, a dog will run around and be excited to see you. A cat will be mad at you because you've come back home and reminded them that you exist. And that alone—your simple human existence—irritates them. Sometimes, cats will weave in between your legs rapidly at the top of stairs. You think, "Oh how cute. They're rubbing my legs." They think, "I hope you trip and fall down the stairs and die."

And you know what? They will not miss you. They will not mourn your passing. They will just shrug and think, "Well, at least I have a giant hunk of food from Fatass McStairFaller. That should last me a few weeks."

Dogs have owners.

Cats have servants.

Listen, I told you I was getting to a point, so let me get to it. Cats do get needy when they get hungry. And now that we're in the Year of Our Lord 2025, there is a solution for that. My friend Shannon bought this robotic, automatic cat feeder. So this thing plugs into a wall, and as long as there is electricity, it will feed your cat. And if there is no electricity, that probably means civilization failed, and cats are like, "Whatever, I never liked humans anyway. Enjoy your robot overlords."

This cat feeder is *fan-cy*. It connects wirelessly to an app, and you can program it, and it will literally feed your cat for you. When the time comes, it makes these whirring noises, and the dry cat food goes down a chute into a ceramic bowl below, making a sound like Froot Loops falling into a cereal bowl.

And when that happens, it does not matter what Dexter is doing in the world. He could be sleeping. He could be about to pounce on a yellow parakeet. He could be in the bathroom of some seedy cat club, doing a line of catnip off a mirror on a dirty cat sink while cat club music[2] pounds through the wall. It doesn't matter. Dexter will stop whatever he is doing and he will run to the food. It short-circuits his animal brain. He is gone. It's a primal response. *The food has fallen, and I must eat now.*

---

2. Probably "Black Cat" by Janet Jackson, or DJ Feline's club remix of "Smelly Cat" by Phoebe.

Now, I don't know what it's like to be Dexter the cat. But in a weird way, I can relate.

After my surgery, I had to install an app from the University of Vanderbilt Medical Center on my phone. It's a portal where I can find out information about my health care, schedule appointments, and even communicate via messaging with my doctors.

And let me tell you, every single time I looked down at my phone and saw a notification from Vanderbilt Medical Center, I had the same reaction that Dexter did. My world just stopped. Whatever I was doing, I was not doing that anymore.

My heart started racing. My stomach dropped. My blood pressure shot up. I started sweating.

And I was struck by a feeling of sheer terror. I'm sure it was some sort of post-traumatic stress disorder.

The worst part about the Vanderbilt app is that it sends notifications pretty regularly, and most of the time, they're innocuous.

"You have a new bill."

Or:

"It's flu season."

Or:

"Halloween candy to avoid if you have peanut allergies."[3]

But sometimes, it says "Dr. Tan's office is reaching out for an appointment." Or "Dr. Tan would like to talk to you about your most recent lab work."

---

3. I gotta say this. When we were young, there was no such thing as peanut allergies. I don't remember food allergies until the early 2000s. When I was growing up, from grades one to four, every single body ate peanut butter and jelly sandwiches at least four times a week. What the genetic nonsense happened to us? Also, man, it would suck to have peanut allergies at Halloween because *every single great* Halloween candy has peanuts. Snickers. Payday. Reese's peanut butter cups. Butterfinger. Peanut M&M's. There's no good candy without peanuts, really... Oh, wait. There is Mounds. Almond Joys have nuts. Mounds don't.

Then, it's high blood pressure time for Tyler.

God, I really hated those notifications.

Dang it. I realize I have something in common with not only cats, but dogs, too. I am like a dog who is so excited to go on a ride in the car, but then, when he gets out of the car he realizes he's at the vet and his tail goes immediately between his legs and his only instinct is:

Wait one cat-gone minute. I've been here before. This is the place with the slippery metal tables. The last time I came here, I woke up and parts of my body were missing and I had to leave with a damn cone around my neck.

Dang it. Maybe I do need a pet.

The Vanderbilt app might make it easier to pay my medical bills online, but it also triggered me like Dexter's cat food machine. It was like an unwanted buzzer of interruption hardwired directly into my brain that short-circuited my mental and emotional life by reminding me that, yes, I have cancer.

And although there are not many moments when I don't hear the countdown, the app's notifications made the ticking extra loud, like an alarm clock stuck in my head.

And all of it was unwanted.

IT TAKES A LITTLE TIME. SOMETIMES.

Believe it or not, there are some real benefits to having a twenty-seven-pound tumor removed in a highly invasive surgery: it causes your world to grind to a halt. Hurry is no longer an option. Time slows waaaaaay down.

This was not something that I was used to. At the time, I drove a super-charged Dodge Challenger, red like Taylor's lipstick,[4] windows tinted as black as my coffee, with a license plate that simply said:

DRIVEN

Not gonna lie, I kinda loved the play on words. I was an ambitious person, and my car needed an operator because I was not an Autobot. And that, my friends, was a *Transformers* joke.[5] Tell me you're an eighties kid without telling me you're an eighties kid.

But now! With my abdomen stapled together, I could barely walk around my house. Do you know what the most difficult part was? Getting up out of bed. My abs were ripped, and not in the good way.[6] I mean ripped as in "medical surgical equipment had literally cut my abdominal muscles to shreds." My abs were so weak, I started calling them SWV.[7]

But the doctors told me I had to move. So as a way to regain abdominal strength, I started taking short walks around the cul-de-sac where I lived. Just a lap around my apartment building. It was now January, and it was quite cold, but I'd bundle up and hobble around. Before the surgery, that walk would have taken me maybe two minutes. Now it took me most of an hour. I started off doing one lap. Then I was able to get my stamina up to 1.5 laps.

---

4. Swifties, you feel me.
5. The Hasbro cartoon, not the Michael Bay movies.
6. I don't mean ripped like Zac Efron in that *Baywatch* movie or Janet Jackson circa 2001. What was up with Zac in that film? He looked like a living human anatomy chart.
7. Shout out to all my nineties R & B heads. IYKYK.

One lap. That may not feel like a lot, but sometimes in our lives when we're starting over, or when we're recovering from something in life that has knocked us all the way down, and when it's time to start over and get going again, it seems like the road ahead is just impossible. And in those moments, the best thing you can do is just...one lap. Sometimes, just one lap is the only thing you can do. And that's okay. It's a start. So go.

This time served my body well. Walking got my blood flowing to my organs, which aided in quicker wound healing. Walking also helped restore the muscle mass I'd lost and trigger better overall cardiovascular health. But for all that walking did for me physically, the real benefit was what it did for my brain.

And my soul.

Walking that slowly—and I'm talking considerably slower than one mile per hour—makes you see the world differently. I had time to do what I call "slow think."

On one of these short-in-distance but time-consuming walks, my literary agent, Erin, called me. This meant a lot to me because I knew she had completed an incredibly difficult battle with cancer herself. "I know it's tough right now," she told me, "but one day, you're going to look up and say, 'I am now finally doing all these things I couldn't do.'" Erin said this to me as I was shuffling around my apartment's parking lot in twenty-nine-degree weather moving at the speed of a glacier.

"That is really hard to believe, Erin," I said. I wanted to believe her, but I didn't. It just didn't seem possible.

There's an old poem from 1648 from the British poet Robert Herrick that famously starts off:

Gather ye rosebuds while ye may,

There's another line from a poet from 1986, Ferris from the House of Bueller, who said:

> Life moves pretty fast.
> If you don't stop and look around once in a while,
>   you could miss it.

After you have extreme surgery or deal with cancer, these kinds of sentiments don't seem so trite anymore. And I know that it sounds like some carpe diem, Robin Williams–standing-on-top-of-the-desks in *Dead Poets Society* kind of stuff here, but it's not untrue.

I started thinking about gathering rosebuds, which for me meant being particular, specific, and mindful about the bright and good things that were happening in my life. So, as I did my ultra-slow snail laps around my apartment's parking lot, I made mental lists about all the people who had made significant sacrifices to help me during this time. I thought about all the people—nurses, doctors, medical teams, friends, family, neighbors, and co-workers—who had gone out of their way to slow down to see me. To help me. These names, and the special, dedicated kindness that each name represented to me, were the rosebuds I gathered on those cold January winter walks.

These were the names of all the people who cared for me. Who sat with me, even when I quite literally couldn't get up and do anything. People who visited me. People who brought me meals. People who spent time with me. And most humbling, people who prioritized me in their life.

Do you know what an honor that is? For people to voluntarily slow down and take time out of their life to meaningfully connect with you? There's nothing like it.

I remember hearing this quote one time. I googled it and found out it was from a business researcher and *New York Times* best-selling author named Jim Collins. His wife had just been diagnosed with breast cancer and had a double mastectomy. And during an interview he said the whole event changed him. He said:

There's no way you could ever say, "You know, in the end cancer's good." You can't say that. But out of that experience we came away with a life mantra: "Life is people and time with people you love." And the more that we began to try to live that idea, and every day we remember that idea, and every day we remember it's not about stuff or adulation or accomplishment—it's about love and people you love and time with people you love . . . it was a defining event that made us better.[8]

There's one line in that quote that sticks out to me:

**"Life is people.
And time spent with people we love."**[9]

Ooof.

Kind of a shame that we only tend to do that when it's suddenly urgent, or an emergency.

So I want to share with you this quick list I made. It would mean the world to me if you would take the time to read it. These people

---

8. "Return on Bad Luck," JimCollins.com, https://www.jimcollins.com/media_top ics/Return-on-Bad-Luck.html.
9. "Being Inspired by Jim Collins," Julia Langkraehr's Blog, Bold Clarity. https:// www.boldclarity.com/jim-collins-quotes/.

took the time to take care of me, and what a joy it is to be afforded the chance to honor them in print. And I know, me asking you to read this is a lot. It's like one of those moments in *The Lord of the Rings* where Tolkien goes into painfully long descriptions of, like, all of Frodo's second cousins. It's like, "Dammit, J. R. R., you know I cannot keep track of all these Hobbits with their weird Hobbit names!"

But check it. These are some people I want to honor here. They saw me. And now I want you to see them. And I know this list doesn't include everybody, so if I forgot you…uh…look, I have cancer, okay. And also you can blame my editor, Beth. Her email is beth@hachette.com. Here we go.

Jerrie
Milton
Shon and Paula
Shannon
Sara
Scott
Bridget
Declan
Zoe
Elysha
Cathleen
Cori and the Theater Bug Board
Laurie
Lisa
Kelly
Michelle and Joy
Wells and Sarah

Nick
Ben
Melinda
James and Dawn
Jimmy and Molly
Sophie
Rob
Reba and Daniel
Mike and Erin
Nakia and my Comcast family
Janet and Jed
Erin and the fam at Folio
Beth, Daisy, and my Hachette family
Lenny and Julie
Chris and Katie

Thanks for reading those with me.

I knew something else was shifting in me during these long, slow, rosebud-gathering walks. I realized that these people had all made a significant impact on me that I would not soon forget, mainly because of their kindness to me.

The way you treat others really does matter in this world.

I know, I know, that lesson sounds as basic as the law of gravity, but unlike the law of gravity, it's easy to forget. The people who make the biggest impact on you in this life—well, it isn't about what they do or accomplish, but who they are.

And now I had some soul-searching to do. As a Black man in the world, how was I going to take the lessons I had learned from all the craziness of the past few months and apply this to my everyday life?

LESSONS FROM MAYA

As I did my painfully slow loops around my apartment building, I did some deep thinking. How (exactly) was I going to concretely change the way I lived, in light of my cancer survival? I knew it had something to do with kindness, as I talked about in the previous chapter. But kindness how? And this is where my experience attempting to rehabilitate from the surgery helped me. I was pretty sure I knew the answer.

Attention.

In our world of distraction, perhaps the biggest gift that you can give someone is the gift of attention. Of slowing down. Of taking the time to actually, truly listen. It communicates, in a digital age of speed, "You matter!" I'm reminded of the famous quote by the Queen Poet herself, Maya Angelou, who said,

> *"I've learned that people will forget what you said, people will forget what you did, but people will never forget how you made them feel."*[10]

Maya is talking about the art of connecting with people in a meaningful way, and that's something that really can only happen when we take the time to slow down and be present.

My long, slow, forced walks had opened my eyes to this reality. The real work of love is done slowly.

And I had to change some things. Now that I was heading back into the real world of real people, and things were starting to normalize, I shifted the way I thought about time. How I typically operated.

---

10. "Maya Angelou and Robert Loomis," video on Facebook. https://www.facebook.com/watch/?v=941503539620059.

Let me give you a real-life example. Most of the people in my life who know me would tell you that from the time I left high school, I have never taken an actual vacation.

Now, I know this sounds crazy, but I will tell you why. I have always worked a day job, nine to five, and so any allotted vacation time (any PTO) would be accrued and used so that I could pursue my acting projects or touring with my band. I took my vacation to shoot TV shows, play music, and do side acting jobs wherever the work took me. This made it so I never planned a proper vacation.

Now, my parents love to go on vacation. Their go-to spot is Hawaii, in particular the island of Oahu. They have been trying to get me to go with them to this island paradise since I graduated high school. They wanted me to go with them so badly, they offered to pay for my plane ticket. For my lodging. For my food. I bet I have said no 100 times to them. I couldn't justify the time away.

Which means...

I have turned down an all-expense paid vacation to Hawaii 100 times...

...in order to...

(Wait for it.)

...work more.

As I did my snail circuit trek around my apartment complex in the bitter Nashville winter air, it suddenly hit me how stupid I had been. There are so many things out in the world that are significant and beautiful and discoverable, things that have nothing to do with work, that are not done simply to further one's career. Things that are just about spending time with people you care about.

Since then, I've been to Hawaii. And it's pretty damn dope. Because after all

"Life is people.
And time spent with people we love."

I began to say yes to a lot more things. I had friends who made plans to go to Isla Mujeres in late spring, a beautiful island off the coast of Cancún that's technically part of Mexico, but also just dangling out there right in the Caribbean. I went with them. And one afternoon, I went for a (very slow) hike, and eventually made my way to a great rock that overlooked the ocean. I watched the waves and water for a long, long time. I remember thinking to myself, "Damn, Tyler. This is always here. It's up to you to come here and experience this." I sat on the rocks, watching the waves come in, listening to one of my all-time favorite songs by Counting Crows:

> It's been so long since I've seen the ocean
> I guess I should

Adam was right. It *had* been a long December. In fact, I had lived through a few long Decembers. I felt that lyric in my soul. And I thought about that line from Jim Collins.

"Life is people.
And time spent with people we love."

CONCRETE JUNGLE WHERE
DREAMS ARE MADE OF

I had another moment, too.

Now, hold tight for a second, I'm about to drop some names. And some of you will be like, "I have no idea who those people are."

But some of you who are theater people (my people!) will know that I have some wickedly talented friends.

You ready, theater nerds?

Don't freak out.

Before my cancer diagnosis, my best friend James Monroe Iglehart was starring in *Hamilton* as Thomas Jefferson/Lafayette on Broadway. I knew he was leaving the show, and I was thinking about possibly going to see him in his closing weekend.

It just so happened that on that same exact weekend, my other friend Megan Hilty—take a breath, theater people—was doing her one-woman show at one of my favorite venues, 54 Below.

And, incredibly, also on that weekend, Jennifer Nettles was playing the lead role in my friend Sara Bareilles's musical *Waitress*. And what I mean by "my friend Sara Bareilles" is that I don't actually know this woman, but I figured that by typing "I am her friend" in a published book, it will now somehow magically happen.

Hit me back, Sara.

Your (future) friend, Tyler.

Honestly, even with everything going on that weekend, I had considered not going. I mean, NYC is expensive. And it's a hassle.

But then I thought about the cancer. And then I heard it again. That damn clock.

Tick.

Tick.

Tick.

And something shifted in my thinking. It became less about what was happening in New York and more about the people that I would get to see and hang out with.

It shouldn't have taken cancer to push me to realize that.

But what can I say?

You live.

You learn.

Thanks, Alanis.

Now, New York City is one of my all-time favorite cities, and honestly, I think it should be yours, too. Okay, listen. I know that there are those of you reading this thinking, "No way. That city is just not for me. Way too much traffic. It's too dirty and smelly. And overpopulated. And way too expensive."

And you know what I would say to you, you New York hater.

You, my friend, are correct.

All that is true. But in your haste of haterism, you forgot one important detail: that ever since they legalized marijuana, it smells like they have a dog problem, and by dog, I mean Snoop Dogg. It smells like weed on every corner.[11]

But, man. I had such a good time.

I hung out with my people there in the city. I went to see all those shows and saw my friends shine. I ate all the slices of pizza from every corner shop. Why is New York pizza so good? Is there crack cocaine in the crust or something? Seriously. Why? Also, I am a vegetarian, and all things considered, I'm a relatively happy vegetarian, but dang if at three o'clock in the morning, those hot dog vendors aren't temping as all get-out. You almost got me, Oscar Mayer. You almost got me.

I went to Carmine's, one of my favorite places to eat in the city. It's an old-school Italian family-style restaurant whose fried zucchini may be the best appetizer I have ever tasted in my entire life. Their simple garlic and oil pasta is so good that I didn't stop eating when

---

11. So here's my proposal. Legalize weed, but make it illegal to smoke. You can only buy marijuana in gummy form. Gummies don't smell. And who doesn't like gummy, in bear format or otherwise?

I was full; I stopped eating when I started to hate myself, in the best way possible.

I will *never* regret that trip.[12]

Now, I know this is all sounding very expensive. And I imagine some of you are like, "Well, that's great, Tyler. I'd love to go to Paris in springtime, too. Wanna let me borrow your jet?"

To which I would say, "I don't like your tone. So no, now you can't borrow my jet."

But my point here is that this time wasn't about the place, it was about the people. Do you have to go to New York or Cancún to meaningfully connect with the people you love? Absolutely not. Sometimes, it's about stopping and slowing down, and realizing how lucky we are to have these people in our lives. And they're right in front of us. Seriously, I want you to take a second and think about when was the last time that you slowed down enough just to watch the people that you care about shine. If it's been a while, trust me when I tell you, this is one of those decisions in life that you'll never regret.

The people you love are always worth it.

**"Life is people.
And time spent with people we love."**

Honestly, some of the best moments from that recovery time were spent locally right here in Nashville, just intentionally connecting with people.

The point I'm trying to make is that my priorities began to shift. I began to see both time and money as not something to be hoarded, but something sacred to be wisely—

---

12. For those of you who are doing the math, this is also the weekend I met one Ms. Jennifer Lynn King. But that's a story for another time.

CHAPTER 9

I'M SORRY

(MS. JACKSON)

I'm sorry.

I need to apologize to you.

I'm sorry that last chapter ended so abruptly.

So you're eight—almost nine—chapters into this book. And I'm so grateful that you've taken this journey with me so far. At this point, you and I are past being mere acquaintances. And I am aware that the very nature of this kind of autobiographical book demands a sacred agreement between author and reader. You picked up this book, and now you're trusting me. But because of that trust—that agreement—I have to be forthright and honest with you. I'm feeling like I've made a mistake here.

Let me explain.

As you know, this whole book has been about a clock. A timeline. An every-six-month cycle that I'm on because of my cancer diagnosis.

Every 180 days or so, Dr. Tan's office messages me in the Vanderbilt University Medical Center app and sets up a time for me to come in and have a series of tests and scans done to check on the progress of my liposarcoma. Then, because everything is done in-house, Dr. Tan comes into the room, reads and interprets the test results, and tells me what's going on with my body.

Every six months.

This six-month cycle is (roughly) early November to early May.

So when I started writing this book, back in late spring/early summer, roughly two and a half years after my initial surgery, I thought an interesting literary framework would be to write the book in real time with you. I'd write these chapters, tell you my cancer story, and you'd walk along with me as I approached my next appointment in November.

I'd do my best to articulate the ticking of that clock, how it overpowers me some days with dread, and how that worry sometimes turns to straight, black, abject fear.

The task was pretty simple: I wanted to take you on that six-month journey with me. I thought it was a good storytelling device.

Listen, I didn't make that up. This *is* my life. I truly do live in six-month chunks between my appointments for scans.

And as I was writing these previous chapters, this upcoming six-month appointment was not a question mark. It wasn't theory. My intentions, both personally and literarily (not a word), were pure.

But there were two problems.

The dates and times didn't line up exactly.

Life didn't wait for Chapter 8. Or Chapter 9.

I didn't finish the book before I got pulled in by Dr. Tan to have my next appointment. I had the scan done.

Today.

Shannon took me to the Vanderbilt Cancer Medical Center.

Shannon goes with me so that she can ask the doctors clarifying questions that she knows I'm afraid to ask. She goes with me so she can share the pertinent medical information with the people who love me that I'm afraid to tell them.

Thank you, Shannon.

But the second problem is the bigger one. Obviously, with my November six-month appointment, I was hoping for a clean bill of health. But Dr. Tan sat across from me and told me that the cancer has grown, or that the indicators they examine every month have moved enough that it's time to go back in and perform another abdominal surgery.

They won't know how much the cancer has grown until they're in there. But they need to open me up. Again.

That monstrous twenty-seven-pound tumor was gone, but the little bits left behind had grown and morphed. Now there were four smaller tumors. Each had to go.

"Four?" I said, shocked.

"Four," Dr. Tan repeated.

Dammit. This thing was like a movie monster that wouldn't die.

Last time, the liposarcoma was wrapped around my organs, and I lost a kidney. I was sure that I wouldn't have to lose anything again this time. But Dr. Tan told me that there's a good chance that I'll lose a portion of my small intestine. Shannon immediately asked what I was thinking and asked for clarification about how much.

"I would estimate about three feet," Dr. Tan said in that Australian accent that I typically found charming and comical but at the moment I hated.

Three feet of my small intestine? That sounded like a lot.

Dr. Tan assured me that losing that much intestine wasn't as big a deal as one might think. I looked down at my phone and quickly googled how much small intestine we have. Twenty-two feet. Okay. Wow. That's way more than I thought. I did the math. Three feet is only 14 percent of my small intestine.

But then I started thinking about the surgery and practically began hyperventilating thinking about going through all of this all over again.

The staples.

The raw pain.

The six-month recovery to even walk properly.

All the unknowns and what-ifs.

The catheters. Those damn catheters.

And most of all, the fear.

As I type these words, it's the end of November. My surgery is scheduled after the start of the New Year.

So I guess I have a new deadline, huh?

Man, I hate that word. Deadline. Why dead?

And so what happened at the end of that chapter was that I just stopped. I was writing. I went to my appointment. And I just stopped.

I just stopped.

I just needed to level with you. I needed you to know that I wasn't trying to employ some sort of trick literary device. This isn't a clever frame for a plot.

I wasn't expecting this news.

And the emotion that I feel more than anything else is the same emotion that I felt when I started writing this book. Fear. I'm afraid. I'm not even sure I care about finishing this book anymore. I don't know if I'll have time.

Also, I have a new clock. A surgery clock. When the doctors are going to cut me open and try to defuse four biological bombs of unknown size and complexity before it detonates, and takes me with it.

So yeah.

I guess the framing of this book now has to change because the framing and focus of my life has changed. My narrative changed, so the book has to as well. It's no longer about the dread of waiting six months to find out my fate. That's already been decided. Depending on schedules and availability, in less than sixty days, I'm going back under the knife.

The same knife that I found out from my mom almost killed me last time.

So.

Yeah.

I just thought that you should know.

CHAPTER 10

WHY DO YOU WRITE LIKE YOU'RE RUNNING OUT OF TIME?

I have ninety-nine problems.

And one of them is *brand*-new.

And it's happening in real time.

For the longest time, it wasn't a matter of if but rather when they were going to have to operate on me. We always knew the cancer was back; we just didn't know when they were going to have to go back in to get it. Well, now we know the when.

It's now.

I have (roughly) sixty days until I go into surgery.

Getting this kind of news can do a number on you. And now, I have some serious heart business to do.

I'm fascinated by how people cope with this type of incredibly frightening and disruptive news. I want to be clear about something. There are levels to cancer news. I'm aware that some people walk into an office and get the news that they have stage four cancer, and they only have years or months left.

This is not my situation. I'm aware that there are people who get the news that they have breast cancer and have to undergo radiation therapy immediately. That's not my situation, either.

My cancer is unique. It's surgical. They can't treat it with radiation. They can't treat it with pills or chemo. They have to perform an invasive surgery where they cut me open and go in and get it.

And look. There are probably a million ways people deal with these kinds of life situations. But I'm not a million people. I'm just me. And so the only thing I can do is share with you my own personal process.

And right now I don't have time to tiptoe around things.

And if I'm being really honest, now that I am forced to stare at some very real existential questions, some really serious stuff, I can't help but lean on my faith.

Which in my case, because I am a Chri…

Man. I have to be honest with you.

I started to type that last sentence and realized how quickly I started to feel all sorts of ways about it. I shouldn't feel this anxious to talk about something so personal and real to me. I just spent nine chapters talking to you about some incredibly personal things, like lament and fear and death. I talked about problems with my penis, for God's sake. But somehow, at this point, I'm afraid to bring up the topic of faith, because I'm afraid I'm going to lose you. Or you're going to shut the book and walk away.

And with the news that I just got, if there's ever been a time I've needed you to stay with me, it's now.

We've come this far, right?

I know that *even bringing up the topic of religion* makes a lot of people uncomfortable. Maybe it even makes *you* uncomfortable.

I don't want that for you. I promise I don't.

But I get it.

Let's be honest: we Americans don't talk about religion. And I don't mean "we Americans don't talk about religion very well." I mean, we Americans legit don't talk about it. And the stats show it.

- According to Pew Research, about half of U.S. adults say they seldom (33 percent) or never (16 percent) talk about religion with people outside their family.
- Roughly 40 percent say they don't even discuss religion with members of their immediate family!
- When asked what to do with someone who disagrees with your religious beliefs, 62 percent of people said, "Try to understand that person's beliefs and agree to disagree."
- Another 33 percent said the best tactic is to "just avoid talking about it."

And again, I get it. I understand why we don't talk about it.

1. This topic is deeply fraught with emotion. The deepest of emotions. Which causes people to overheat, like Yosemite Sam with steam coming out of his ears. I get that.
2. The topic of religion is incredibly personal, requiring a level of vulnerability that is so white-hot that most people can't go there. Vulnerability requires real risk, which means someone could take your words and hurt you. It's safer to just keep your thoughts to yourself.
3. Religion is also very complex. And our society isn't into doing "complex" well. We don't do nuance much. But we'll click the mess out of some clickbait. Outrage. Black-

and-white, I'm right and you're wrong. I'm the hero, and you're George Santos.

But—and maybe I don't know you—but I bet for a lot of you reading this, it goes deeper than statistics and emotional complexity. A lot of people just haven't had positive experiences regarding faith.

And real talk, people. I just changed the word "religion" to the word "faith" in that last sentence because I didn't know which one would be less off-putting.

See! This is so tough to talk about. Even what words we use. So I'm going to use the words "religion" and "religious" going forward because...I guess...they're the most clear.

Maybe you're not particularly religious, and you feel a bit like I've gone and done a bait-and-switch on you. Maybe you're saying, "Look, I didn't buy this book to have it turn into a religious thing. I came here for verses from New Edition, not the Twelve Disciples!"

Maybe you're irreligious, and think nearly all of religion is just kinda made-up nonsense. Or you're science-y and have experience with religious people being anti-science, or have seen science and faith pitted against each other, like a zero-sum game.

Or maybe you've had bad experiences with church, or religion, or Christians. And so all that trauma is flooding forward, even as you read this.

Maybe you're part of the LGBTQ+ community, or you have people you deeply love in that community, and the way that society has gone the past decade or so, you've watched the rhetoric from religious folks get ratcheted up, and it hasn't been particularly kind or loving. You, or your loved ones, feel like casualties in the culture wars. And if someone was going to force you to choose sides, you know what side you'd be on. You'd choose your peoples over steeples.

Or maybe you've been an observer, and over the past few years, you've seen religion be used as a political tool in ways that make you profoundly uncomfortable, or even angry. When you hear the word "Christian," you feel that word now has more of a political edge to it than a religious one. And one you find more than distasteful. Offensive, even.

Again, my friends, I get it.

It sucks because I can't even talk about my faith without all that baggage.

But there's another side of the coin: I don't have time to *not* talk about this topic. When you face death, or an unknown future, things get real. You have to figure out what you're going to lean on, and what matters to you. And a person's religious views—whatever they may be—determine that.

So I don't have time to *not* talk about this.

And one more thing: maybe you can look at it like this. There's a lot of you reading this who are not a six-foot-two Black man, but you've trusted me enough to walk you through my experience as a Black man in America. And I want to thank you for that. Because I believe that it's brought us closer. That's what proximity is all about. For those of you who aren't religious, respectfully, I'm going to ask you to let me talk about my experience, even if it's very different from yours. What you're going to read here in the next bit is about me. This is also who I am.

YOU GOTTA HAVE FAITH, FAITH, FAITH

So how did we get here? Well, as you may or may not know, I came to faith in high school. I went to a small Bible college in the Santa Cruz mountains in California. I'm also a churchgoing man. For a while, I was a youth pastor. I was also a spiritual coach for a local high school football team. I was the narrator and host for *The Gospel Project*, a series of videos for kids that explained the story of the Bible and was distributed to more than 47,000 churches in the US. I wrote at some length about my religious journey in my previous book. There was a transcendent moment for me when I was in high school at a summer church camp. Rather than retelling the whole story, let me recount for you some of that moment.

Chapel ended, and we had thirty minutes until curfew.

That walk from the chapel back to the cabin was my own personal spiritual pilgrimage. As I took that walk back, tears flowed down my face.

There was no doubt in my mind that there was a God in this Universe, and that for some reason, He'd broken through reality to get to me. This was not like the fleeting feeling when a girl liked me. This was not like hitting a home run. This was so much bigger.

Some friends asked if I wanted to walk with them, but I hung back. I couldn't. I needed this moment to be alone.

As I walked by myself, I had a deep sense, down in my bones, that my life had been changed forever, and I was trying to grapple with what that meant.

The air felt different.

The sky looked different.

The stars had a different meaning.

God was going to walk with me, now, for the rest of my life.

I knew I was never going to be the same.

I was not wrong.

The point is, I'm not an expert in religion, by any means, but I am serious about it. So when I got the frightening news from Dr. Tan that it was time for him to operate again, I knew that I'd immediately need to lean on the resources of my faith tradition to help me process this. To help me through this. I knew what I needed.

I needed Jesus.

There.

I said it.

Jesus.

And I know in our current cultural climate, even saying the name *Jesus* in a book like this can cause problems.

And I'm going to be honest with you, this makes me angry. I feel like something very personal and important to me—my faith, Jesus, Christianity, whatever you want to call it or however you want to say it—has been hijacked in the past several years.

It's been stolen.

It's been co-opted.

Or maybe the right term is that it's been vandalized.

To the point where for a lot of people, when they even hear someone start to talk about Jesus, they shut down.

And again, I get it.

WE DON'T TALK ABOUT BRUNO.
NO. NO. NO.

There's a story I've told some of my close friends about when I was writing my previous book. The original title and subhead for the book was slated to be *I Take My Coffee Black: Reflections on Tupac, Musical Theater, Jesus, and Being Black in America.*

But at one point, as I was sending out the early advance reader copies to the group of beta readers, I got some interesting feedback. A woman in the reader group named Julie wrote a comment, saying,

"If I saw Jesus on the title of the cover, I would have immediately cringed. But then I remembered, Tyler, there's the white Jesus and the black Jesus. And, well, I like the black Jesus."

Now, look. Some of you might be confused by Julie's comment. Two Jesuses? But I was not. I knew exactly what she was talking about. Say less, sis.

I think she was trying to say, "As I listen to how people talk about Jesus and Christianity, I hear two versions of the same faith, and that's confusing."

Let's get real with some examples. When I think about Jesus and Christianity, I think of all sorts of things, but I think about that epic song "We Shall Overcome." This song was sung by Mahalia Jackson, one of the central voices in the Civil Rights Movement. At the time, Mahalia Jackson was the most famous Black singer in the world, and she would often travel with Dr. King, using her powerful, beautiful voice to sing old spiritual songs to remind the crowds that the battle being fought was much deeper than politics. Her voice and her songs reminded the gathered folks that though the world at large might not have known, experienced, or understood the profound suffering and pain inflicted upon the Black community, God did.

Mahalia Jackson was right behind Dr. King during his most famous speech, on the steps of the Lincoln Memorial during the March on Washington on August 28, 1963. Mahalia had heard Martin Luther King speak dozens of times. She'd heard him deliver words that inspired Black folks to endure suffering and not lose hope. She'd heard King talk behind closed doors, with the freedom that only comes when you're in the company of friends. And twelve minutes in, Mahalia Jackson knew that King wasn't being…fully King. That something was off. And if you listen to the speech, she's right. Keeping it real, the first twelve minutes, well…it's filled with weird, bland Constitutional language. King uses an extended banking metaphor about "insufficient funds." A banking metaphor! Not his hottest bars.

So Mahalia yelled something to him.

"Tell them about the dream, Martin."

Then, there, at the 12:20 mark of the speech, and for the remaining five minutes, something in King fundamentally changes. King goes into rarefied air, delivering—extemporaneously—one of the finest speeches we'll ever hear.

It's stunning, how poetic and effective the remaining 297 seconds are. From an oratory standpoint, it's like watching Michael Jordan score thirty-seven points in five minutes. King repeats the phrase "I have a dream" nine times, each time articulating a powerful emotional picture of a reality that had yet to be realized in racially divided America. He paints a picture of America not of tolerance, or beleaguered coexistence, but brotherhood. White men and Black men sitting down with their families at the dinner table. Black boys and girls playing as friends with white boys and girls. It's relational. It's friendship. It's a picture of the future we can all long for.

Then King goes into another repetition, saying, "Let freedom ring" eleven times, and while he does it, King rhetorically marches through the nation, touching several Southern states and their most powerful geographic feature. It's mesmerizingly beautiful.

And King knows it. His voice gains power. His words are punctuated with clarity. With certainty. Gone are the pauses and the slow pacing. King is no longer calculating his words. They are pouring out of his essence. He's not delivering a talk. He's preaching to a nation the deepest truths that he's ever known.

He's preaching.

Look at his body language at the end of the speech. He practically levitates when he says the line:

> "All *of God's children, Black men and white men, Jews and Gentiles, Protestants and Catholics.*"

And then that final line:

> "*Free at last. Free at last. Thank God almighty, we're free at last.*"

!!!!!!!!!!!!!

This speech isn't just a speech. It's a sacred moment of historical proportions. I don't use the word "sacred" lightly. It means that it had religious or transcendent implications. And it did. After all, folks tend to forget that Dr. Martin Luther King was a pastor. A minister. He was a reverend. A Christian. A follower of Jesus. And he was preaching. Preaching! To a nation. A nation that needed it, more than ever.

"Tell them about the dream, Martin."

After that speech, Mahalia got up and sang "We Shall Overcome," which was like the anthem for the Civil Rights Movement.

> We are not afraid (oh Lord)
> We are not afraid (oh Lord)
> We are not afraid, today

> Oh, deep in my heart
> I know that I do believe
> We shall overcome, someday.

That's what I think about.

Or I think about another moment that's less historical and more personal involving the Queen of Soul, Ms. Aretha Franklin. Many people do not know that her most famous and best-selling album was a live recording of her singing gospel music. Aretha struggled with some demons, including years of oppressive and abusive relationships with the men in her life, including her husband, which led her to abuse alcohol. But when life fell apart for her, Aretha (whose daddy was a pastor) knew how to come home. Home was church, because God was in church, and God would help her, no matter how messy things got. And in that recording, Aretha is singing with her entire body and soul. She is, literally, dripping with sweat. And I think about her, singing a famous song written by Thomas Dorsey after the death of his infant son. It's called "Precious Lord, Take My Hand."

> Precious Lord, take my hand
> Through the storm, through the night
> Lead me on to the light
> Take my hand precious Lord, lead me home.

That's what I think about.

In so many words, that's what my friend Julie meant when she referred to the "black Jesus." And I want to be clear. Though her sentiment was about race, this version of Jesus is not limited to one race. It's not about race at all. It's much, much more about theology.

So there's that version of the Christian faith.

But then there's another version. That one is highly politicized. It uses extreme language, often infused with lots of fear-mongering. And there's a lot of triumphal and apocalyptic language. You saw it back on January 6, 2021, when a group of political dissidents stormed the Capitol building.

That assault was accompanied by a lot of explicitly Christian symbols, like Jesus flags, Bible quotes, and sermons delivered via loudspeakers. And for many of the 2,000-plus attackers, it was done in Christianity's name.

For example, Michael Sparks of Kentucky (who was later charged by the FBI as one of the first to enter the Capitol) wrote on social media that "Trump will be your president four more years in Jesus name."

Or this quote, from evangelical leader Franklin Graham, who had this to say when he was asked by David Brody of the Christian Broadcast Network (CBN) about what would happen if Donald Trump lost the 2020 presidential election:

> *I'm just asking that God would spare this country for another four years to give us a little bit more time to do the work before the storm hits. I believe the storm is coming. You're going to see Christians attacked; you're going to see churches close; you're going to see a real hatred expressed toward people of faith. That's coming... God has put him [Donald Trump] in this position to defend Western civilization as we have known it.*[1]

1.　David Brody, "Exclusive: Franklin Graham Tells CBN News He Thinks the Democratic Party Is 'Opposed to Faith,'" CBN, August 28, 2020. https://www2.cbn.com /news/us/exclusive-franklin-graham-tells-cbn-news-he-thinks-democratic-party -opposed-faith.

At the storming of the Capitol, we saw signs that read "Jesus is my Savior, Trump is my President." This was religiously sanctioned violence, done by a "righteous" mob holding the Bible high above their heads.

Which for me—as a Black man and a Christian—is absolutely asinine.

It makes me feel that you are hijacking the name of Jesus.

My Jesus.

Co-opting Him.

Stealing Him.

That my faith has been vandalized.

Because those two versions of Christianity are *very different* from each other.

I've been asked why I, as a Black man in America, would even *want* to associate myself with this religion, marred as it is. And to be fair, I've been given a plethora of reasons to reject it all. After all, as a Black man in the United States, the Bible, Jesus, and Christianity have had both a troubling and glorious role in my own people's history.

Let me outline this for you so you can simply see it. At the exact same time, all of these statements are true:

- The Bible was used to prop up and justify slavery in the South.
- The Bible was used by abolitionists as the moral and philosophical basis to oppose slavery.
- *Uncle Tom's Cabin*, arguably the most influential work of fiction in US history, exposed the evils of slavery and dramatically shifted Northern US attitudes toward slavery. It was written by Harriet Beecher Stowe, the daughter of

a preacher and a deeply religious woman, who said that the book came to her "in visions" and that she did not so much write it as receive it from God.

- That same book, according to one historian, "stiffened the South's resolve to defend slavery and demonize the North." Southern preachers used the pulpits to offer the country a new vision of slavery, as a positive good ordained by God and sanctioned by Scripture.

- Later, in the fifties and sixties, the Bible was used to justify Jim Crow and de facto segregation.

- The local church and the Bible were central to the message and method of the entire Civil Rights Movement.

- Martin Luther King Jr. was a preacher, was trained at a seminary, and was a pastor at Dexter Avenue King Memorial Baptist Church. Some of his most famous speeches were actually sermons given in churches.

- Famous segregationist and senator Strom Thurmond was not only a member of the First Baptist Church in Edgefield, South Carolina, but he was the superintendent of Sunday school for that church.

So damn. Which is it? Was the Bible (and Christianity and Jesus) a liberating force for my people? Or was it an instrument used to keep the status quo?

Has the name of Jesus been hijacked?

In the big picture, all of these questions really matter. But for me, with sixty days left before my surgery, I don't have the time. I don't have time to get into those questions.

I needed to get to the thing.

The thing that I knew for sure.

The thing that changed my life.

The thing that started at a summer camp back in high school.

YOU CAN GET WITH THIS.
OR YOU CAN GET WITH THAT.

So back to my friend Julie who was talking about the two different types of Jesus.

I think she was trying (in her own way) to articulate a truth: how you experience the world (especially in the United States) is shaped by a lot of things, including your race. Your race affects and impacts your experiences. Although "being Black" or "being a minority" is not a uniform experience (by any means!), there are parts of that "being Black in the United States of America" Venn diagram that *for sure* overlap. Just like how "experiencing the world as a woman" is going to be different than "experiencing the world as a man." Is it the same for *every* woman? No. But there is some real overlap and shared experience. "Watching Jason Momoa on the silver screen makes me feel a certain type of way," for example, is something universally shared by females. Also males. Hell, this applies to women who aren't even attracted to males. In fact, if you have a beating heart, you're attracted to Jason Momoa. Dang, he's hot.

And look, when you're part of a minority group that was enslaved for several hundred years, and viewed for roughly 400 years as less than human by the dominant culture, that impacts how you read the Bible's stories, because it impacts how you see things like power, money, justice, and hope. There is a unique thing that Black folk bring to reading and understanding the Bible, and Black scholars and theologians have pointed this out, both historically and recently.

It's not just based on race, of course. But I think this is what Julie might have been trying to articulate.

And this tension is not new.

Interestingly enough, whenever I feel isolated and alone as a Black man thinking about "will things ever change" or "am I the only one who sees this," it's incredibly tragic how simple it is for me to go back in history and find Black writers who articulated the *exact* same things I'm feeling (but in *their* time period).

I want to ask you to do something for me, to share an experience with me. I want you to read something written by Frederick Douglass, the famous American abolitionist and writer who wrote about this very issue more than 150 years ago.

In his famous memoir *Life as an American Slave*, Douglass talked about the "two Christianities." He was such a vocal opponent of Southern Christianity (which used the Bible's teachings to prop up slaveholding) that people began to wonder if Douglass was anti-religious. After all, why wouldn't a Black man be opposed to Christianity if it were the theological and societal basis for the enslavement and torture of him and his people?

So this is what I want to ask you to do. Read his words and see how simple it was for me to find another Black man in history who felt the exact same way as I do today. It shouldn't have been this easy. Also, this is spot-on.

> *Those unacquainted with my religious views may suppose me an opponent of all religion . . . what I have said respecting and against religion, I mean strictly to apply to the slaveholding religion of this land, and with no possible reference to Christianity proper; for, between the Christianity of this land, and the Christianity of Christ, I recognize the widest possible*

difference—so wide, that to receive the one as good, pure, and holy, is of necessity to reject the other as bad, corrupt, and wicked.

To be the friend of the one, is of necessity to be the enemy of the other. I love the pure, peaceable, and impartial Christianity of Christ: I therefore hate the corrupt, slaveholding, women-whipping, cradle-plundering, partial and hypocritical Christianity of this land. Indeed, I can see no reason, but the most deceitful one, for calling the religion of this land Christianity. I look upon it as the climax of all misnomers, the boldest of all frauds, and the grossest of all libels.

Douglass was saying, "These two things are not the same thing." And he's also saying, "Y'all have to choose."

AM I LIVING IT RIGHT?

When you face a serious threat to your life, or an uncertainty, like cancer, the questions and things you think about shift pretty rapidly.

People sometimes ask me if I think about death a lot. If we're being honest, ever since my cancer diagnosis, I kind of do. But thinking about it and worrying about are two different things. Honestly, there are some parts of death that I'm not too concerned about. And if that seems glib, I don't mean it to be. The afterlife part? That may be complicated for some, but I rest on my faith. As the Bible says,

I'm here to tell you, there's something else
The afterworld, a world of never-ending happiness
You can always see the sun, day or night

Wait. Is that the Bible or is that Prince? Alexa? Play "Let's Go Crazy" by Prince.

Yep, okay, so that's definitely Prince. My bad. My bad. But the sentiment still applies. And oddly enough, some of the descriptions of the Bible aren't that different. In the famous words of one of the most famous Negro spirituals:

> Swing low, sweet chariot
> Coming for to carry me home.

When you're part of a historically enslaved people, there's a great need to believe that A) God still sees you despite your suffering, and that B) He's going to do something to make this all right someday. A lot of Negro spirituals contain promises about something better coming, and God setting all things right someday. There's a lot about Heaven in those old Negro spirituals. Heaven as a consolation, as a way of hope, as a form of justice for those who really need it.

A while ago in church, I heard a guest preacher use the entirety of his thirty-five-minute block to pull out of the Bible all the things we know about the afterlife, about Heaven, and what life after death is going to be like. He was essentially trying to paint a picture of what Heaven was going to look and feel like. All due respect to this man, this seemed like a fool's errand to me. There's a verse in the Bible where the apostle Paul says:

> What no eye has seen, nor ear heard,
> nor the heart of man imagined,
> what God has prepared for those who love Him.[2]

---

2. 1 Corinthians 2:9 ESV.

Well, Paul, lemme tell you what I've seen in my multiple trips around the sun, buddy. Have you ever seen *Willy Wonka and the Chocolate Factory*, Paul? Well, I have. So I can imagine some pretty glorious ish. Have you been to Disneyland at Christmastime, Paul? I have. What about Hawaii? You been to Hawaii, Paul? Have you dangled your toes in the surf at the Waikaiakaieeoneweona Beach? Did I just make up that name by typing a whole bunch of vowels and throwing in some K's, M's, and W's? You bet I did! Look, I suck at geography. The point is, Paul, that I've been somewhere in Hawaii that I can't spell but was magnificent! Oh, and what about what my ears have heard, Paul? Have you ever seen Jay-Z, Garth Brooks, Dave Matthews Band, and Taylor Swift in concert, Paul? I'm going to guess *no* since they didn't tour in Athens or Philippi, and, well, you've been dead since the first century. The point is, Paul, these eyes have seen some stuff, and these ears have heard some things.

Whoa.

Take a breath, Tyler.

I don't know why I got so aggressive with Paul there. He's actually trying to help me out and was making the same point that I was: that whatever God is cooking up is better than all that, and Heaven's going to be incredible.

So. Yeah, not really worried about that part of dying.

But I will tell you what I'm fixated on.

I'm fixated on right here and right now.

I'm focused on the time I have remaining.

I'm focused on today. Because I don't know how many more todays I am going to have.

This is why I needed to talk to you all about Jesus. The time that Jesus was in the public spotlight during His time on Earth was pretty short. Three years, most scholars tell us. So most of the words, the teachings, and the miracles that Jesus did were done in those three years. That's not a lot of time. And during that time, Jesus was shockingly intentional about how He interacted with and loved people. He loved in ways that seemed extreme to some people. He loved in ways that seemed crazy to some people. He loved in ways that seemed outrageous to some people. He loved in ways that seemed heretical and blasphemous to some people.

He loved in ways that got Him killed.

And the night before His death, in the Garden of Gethsemane, the Bible says that Jesus was afraid. So afraid that He sweated blood and asked God to not let happen what was about to happen to Him. I'm not exactly sure what specifically Jesus had in His mind that He was afraid of, and the text doesn't completely tell us, but it does tell us that He didn't want to be alone. At the Last Supper, He said it was His "deep, deep desire" to eat that meal with His friends. He begged His friends, the Disciples, to stay up with Him, talk with Him, pray with Him.

Jesus seemed to really love loving people.

And I want to live and love like that. And so how I live today is what matters most to me. How do I treat people? And not just am I loving people well, but are they actually feeling the love that I'm attempting to communicate?

To quote my man John Mayer:

> Either way I wonder sometimes
> About the outcome
> Of a still verdict-less life
> Am I living it right?

> How do I know?

And for that, I want to go back to the question before us about the two Christianities. For me, honestly, it's not all that complex.

Even a cursory reading of the Bible and the teachings of Jesus will reveal that the highest ethic is to love God and love others. And this is the key: those two are *combined*.

There is a critical moment that's so important it's recorded in Matthew, Mark, and Luke. Jesus is asked a pointed question about what the most important law is to God. Basically a dude asks, "What does God think is the most important thing that people can do with their lives?" And then Jesus clarifies what God most wants from people. Jesus answers in a two-part response: Love God and love others.

Love God.

And love others.

And this clarification has vast implications. Jesus is clearly saying, "If you love God, it will always lead to an expression of how you love other people. Now, if you love God and that doesn't make you love people more, you're missing the whole point. You're doing it wrong."

Doing what wrong?

Everything.

Jesus is saying, "You can't say you're a serious follower of me and treat your neighbor like trash." Loving God and loving others are tied. Love is the highest ethic in the Bible.

This isn't confusing. Look, my friends, words have meaning. They just do.

Let me give you an example. Heck, I don't know, uh . . . when Sir Mix-a-Lot says that he likes "big butts" and then insists, emphatically, that he is not lying, we cannot, in good faith, turn around and say, "Sir-Mix-a-Lot is anti-big-booty."

That's not 👏 how 👏 words 👏 work.

When Salt-N-Pepa and En Vogue team up and *all six voices* sing in unison to extol the virtues of their "man"—in the process calling him a "mighty, mighty good man" more than twenty-three times, one simply cannot say that these ladies find their man puny, wimpy, below average, and less than desirable.

That's not 👏 how 👏 words 👏 work.

When Queen Whitney articulates clearly that she wants to run to you, and then *repeats this desire explicitly more than a dozen times*, we cannot honestly surmise that what she *really* wants is to be all alone, and that she does not want anyone to hold her in their arms, thereby keeping her safe from harm.

That's not 👏 how 👏 words 👏 work.

So when Jesus is asked, point-blank, "What's most important?" and He purposely and intentionally combines the long-standing Jewish commandment to "love God with all your heart and soul and mind and strength" with "love your neighbor"—that's not opaque. That's not confusing.

Love God.

Love other people.

And…as Jesus would go on to show with the rest of His life, this kind of love is nearly always self-sacrificing and nearly always costly. And nearly always given freely to people who don't deserve it.

The model of Jesus was to offer radical, self-sacrificial, deeply controversial love to everyone, even one's enemies. This is called Grace. It's to be distributed freely, like samples at Costco.

Friends, look, I live in the South. Which is my choice. But during the past several years, there are times when I haven't seen this type of humble Jesus love from some of my white brothers and sisters in the faith. I know I've said it already, but I mean it when I tell you that I feel like the name of Jesus was vandalized. Since 2016, I've seen an uptick from self-professing Christians in these things:

- An unwillingness or lack of desire to connect with people of different political persuasions and the tendency to view them as "immoral" or "against God."
- An unwillingness to connect with, get close to, or hear the life stories of people who are sexual minorities, instead viewing them as "opponents" or, worse, an "enemy."
- Ambivalence of many Christians toward issues of injustice that face people of color.
- Outward antagonism and character assassination toward Christian leaders of color—who happen to be your brothers and sisters in the faith—who bring up issues of injustice.
- Weaponization of the Bible and faith to call those who disagree with you "not real Christians."
- Overuse of the pejorative and dismissive word "woke" as a label to disregard all perspectives and arguments about politics and history that point out systemic, baked-in injustices.
- Utter lack of humility of some people to even listen to people of color—people who happen to be your brothers and sisters in the faith—about issues that affect real people in real communities (even if it's not yours).
- A wholesale inability to lament with people of color for even one second when injustice happens to minority communities.

Are we serving the same Jesus or not?

Love God.

Love other people.

Is it that complicated?

I don't know, y'all. I don't see a lot of "love your neighbor" in there.

I'm just saying, don't lose the plot.

I'm just saying, the words in the Bible mean something.

The model of Jesus was to offer radical, self-sacrificial, deeply controversial love to everyone, even one's enemies. Grace.

So whenever you see *that*, I think you know, "Oh, that's the real thing."

And to be clear, I don't just mean "whenever I see this at work in other people."

I mean "whenever I see this at work in *me*."

And this isn't theory to me. It's not academic.

I think this is life or death.

Actually.

I *know* this is life or death.

Look, there are a lot of people out there who claim the name of Jesus and claim to be Christians. But in the end, it's not even about what *others* do.

In the end, it's about what *I* choose to do.

With this time that I have left, I'm choosing to live and love like the Jesus I know.

Friends, it's been a long, exhausting few years, and I simply don't have time. I don't have time for these arguments about, or to wade into, the culture wars. I don't have time to explain to Christians why "loving your neighbor" is something Christians should take seriously because Jesus said it. And brothers and sisters, if you don't listen to Him, then you probably aren't going to listen to me.

But I sure wish you would listen to Him.

And if you're out there, and you're not religious at all, and this is not part of your story at all, well, good news. You are a human, which means you're a part of the group of people that I believe my God has told me to love.

And I'll do my very best to love you and welcome you.

No matter who you are.

Or what you believe.

Because that's what Grace is.

Love poured out on the undeserving.

And that?

That is something I know a whole lot about.

CHAPTER 11

THEY FORGOT ABOUT DRE

<Exhale>

I remember the day like it was yesterday.

January 26.

It was a Sunday. Early afternoon. Some friends from church and I were eating at Mojo's Tacos right outside of Nashville. Mojo's is probably my favorite taqueria in the greater Nashville area. To be fair, most of the time, my favorite taqueria is the one that is serving tacos. But this place is its own kind of special.

You guys, they have these Korean fried cauliflower tacos. They're topped with this fresh ginger slaw and finished with toasted sesame seeds and something called "Gochujang Sauce." It's the kind of food that's so good, it renders you speechless. It does not matter how great the conversation is with the people at your table, when the food comes, all talking ceases. It turns into a silent movie. I don't care if you were at a table with Tom Cruise, Tom Hanks, and Tom Brady, when those Korean fried cauliflower tacos come, those Toms better turn into some Charlie Chaplins, I'll tell you that much.

But I digress.

Dang it. Tacos.

Anyway, the giant TV above Mojo's bar showed an image of Kobe Bryant. The caption read "Kobe Bryant 1978–2020." And I thought, "Okay. What record of Kobe's did LeBron break this time?" I thought ESPN was making some sort of joke. Like LeBron killed Kobe's assist record or something. Ha. Ha.

Do you know what I absolutely *did not* think?

Do you know where my mind absolutely did not go?

I pulled out my phone and went to Twitter and clicked over to see the top trending topics. Kobe was at the top. Why were people talking about Kobe?

I clicked on it.

And then I saw the news story.

And found out about the helicopter.

And the fog.

And the crash.

And his daughter.

And it felt like my heart stopped.

I looked around at the table I was sitting at, and I needed so badly for them to tell me that it was a joke.

But it wasn't.

For the next few weeks, people all over the nation, especially people in the greater Los Angeles area, mourned the loss of an icon. Thousands of people flocked to the Staples Center (where the Lakers played) to find solace by being together and grieving together. Across the plaza, mourners left posters, notes, flowers, and jerseys. Folks made makeshift memorials to pay their respects.

For only the second time that decade, the NBA delayed a game, postponing the Lakers' next game. When the game was finally played, the Lakers left two courtside seats empty for Kobe and his daughter Gianna. Before the game, LeBron James (who at that time was playing for the Lakers) tried to read a prepared statement but then tossed his notes to the side as he attempted to communicate what Kobe meant to the sport, to the city, and to him. During the National Anthem, sung by R & B legends Boyz II Men, who were dressed in yellow Kobe Bryant jerseys, LeBron could be seen openly weeping.

We all were.

Then R & B artist Usher, dressed in all black, stood in front of a wreath of yellow roses fashioned into Kobe's number and sang a moving rendition of "Amazing Grace." As he sang, eyes closed in reverence, the scoreboard showed clips of every NBA team starting off their games by grabbing the tip-off and putting the ball on the ground for a twenty-four-second shot clock violation, in honor of Kobe's number 24.

Every.

Single.

Team.

Near the end of the song, Usher improvised:

> Amazing grace
> Oh, we need your amazing grace.
> Lord, send your amazing grace
> to every man, woman, and child that's hurting
>   right now.

And then each starting player was introduced by the public address announcer as "Kobe Bryant."

This wasn't a basketball game.

We were watching a memorial service.

Just thinking about all that gets me emotional. I think about the shining photos of Kobe with his family, of that one famous photo of him and Gianna sitting courtside at the Staples Center; he is wearing a bright orange hoodie with the WNBA logo emblazoned on it, his arm around his teenage girl, as they both look up at the scoreboard, smiling. Pure joy.

I think about the story sports journalist Elle Duncan shared about a time when she met Kobe backstage at an ESPN event. She was eight months pregnant at the time (and showing!), and Kobe immediately began talking to her about parenting. When she told Kobe that she was expecting a daughter, Kobe high-fived her.

"I'm a girl-dad," Kobe said, noting that he had only daughters. He then added, "Girls are the best."

This fierce competitor, known so much for his relentless intensity that his nickname was Black Mamba, was a huge softie for his four daughters.

Sometimes, despite all my efforts to not think about it, I do imagine what Kobe said to his girl in their final moments, or how desperately he must have tried to protect Gigi as that helicopter went down.

God, I try not to think about that. It's too much.

DON'T YOU...FORGET ABOUT ME

The tragic death of Kobe and his thirteen-year-old daughter, Gianna, was a national story that produced a deep sense of shock and grief in people. It impacted me so much that when I wrote my children's book *A Door Made for Me*, I had the illustrator dress the main character in a yellow number 24 Lakers jersey, in honor of him.

And maybe you're like me. Maybe you remember exactly where you were, too, when you heard that Kobe died.

It's a moment I won't soon forget.

But there's another side to this. That helicopter crash didn't only claim the lives of an NBA superstar and his beloved daughter.

Nine people were killed on that flight.

Nine.

This group was all headed to a basketball game at Kobe's Mamba Sports Academy in Newbury Park, California, where Kobe was scheduled to coach Gianna's team. The other crash victims were:

- Alyssa Altobelli, a teammate of Gianna's
- Her father, John Altobelli
- Her mother, Keri Altobelli
- Payton Chester, a teammate of Gianna's
- Her mother, Sarah Chester
- Basketball coach Christina Mauser
- The pilot, Ara Zobayan

But those names aren't household names. And, understandably, the death of a sports celebrity overshadowed those people in the national news. But there's a whole lot of people who loved the Altobelli family and the Chester family, and Coach Mauser, and the pilot, Ara Zobayan. And for them, January 26, 2020, is not the day Kobe died.

It's the day their world caved in.

It's the day someone they loved left this world forever.

Their mom.

Their dad.

Their sister.

Their friend.

And although those other seven names might have been forgotten by most of us, they will never be forgotten by those who loved them.

No one deserves to be forgotten.

BABY, REMEMBER MY NAME

It's funny—for most of my life, I never thought about death. Actually that's not true. When I was younger, I used to think that I would die before I turned twenty-five. Why? I don't know. It was something I told my friends, even. When I turned twenty-six, they were like, "Well, you made it," and we moved on. But after that, it was like the curse was broken and I didn't think about dying. Like ever again. If I did think about it, it was concerning *other* people. But here's the deal—now, in real time, as I sit here and write this, and this appointment for my second cancer surgery approaches, I think about dying a whole lot more.

All the time, actually.

I'm not saying there's a high chance that I could die during this operation.

But...

...the percentage is not zero...

...and it's far more likely than it was a few years ago.

Or even a few months ago.

And that's the truth.

And as I penned this chapter, and tried to share with you what was going on in my heart and head, I thought that the majority of it would be about my fear of being forgotten. Which—I think—is mostly a fear of not making a lasting difference in the world.

So I guess in some ways, everyone is afraid of being forgotten.

I wrote about this in my previous book, but some of you might remember that for my final year of high school, I changed schools so that I could attend the newly opened Las Vegas Academy for the Performing Arts. Some of you thought that you were going to make it through this book without me talking Las Vegas Academy. Well, I love that school too much to let that happen to any of y'all.

LVA was a performing arts magnet high school that drew upon students from the thirty-plus high schools in the greater Las Vegas area. It was a school dedicated to training students who had demonstrated skill in the areas of orchestra, music, dance, theater, and theater tech.

Now, the de facto leader of this new school was not the principal, but Ms. Pattie Emmett, a veteran teacher who was in charge of the school's entire theater department. And Ms. Emmett decided that our high school's first production would be the musical *Fame*, based on the 1980 movie that chronicles the lives of students at a performing arts high school in New York City.

That's right.

A performing arts school.

Doing a musical.

About a performing arts school.

The title song in that musical is the song "Fame," originally performed by Irene Cara, who played the role of Coco in the 1980 film. The song was a sensation in 1980, topping the charts and even winning an Oscar for Best Song. Here are the lyrics. Feel free to sing along in your head. Or better yet, just stop reading this book for a second and stream the song. You'll have to push past the early-eighties synthesizers for the first thirty seconds, but when Irene Cara starts singing, this song turns *transcendent*.

Alexa, play the song "Fame."

(FAME!) I'm gonna make it to Heaven
Light up the sky like a flame
(FAME!) I'm gonna live forever
Baby, remember my name

The whole point of this musical is that chasing after fame is really about chasing after immortality. Although this was decades before social media, the seeds of this idea were planted and sprouted. I think about the film *La La Land, which won the award for Best Picture in 2017*. The dazzlingly shot second number "Someone in the Crowd" follows the main character, Mia (Emma Stone), and her roommates as they dress up and prepare to go to a party, where they hope to be "discovered" and elevated to starring roles in the movies. Mia and her girls sing:

Someone in the crowd could
Take you where you wanna go
If you're the someone ready to be found.

Don't sleep on *La La Land*. That movie is dope. But check it, it's the same idea. If the girls get "discovered"—then (and perhaps only then?) will they finally be someone. Then they will finally have their existence validated. "Fame" is what stamps a human being as being truly worthwhile.

And in our modern social media world, the concept of fame has only intensified, with popularity being numerically trackable. In his documentary *Fake Famous*, filmographer and author Nick Bilton talked about this, saying, "*Likes* translate to more followers, which is the current currency of the most important thing on Earth today— what everyone seems obsessed with—being famous."

And not to get too morbid, but hey, I have cancer and I think about this stuff a lot more than most people, and I think I know why we all go after fame. I think it's because fame gives us a sense that you will live on.

It's an antidote to one of our biggest fears, as people: that no one will remember us.

Rumbling in the background for all of us is an unspoken reality. We're all on a timeline. And I'm going to say something that should not be controversial one single bit because it is absolutely true. We are all going to die. We come into the world, and we're not permanent. I think about Mother Teresa of Calcutta, who once wrote:

> *"There are two guarantees in life: Death is for certain and Michael Jordan will not lose in a game seven in the Finals."*

Wait.

There's a *chance* that I might be a teensy bit off with that quote.

See? I'm joking. Why? Because of emotional preservation. Even now, after all that I have been through, I find it difficult to lean into the truth that all of us will die.

<Exhale>

And the truth is, most of us will be forgotten unless we are:

- A massively important world leader who effectively led through a time of crisis (think: Washington, Lincoln, Napoleon, Bill Pullman as President Thomas J. Whitmore, whose rousing speech inspired the humans to win against the aliens in *Independence Day*)

- A billionaire who put their last name on a whole slew of buildings (think Rockefeller, Carnegie, Sam "Walmart" Walton)
- An evil dictator who unleashed untold suffering on thousands or millions of people (Genghis Khan, Hitler, Stalin, Pol Pot, whoever wrote the song "Baby Shark")

Yes, my friends, I hate to say it, but the vast majority of people who have ever lived or will ever live will have their names lost to the fickle sands of history. But also, I live in the South, where there are statues of people who fought to keep my people enslaved. Whole statues of slave owners!

And these statues are up because of that desire of people to not want to be forgotten.

I guess this is what it means to be human.

This is life.

That being said, as an aside, I do have one request. I don't need a giant statue of me (I'm already chiseled! Hey girl!). I don't need to have a theater named after me, or some side street in Nashville. But there is something I want.

Every day, I try to exercise. I have a five-mile route that takes me down my block, through some city streets, and then out to the J. Percy Priest Dam, where I can look out over the lake and the water.

There's a bench along that route that is my bench.

I even call it that.

When I see it, I say to myself, "That's my bench."

Sometimes, when I see people sitting on it, I get a bit indignant. "Yo. Why are you sitting on my bench?" Now, I don't say this *out loud*. It's not like I go around chasing people away from my bench like an angry goose or something.

But I want to be clear: this bench *is* my bench.

I have done some of my deepest thinking on that bench, and although it's a common bench, I've had some uncommon moments on that bench. I don't ask for much, but I want the City of Nashville to make this bench my bench. That's all. Just a major municipality to honor me. Again, I don't ask for much. I want this to be the *Tyler Merritt Memorial Sit Yo Ass Down and Rest and Think for as Long as You Need Bench.*

The *Tyler Merritt Memorial Sit Yo Ass Down and Rest and Think for as Long as You Need Bench* (or the TMMSYADARATFALAYN Bench, for short) will give support to people's tired bodies, and with its stellar view of the lake, peace to people's souls as they sit. In good weather and bad, that bench will always be there for people.

That's what I want, if I'm being honest. I want a bench. City of Nashville, don't let me down. Your citizens and their tired posteriors need—nay, they deserve!—the *Tyler Merritt Memorial Sit Yo Ass Down and Rest and Think for as Long as You Need Bench.*

Dear Beautiful Black Baby Jesus. Please make this happen, in Your Name. Amen.

AND WHEN I'M GONE, JUST CARRY ON, DON'T MOURN

And yet.

Even though there are no guarantees that anything we do carries on with us, that is not what I'm finding is bothering me the most these days. As I said, I thought this chapter would have something to do with "legacy." I figured, as I sat down to think about this chapter, that I'd be fixated on leaving something behind for people to remember me by.

But that's not it.

That's not the bull's-eye of my fear.

What I'm most afraid of, beyond a shadow of a doubt, is that the people I love most in this world when I'm gone will forget how much they meant to me.

That they won't have the encouragement they need to make it through the tough days.

That they won't have me there to remind them of who they are when life beats them up.

So much of what I try to do in my day-to-day life, so much of my existence, is that. Notes, emails, texts, posts, phone calls, visits, meals, and face-to-face conversations. All of them done...

To encourage.

To uplift.

To make sure my people are okay.

That's who I am. That's what I do. But what if I weren't around? Would they remember my voice? My heart? My words?

In the quietness of my room, in the evening, when the distractions of the day have ceased, and I'm left alone to think, alone in the silence, that's what I think about. That's what I worry about.

Remember the quote from Maya Angelou, "I've learned that people will forget what you said, people will forget what you did, but people will never forget how you made them feel."

I think there is a great deal of truth in this. And I think if we are reflective, we will see it's even more true than we initially thought. For example, at the risk of being a super Debbie Downer, I want to focus on the negative side of this. I promise, we'll only stay here for a second and move on after I make my point! I don't know why I wrote that. Why am I worried about killing the upbeat vibe of this chapter? This is literally a book about cancer.

CANCER! Practically any subject I bring up is going to be a positive mood-changer.

Hey, guys, let's talk about the leading cause of death in cats! Feline AIDS?

Okay, back to bullies and meanies. We all have people in our lives who made us feel small. Maybe someone comes to mind for you right now. Someone who belittled you, who made you feel excluded, or worthless, or dumb. Maybe it was a teacher or a bad coach. Maybe in high school, you basically lived in the plot of *Mean Girls*. But I bet you remember those people's names. And I bet the feeling you have right now isn't a very positive one.

This is the power of our lives. This is how we can affect one another. Maya is right: we remember how people made us feel.

But the converse is true as well. And this is where I want to park for a bit. We really can affect each other positively. There are times when my mom will just call and leave me a voice mail. "Hey, Ty. Just thinking about you. Call me back. Love you."

I wish my mama could do this for every single person on the planet. I think the world would instantly be better, with my mama leaving everyone voice mails. I bet even Auburn fans would be tolerable if they got a call every day from my mama. I mean, it's possible. This is the power of loving encouragement.

And Maya's right. I'll never forget it.

Of course, there are times when I do the same for my mom. I'll call her or send her a text saying, "You're on my mind, Mom. I love you!" I know what that means to her. I know how that makes her feel.

And the thing is, I know this truth deep in my bones because it *is not new*. I've seen the power of loving encouragement since I was a little boy.

POUR SOME SUGAR ON ME
(IN THE NAME OF LOVE)

As I've shared, both my parents were from a small, rural town in Alabama called Eutaw. And about twice a year, my parents would figure out a way to go back home to visit with their parents and their family. My grandma on my dad's side still lived in the same house she did when my dad was growing up. And even though my grandma had other grandchildren, you wouldn't know it by watching her interact with me.

She always made me feel like I was her favorite person in the whole wide world. She always said the same thing to me when I showed up at her house. She'd open the door, take a look at me, and say, "Boy, you look like you've put on some weight."

She said this no matter what. I could have lost twenty pounds and she'd still say it.

For a while, this confused me. "Wait one second. Is my grandmama bullying me? Is she calling me fat? I'm not fat. In fact, I will have you know, *Grandma*, because of baseball conditioning, I have slimmed down *three holes in my belt*, thank you very much. What the actual hell, Grandma?"

Later on, my mom explained that because Grandma lived through the Great Depression, there were times when there simply wasn't enough food to go around. Being skinny during the Depression was decidedly *not* a good thing. For my grandma, having her grandson show up to her house *not* overly skinny was like a giant sigh of relief. It meant her grandson was eating enough, that he was safe, for now. Man, that Great Depression laid out some long-lasting generational trauma, huh?

Okay, also my grandma was kind of mean sometimes. But I digress.

I would remember sitting in her house, whose walls were filled with picture after picture of her beloved family and extended family. We'd sit there, surrounding her tiny TV. It didn't even matter what was on. Naw. It was just an excuse to talk, and Grandma would pepper me with a never-ending litany of questions about school, about my friends, about everything.

But although I remember sitting in her house (and those grandmother interrogations), those aren't the most important and precious memories to me. Here's what was. Each time, as we prepared to leave Eutaw and go back home to Las Vegas, my grandma would pull me aside.

Just me.

Me alone.

No one else.

And she'd give me a present to take home.

It would be a loaf of pound cake, made from scratch the night before in her kitchen. And it wasn't just regular pound cake. It was *lemon* pound cake, made (I could only assume) from the fresh lemons picked from the trees out back. It was covered with a sweet, sugary lemon glaze, and sometimes, when she handed it to me, it was still warm.

"This is for you," she'd say with a wink.

I don't know if I was her favorite grandchild. Knowing my grandma, her heart was big enough for each of us—all of us—to be her favorite grandchild. But I know what I felt each time she handed me that loaf of fresh lemon pound cake.

I felt like I was her favorite.

That's how she made me feel. Like a treasured grandson who mattered more than anything else in the world.

And Maya is right.

I will never forget how that made me feel.

Never.

Also, Grandma, God rest her soul, did you ever think that maybe I put on a little weight because of your damn pound cake?

EMPTY CHAIRS AND EMPTY TABLES

I want to go back to another tragic day: August 31, 1997. It was the day the world learned that Princess Diana of Wales had died in a tragic car accident in Paris.

The world mourned, not because she was a celebrity, or was young and beautiful, or was a fashion icon (and she was all those things), but because of her humanity. They mourned her because of how she made them feel.

Two moments stand out in my memory. The first is an outfit. No, I'm not talking about a glamorous dress or an elegant ensemble. It's her, wearing simple khaki pants, a white shirt, and a heavy flak jacket as she walked through a former minefield in Angola, where a civil war left thousands of mines that endangered children.

A princess.

Walking through a minefield.

To bring attention to a deadly place filled with deadly mines, and that someone should do something about it.

She brought much-needed publicity to an obscure place that needed help clearing away the deadly landmines, and she also helped galvanize the political will of leaders to make international agreements that outlawed these weapons (which disproportionately affect citizens, and remain long after the conflict is over).

A princess.

Braving landmines.

To make fields and roads safe for kids.

That's gangsta.

The second is a moment in the US back in 1989. During this trip, Princess Diana toured Harlem Hospital's pediatric AIDS unit. During the tour, the doctors led her through a ward of young children, most of whom were in foster care. "Why?" Diana asked. The doctor explained that their families abandoned them, and no one would care for them "because of the stigma of the disease." During that time, the stigma around AIDS and the general (erroneous) public belief was that it could be spread easily by casual contact.

And in that moment, Diana (herself a mother) saw a seven-year-old Black boy in blue pajamas, and overcome with compassion, she bent down to hug him, burying her face in his neck and holding on to him for several seconds.

Diana's hug was a hug heard around the world. It not only shifted attitudes toward AIDS, but cemented Diana as "the people's princess."

Five days after Diana's death, in the middle of the massive headlines surrounding Princess Diana's death, the grieving of the international community, and the plans for her royal funeral, I remember that there was another death.

Mother Teresa died.

Not nearly as much fanfare.

And yet, this woman who spent most of her life helping the poorest of the poor, and helping people with terminal diseases die with dignity and care, might not have been a celebrity, but she taught us all lessons about what it means to live.

"Not all of us can do great things," Mother Teresa said, "but we can do small things with great love."

Small things.

With great love.

And that love ripples out.

That's the one legacy we all can leave—how we made people feel.

HAVE I TOLD YOU LATELY
THAT I LOVE YOU?

Honest to goodness, it's tough to think about dying. I often use euphemisms to shield me from saying what I mean. I'll say, "once I leave Earth" or "when I'm not around as much anymore."

Around as much?

Well, that's an understatement. Tyler, you're not gonna be around *at all*. Use precise language, my brother.

But the most emotional I get when I think about dying is when I think about Zoe. Zoe is the oldest child of two of my oldest and closest friends, Bridget and Scott. I met Bridget when I first moved to Nashville. She lived upstairs in the apartment above me, and her roommates and mine quickly became fast friends. Now, every Sunday, to this day, I go over to their house for dinner.

I watched as Scott and Bridget became a couple. Then I watched as they became parents, first to Zoe, and then, a few years later, to her little brother, Declan.

I think about all those Sundays, hanging out in their playroom, which was packed with doll houses and books and princess dresses. How many random games did we play there on the floor? How many times did I intentionally lose, just to hear her squeal with laughter that she won? How many times did Zoe twirl around in whatever princess costume she most felt like that day, as I sang along with her like Elsa that the "cold never bothered me anyway" or like Tiana that

I am "almost there" or like Moana that "line where the sky meets the sea," well, dammit, it calls me.

I think about the dozens (hundreds?) of times she'd run into the room, hair still damp from her evening bathtime, wearing colorful pajamas. It was time for bed, yes, but she knew that first she got to hear Uncle Ty Ty read her a book. Or maybe more than one, if she was good. And she was always good. (For me at least.)

I think about our Sunday nights with spaghetti dinners, and wearing matching LeBron James jerseys as we cheered on the Heat in the NBA Finals together. Or the crunch the piles of fall leaves would make as she and her brother took turns jumping into them. Or the mittens, hats, and scarves we had to keep track of when we went strolling from house to house on crisp Halloween nights.

Now Zoe isn't so little. She's thirteen. She plays sports, so now my afternoons are often spent in a gym, yelling very loudly and cheering with probably too much passion for middle school volleyball games.

Zoe isn't biologically my niece, but she's my niece. I don't have kids. I don't have a daughter. But I sorta get the hype. I've known Zoe since she was in utero, being "fearfully and wonderfully" knit together by God. I remember holding her in the hospital. I remember when I used to enter the house, she would run to me and scream "Uncle Ty Ty" and demand that I pick her up. I remember her giving me good night hugs, squeezing me with her little arms as though I was her favorite person in the entire world. I've loved watching her grow up.

The idea of her walking across the stage in her cap and gown, or going off to college, or having someone special that she wants her family to meet because it's just that serious—the idea of me missing that? The idea of not getting to see her grow up? That makes me so angry and sad. Why, God? Why would you put this incredible person in my life and make me love her so much to not be around to love them their entire life?

<Exhale>

It's almost too much.

So that's who I think about. Zoe.

Zoe makes me think, "Did I do enough when I was here? Is Zoe gonna remember how I made her feel?" Yeah, yeah, I know. I'm not her parent. I'm not the end-all, be-all in Zoe's life. But this girl matters to me. And in thinking about her, I also think about all these other lives that are precious to me.

Have I left her with something that will help her through all the ups and downs of life?

Author and *New York Times* columnist David Brooks once wrote, "It occurred to me that there were two sets of virtues, the résumé virtues and the eulogy virtues. The résumé virtues are the skills you bring to the marketplace. The eulogy virtues are the ones that are talked about at your funeral"[1]

He's right. And there's great hope in this. You and I might not be able to change the destinies of whole nations, but with our quiet, boring, maybe even small or even mundane right-here lives, you and I can have a real impact on the people right in front of us.

Not fame.

---

1. This quote is from this article: "The Moral Bucket List," *New York Times*, April 12, 2015, https://www.nytimes.com/2015/04/12/opinion/sunday/david-brooks -the-moral-bucket-list.html. The idea is also expanded upon in Brooks's 2015 book, *The Road to Character.*

But impact.

Which is always better.

And if we do that, then we will have succeeded. I feel like this makes me hopeful, because it means that you and I can create real, honest-to-goodness legacy for the people right in front of us.

So regardless of my résumé, what I most want at my funeral is Zoe, choking back tears because she misses me, telling the people who are gathered there, "Uncle Ty Ty loved me, and I will never forget him."

I want her to remember "the lemon pound cake."

And how that made her feel.

That's the only legacy I find myself caring about.

I don't want the people I love to ever forget how I made them feel.

Also, I want my damn bench.

CHAPTER 12

STOP THIS TRAIN

(THE ONE ABOUT ACCEPTANCE)

So scared of getting older.
I'm only good at being young.
So I play the numbers game
To find a way to say that life has just begun.

—John Mayer, "Stop This Train"

I can't lie. I was about three-quarters of the way done with writing this chapter and decided to come back up to the top and insert this disclaimer. We're almost at the end of this book that we've now walked through together, and if I'm keeping it 100, I just don't want it to end.

I don't know what it is. I don't know if it's your companionship while I write this. If it's you walking with me as I face my fears—as I lament—as I find a surprising amount of humor in something that, in my bones, I find no humor in at all. At all.

Listen. I need you to know this. You walking with me through this has brought me a surprising amount of comfort that I just didn't expect. Thank you.

<Exhale>

I now have about twelve days until the surgery.

Twelve.

That's how long until Dr. Barocas and Dr. Tan (my Jordan and my Pippen) and the team at Vanderbilt open up my abdomen (again) and remove as much of this cancer as they can.

A little less than two weeks.

And that clock? My internal clock? It's deafening to me right now. It's nearly all I can hear, at any moment.

Tick.

Tick.

Tick.

My mother has booked her flight out here to Nashville, which has stamped a certain finality to this date on the calendar. In twelve days, she'll be the one to drive me to the hospital. She'll be there, too, when they wheel me out of my hospital room into the surgery prep room. She'll be the last person to see me before I go under (doctors and nurses excepted).

I'm already planning in my head what kind of disturbing joke I will make to my mother about how this may be the last time she sees me. It wasn't funny the last time. I'm not sure why I think it will be funny this time.

I'm learning this kind of joke is never funny.

Burying a child, I am told, is one of the worst things that a human can face. There are words in our English language for a person who loses their parents (orphan) or their spouse (widow). There's not even a word for a parent who loses a child. For my mother's (and my father's) heart's sake—I hope I wake up from this surgery.

Yes, for them.

But also, for me.

These are the kinds of things I think about nowadays.

Twelve days.

Tick.

Tick.

Tick.

IN CASE YOU DON'T LIVE FOREVER

Okay, I need to stop.

I was driving. It was 10:11 a.m. here in Nashville on a Saturday morning. I was just driving and listening to a playlist of songs that makes it quite literally impossible for me to be in a bad mood.

Can you be in a bad mood listening to "Could You Be Loved" by Bob Marley? Or "If It Isn't Love" by New Edition? Empirically, I think the science is in. It's impossible.

I was on my way to the Great Smoky Mountains in East Tennessee to spend some time with someone very special to me when my cousin Kayla called.

But I was in road trip mode, singing a *stirring* rendition of "Defying Gravity" from *Wicked* as I harmonized with Kristin Chenoweth and did my best Adele Dazeem impression. And once one starts the act, one *has* to finish the act. So I ignored the call.

Then Kayla called me back.

Shit.

There are only a few reasons why people call back twice. And none of them are good.

"Hey, Tyler," she said. And I knew immediately something was wrong.

"What's wrong, cousin?" I said.

"I had a feeling you may not have heard yet," she said.

"Heard what?"

"Mason died," she said.

I felt my heart sink.

I need you all to know about my Uncle Mason. Because he's important in the life of my family.

Uncle Mason was not, technically, my uncle. But for the last forty years of my life, he's been my father's very best friend. Uncle Mason might be the closest person in the world to my father, and my father quite literally has a twin brother.

I first met Uncle Mason when I was seven or eight years old when my family first moved to Las Vegas for my dad's job at Nellis AFB. Uncle Mason was in the Air Force with my father. They quickly became fast friends. Perhaps it was because Mason was another Black man in the Air Force, which at that time was only about 15 percent Black.[1] Or perhaps it was because Mason had an easygoing lightness and joviality to his personality that counterbalanced my father's intensity. Or maybe it was because Mason was a man of extraordinary patience, and being friends with someone as particular, feisty, and ornery as my father takes the patience of Job.

Whatever the reason, and I mean this when I say it, Uncle Mason was family. There's a Hebrew proverb that says that "there is a friend who sticks closer than a brother,"[2] and that's what Uncle

---

1. https://www.airforcetimes.com/news/your-air-force/2023/08/29/study-eligibility-rules-hamper-minority-representation-in-air-force.
2. Proverbs 18:24.

Mason was. I don't know some of my biological family members as well as I know Uncle Mason.

Sorry.

Knew.

As well as I knew *Uncle Mason.*

Damn.

When I first met Uncle Mason, he drove an orange Corvette. He might as well have been driving a real-life, life-size Hot Wheels car. He was the coolest person ever. To this day, he is the main reason I think Corvettes are the coolest car in the world.

To be fair, I suppose I was also influenced by those bad dudes from *The Karate Kid* who showed up at the Golf n' Stuff Family Fun Center in that awesome white Corvette to try to mess with Ralph Macchio, aka Daniel LaRusso, who was on a date with super hottie Elisabeth Shue.[3] Sure, Cobra Kai was a bastion of toxic masculinity—but that car was dope. I also *may* have been influenced by Jason Bateman, who drove a red Corvette in the 1987 cinematic masterpiece *Teen Wolf Too*. Also, I see you, *Teen Wolf Too*—making the bold title choice to replace the number "2" with its homonym "Too" meaning "also." Nice play on words there. Also, I think we can all agree: *Teen Wolf Too* is easily one of the top five teenage were-wolf boxing movies in US film history.

But listen, all those movies aside,[4] my real-life Uncle Mason drove a Corvette, and that was the coolest.

When I was in middle school, Uncle Mason got married to a woman named Valeria, who had a daughter named Kayla who was

---

3. Fun fact: the song "Goodnight Elisabeth" by Counting Crows? Yep. It's about Elisabeth Shue. Looks like Adam Duritz had a massive crush on her, too.

4. "A List of Movies with Vettes," Corvette Forum. https://www.corvetteforum.com /forums/c4-general-discussion/989655-a-list-of-movies-with-vettes.html.

my age. They moved into the house directly across the street from us. Soon, Kayla and I became...well...cousins. Summer in Vegas is scorching and meant you had to be in the water. So half the time all of us neighborhood kids would be playing in *my* pool, and the other half, we'd make our way across the street to Kayla's house to swim in *her* pool.

Again, Kayla wasn't a biological cousin.

But try to tell either one of us any different.

I have so many memories with that family.

You know, it's funny to me. In the previous chapter, I was reflecting on my own mortality and I wrote this sentence:

And I'm going to say something that should not be controversial one single bit because it is absolutely true. We are all going to die.

I *literally just* wrote that in the previous chapter. I wrote that. But I wrote it before Kayla called me. Finding out that Mason died hit me like a concrete cinder block. I'm in shock and disbelief. When death happens, when it's in my face, I forget my own words. Death is like an invader. It's foreign. It's not supposed to be here.

And yet, here it is.

I could try to tell myself that this outcome wasn't terribly surprising. The truth is Uncle Mason was sixty-four years old (relatively speaking, still pretty young), but he wasn't in the best of health. The last time I saw Uncle Mason, this past Christmas, he looked okay. He was more thin than he should have been. Thinner than a healthy person should be. And this past week, he'd had some outpatient surgery and was home recovering.

All this should have mentally prepared me for the news from Kayla. I should not have been surprised.

But I was.

That morning, mere hours ago, around five a.m., his daughter Nia, who had come to town to help him as he recovered from his surgery, found him. His body was freezing to the touch. Nia knew he was gone.

C. S. Lewis once wrote that "the death of a beloved feels like an amputation."

Pain.

I had to stop. I pulled my car over, got off an exit on a busy Tennessee highway, and as the rain fell, I sat in my car and sobbed. I cried for Nia. I cried for Kayla. I cried for my dad. And I cried because I would never see my Uncle Mason again.

How was it possible that I already missed him?

He hadn't even been gone for five hours.

GET RIGHT TO THE HEART OF MATTER— IT'S THE HEART THAT MATTERS MORE

Last chapter, I referenced an author named David Brooks who said, "Most of us are too focused on résumé virtues. We need to be focused on eulogy virtues."

One of my people who read the draft chapter gave me some feedback, saying "That's a great quote. What does it mean, practically? What should I add to my life? What should I stop?"

That was a *great* note.

And it seems all the more pressing today, as I think about the fact that, sometime soon, there will be a memorial service, where people are listening to other people talk about Uncle Mason. Someone will deliver a eulogy about his life and try to sum up his existence and impact on this Earth in a three-minute speech.

This topic is probably worth a whole book by itself, but I want to share with you two thoughts that I have, and both come from the real-time emotions that have flowed from my uncle's death.

Thought 1: We Don't Have as Much Time as We Think

As I was grieving in my car, as I was processing with Kayla, my heart began to break as I realized something. A few years ago, Valeria, Kayla's mother, had passed away. And due to a complicated relationship (so many of us have our own "complicated relationships"—don't we?) Kayla and Val hadn't really been speaking when Val passed. And things weren't much better between Kayla and Mason. She hadn't talked to him in quite some time. As I was thinking about this, Kayla began to talk about the guilt she felt. This was now the second parent who had passed before she was able to reconcile and make things right.

Without getting too much into family drama, this had caused an understandable resentment between Kayla and Mason's biological daughter, Nia. Nia had been taking care of her father before and after his surgery, and because of that, Kayla's absence felt like abandonment.

As I was on the phone with Kayla, I asked her, "Where are you right now?"

"I'm standing in a Home Depot," she said. "And I am frozen. I don't know what to do. I can't move."

I couldn't tell if my cousin was crying. Somehow, though, the pain in her voice seemed deeper than crying.

"Again, Tyler? Again?"

I knew this was not how she wanted things to have gone.

"I want to go over to the house, but I don't know what people will think," she said, her voice breaking. "What if they're mad? What if they're upset that I just showed up at the house that I haven't been to in a minute?"

"Kayla. Listen to me. You need to go over," I told her. "Go to your father's house. My mom and dad are there. You have a place there."

Looking back at it, I think Kayla was trying to tell me that she was worried about Nia's reaction.

After we hung up, I called my mom. She didn't pick up. I called my dad. He answered. Everyone was over at Mason's house, he told me. I knew for a fact that my parents would embrace Kayla the second they saw her. I just wanted Kayla to know that, too.

"Dad," I said, through my own tears. I hate crying in front of my dad, because he's so stoic. But I couldn't help it. "Can you please reach out to Kayla, to let her know that she has a place with the family during this time?"

"Of course, son. Your mother and I can reach out to Kayla," my father said.

And as he said that, I could hear Nia in the background. I asked my dad to pass the phone to her. I was just wanting to offer my condolences. I wasn't ready for what she had to say to me. She'd heard my father say Kayla's name, and as she spoke to me, the pain and hurt flowed out. "Tyler, I was here with dad. Kayla was not," she said.

Listen, I don't feel comfortable sharing all of the details of the conversation that Nia and I had, but I listened to her as she poured out her hurt and her rage and her reasons why she didn't want to see Kayla in that moment.

I sighed deeply. I understood Nia's hurt. I tried to talk to her, to play peacemaker, but the emotions were too raw. Too soon.

I hung up not knowing how to fix things. I thought about Nia, grieving her dad, and harboring hurt and resentment. I thought about Kayla, grieving her dad, and filled with regret. All this swirling pain. How could any of this be mended?

Because of the words I'd just written in the last chapter, this question was in the front of my mind: what would it mean in this situation to live a "eulogy" life?

Ironically, even though the word "eulogy" is something people say about you when you're dead, really, it has to do with how you live. It has to do with our hearts and how we feel about the people who are still on this Earth right in front of us right now.

I think about that line from Jim Collins from just a few chapters back:

"Life is people.
And time spent with people we love."

This is what I know. It's likely, statistically, that there are people in your life right now whom you haven't talked to in months or years or decades. And maybe this is because things just drifted. Or maybe it's because things got broken. And maybe there's a mountain of wouldas and couldas and shouldas, and a moat full of hurt feelings and misunderstandings. And you keep saying in the back of your mind, "I need to get this right." You know, deep in your bones, that love means fighting for connection. And at your best moments, when you're right in your heart and head, you hear a voice saying to you, "Look, you need to lay it all down. You need to move to make amends." This is what you want.

Let me tell you, friend, every second that goes by that you're *not* doing that, you're fighting against living this "eulogy" life.

Again, this shouldn't be that surprising to anyone, but once they're gone, it's too late. And once they're gone, at some point—and I am speaking from personal experience here—you are going to have a moment of searing clarity and you are going to remember, in vivid color, why you loved that person and how very deep the connections were that connected you to them. And you're going to wish against death that you'd moved to lay down your own hurt. That you'd moved, before it was too late, to attempt to reconnect.

Look, I want to be clear: I am *not* saying that you should enter back into toxic or abusive or harmful relationships. I think about steps eight and nine of the twelve steps of AA, which are technically about substance abuse, but I've found the principles to be wildly helpful just in everyday, general life, too. Those steps outline some boundaries around reconciliation:

STEP 8. I made a list of all persons I had harmed, and became willing to make amends to them all.

STEP 9. I made direct amends to such people wherever possible, except when to do so would injure them or others.

That last line is key. Make amends, unless it's going to hurt the other person or someone else. Guess who that someone else is? Yep. It's you. So boundaries are good and fine. Please hear me: this is not about guilting you into putting yourself in a position where you'll be harmed.

This isn't about guilt.

It's about regret.

Will you regret this?

"Do not repay anyone evil for evil. If it is possible, as far as it depends on you, live at peace with everyone."[5]

These are famous words from the apostle Paul, but he smoothly puts all those caveats in there.

If it's possible.
*As far as it depends **on you**.*
Live at peace with everyone.

Don't live with regrets.

If it's possible. Do it. If there's any way. Do it.

As far as it depends on you. You. You. Be the first one to move. This doesn't mean that you're admitting fault in the situation. All you're saying is, "I don't want this distance between us."

Live at peace with everyone. Everyone.

I think this is part of what it means to live a eulogy life. I think this is a big part of what it means to love. I don't mean "feel the emotion of love." I mean love. The action of loving someone.

And here's something that's difficult for me to admit, but I'm too far deep in my own life now, and I feel closer to this thing called Death than I would like to recognize. And I guarantee that I've been the villain in someone else's story. And if—by some odd chance—you are reading these words and I was the one who hurt you, wounded you, in any way, by what I said or did (or what I left unsaid or didn't do)—then I hope we can make amends.

I want to "make direct amends to such people wherever possible."

And on the other side of the coin, if you're reading this and

---

5. Romans 12:17–18.

someone comes to your mind…someone who has hurt you. Someone you have relational strains with. Someone you're finding it difficult to forgive, well, as much as I want you to love this book, put it down. Put this book down, right now, and go make that phone call. Or send that text.

Because skip the fame.

Skip the monuments.

Skip the accolades.

Skip your name up in lights.

The real legacy of a life is your relationships.

Don't leave any important ones broken, if you can possibly help it.

A eulogy life.

We have to stop living like we have unlimited time, because trust me, my friends, as I sit here thinking about my Uncle Mason, who was with us yesterday but as of this morning is no longer, we don't.

We just don't.

I JUST WANT TO LIVE WHILE I'M ALIVE

It's raining as I drive through eastern Tennessee. The gray matches my mood.

My mom called me back to tell me she's reached out to Kayla, trying to welcome her, encourage her to come over. I thank God for my mother, for about the millionth time in life. I swear, everyone on Earth would be better if they knew my mama.

Then my mother told me something I didn't know.

"Mason had cancer," she said.

The word hit me.

It all made a little more sense to me. Mason was sixty-four years old, but things in his body seemed to be falling apart more quickly than his age indicated. Mom told me that Mason never used the word "cancer." It wasn't something he wanted to say or talk about. Sometimes, just the word "cancer" is too much to utter. So we avoid it, thinking that if we say it too much, we'll somehow summon it—like it's a monster. Or we think that if we don't say its proper name, it will slink away, angry no one is paying attention to it, like a childish pop star.

Regardless, Mason never talked about having cancer. And no one was ever around with him in the doctor's appointments to hear any medical professional say that word out loud. Mason carried the truth of his sickness like he carried the cancer itself: inside him.

My mother told me something that bothered her.

After she got the tragic news of Mason's passing, she and Dad went next door to comfort Nia and to help her clean up after the ambulance left. Mom told me that on Mason's desk, in his bedroom, there was an insulated tumbler. And inside was some Crown Royal, still chilled, with ice cubes gently clinking against the metal sides of the cup.

"And earlier that morning, he'd gotten up to go smoke," my mother said. "I can't believe he was still smoking and drinking in light of his health concerns."

"Mom," I said, as respectfully and firmly as I could to the source of my own life, "what this man decided to do when he knew that he didn't have much time left just shouldn't be your concern."

As I said before, there are a small number of people in this world who have sat in a room with a doctor and heard that diagnosis, "You have cancer."

Once somebody says that to you, it changes everything.

Earlier that day, mere minutes before, you had walked into a medical building and your life was going one way. But now? Now you walk out of those doors and everything is completely different.

I know what that's like.

And so did Mason, even if he didn't tell other people about it. The thing he couldn't quite bring himself to name was going to kill him.

I understand my mother's point. Yes, there is such a thing as general health and well-being. And there are ways to fight cancer. But there are also things you can't do.

And this.

This is the final stage of the disease. The final stage of cancer.

Acceptance.

Thought 2: Sometimes, with Cancer, There's Nothing You Can Do

This is going to sound strange, but it's oddly comforting to know that someone like Steve Jobs could die of cancer. He had one of the worst kinds of cancer, that deadly assassin ninja kind. Pancreatic cancer. The five-year survival rate for pancreatic cancer is only 10 percent. Steve Jobs was a titan of industry, a genius, with nearly unlimited money and resources to pour into beating this disease.

But cancer is no respecter of persons.[6]

And in the end, there was nothing that Steve Jobs could do.

I don't know. Maybe it shouldn't be comforting to me, but it helps me realize I'm not in control. That there are things over which I have no say.

Acceptance.

---

6. I almost wrote, "Like honey badger, cancer don't care." But I figured that would pull you out of the prose. But seriously, honey badger and cancer don't give a _____.

I'm not saying you don't fight. I have watched dear friends undergo radical radiation treatments and take years-long chemotherapy sessions. It's quite a thing to have to pour poison into your body to try to kill the thing that's killing your body without killing your body. Sometimes, doctors say, "There's not a lot we can do, even with treatment." And sometimes people decide to live out their final days without the treatment.

I don't pretend to understand what that decision is like.

But I understand it.

Sometimes, there are no more options. And the only thing left is reality.

Acceptance.

So if Mason, knowing what he must have known about his own situation, wanted to drink his favorite blended Canadian whiskey— if that gave him some peace or joy or solace or comfort—then who am I to say anything? Here's what I can bet for certain. Whether or not he sipped some Crown Royal had nothing to do with Mason's death.

On his death certificate, the coroner will not write "Crown Royal." No. This was all cancer's doing.

I know a little something about this.

My cancer? Well, it's what they call a "fatty cancer," which is a pretty unflattering name. Dr. Tan told me that losing weight would help. There would be less pressure on my interior organs. Less interior fat for him to have to cut and slice through.

But up until a few months ago, if you asked me if I was going to go on a strict diet, denying myself tacos and pizza and light, flaky, buttery biscuits with blackberry jam from Puckett's, I would have responded with four simple words.

Hell.

To the.

Naw.

If I was going to die, I was going to die well fed with some deliciousness. That was what I thought.

But that's not my reality now. A few months ago, I hired a personal trainer named Justin, who kicks my butt twice a week. He's also put me on an incredibly regimented diet. For months now, this is what I have been eating.

THE TYLER DIET PROJECT

Each morning I have one single cup of black coffee. I think Justin added that in there as a joke, based on the title of my first book. Then I eat a cup of oats, with one packet of Splenda and some cinnamon. I then add a cup of fresh blueberries. Then, I make an omelet with six egg whites and some peppers. That's breakfast.

Then, usually I work out.

Afterward, I can have a protein shake, made with protein powder mixed with unsweetened vanilla almond milk.

For lunch, I have two cups of broccoli, spinach, or other mixed vegetables, fourteen asparagus spears, a half cup of chickpeas, and about five ounces of plant-based chicken substitute.

For dinner, it's one cup of quinoa, two to three cups of spinach leaves and edamame, two boiled eggs, cucumber, and some balsamic vinegar dressing.

Then for an after-dinner dessert, I get a cup of plain Greek yogurt and add one cup of fresh blueberries and twenty-four almonds.

That's my life.

My trainer Justin asked me what my goals are.

"Is it to be as healthy as possible for the surgery?" he asked me.

Honestly, no. That's not it.

I am not doing all this to give myself the best chance to survive this surgery. At the end of the day, when Dr. Barocas and Dr. Tan open me up in twelve days, I've got no control. Who knows what they'll find with the cancer?

Here's what I do know.

There's no way my doctors are going to be staring into my chest cavity, saying to each other, "Oh, man. Marcus. This cancer is bad. If only Tyler hadn't eaten those sweet potato fries with the garlic aioli dipping sauce back in December. Dammit, guys, we could have made this surgery work. Someone pass me some spinach, stat!"

As soon as they put me under, it's all out of my control.

That's what I mean.

Acceptance.

You've got no control. There are no assurances. There just aren't. And I've watched quite a bit as people I know around me struggle with this reality. Honestly, sometimes, because we as humans don't like things to be out of our control, we try to grab it. We think that we can dictate the outcome if we just do X or Y or Z.

"If I work out intensely, lose eighty pounds, and only eat kale from now until the surgery, my blood will be so full of antioxidants and my organs will be so clean that I will for sure *survive this cancer operation."*

Uh. No.

And this is where religious people can sometimes be annoying. I know, they don't mean to be. But sometimes, they are. Look, I love it when people say that they are praying for me. I will take it, friends!

But what's unnerving is when people say things like, "Just know that you got a *lot* of people praying for you, Tyler."

Like that's some sort of divine guarantee? Some way to force God's hand? Does the sheer number of people praying for me help my cancer survival odds? Is this a numbers game? Are prayers like an annoying chiming motion-sensor doorbell over the entry of a 7-Eleven that gives off that singsongy *ding-dong* every time someone walks under it, and if enough people pray, it's just nonstop noise and God is like, "*Enough* with the noise. Fine! I'll heal him."

Also, what kind of God would I serve if He didn't heal me because I didn't have *quite* enough people praying fervently enough for me?

"Oh, man, Gabriel. Tyler's prayer team is only nineteen people, and one of them is a grade-A dunce whose prayers are basically unintelligible.[7] *If it'd been twenty-two people, maybe I'd heal him. Dang it. Guess he's a goner."*

Nowhere in Christianity does it teach that prayer is a way to control outcomes.

Here are some other annoying Christian platitudes that well-meaning people say to me. Again, I know these folks don't mean ill. But it's irritating when someone says:

God didn't bring you this far just to let you die . . .
or
Remember, Tyler, our God is a healer.

I don't get this, either. This seems to me to be like some sort of biological Health and Wealth Gospel. God is not obligated to heal

---

7. I'm looking at you, Tieche.

me. Respectfully, ma'am, you are not God, and you do not know the outcome of my life. Also, respectfully, ma'am, there are lots and lots of people far more devout than me, and if I'm keeping it real, a lot more deserving to live—who have died of cancer.

You and I can't control this with religious activity. Or biological activity.

Also, what kind of God do I serve if He's not good enough to trust Him with my life, including before, during, and after the surgery?

Read that again.

Acceptance.

So, no, that's not why I eat the way I eat and let my trainer Justin kick my Black butt twice a week. I am at the age where eating good, healthy food makes me feel a *whole* lot better than downing a whole bag of salt and vinegar Kettle Chips[8] at midnight. I want to eat healthy so that I can feel the absolute best that I can feel in the time that I know for sure that I have left.

I don't have many guarantees. But I'm alive now. And for the next twelve days, I don't want to be in a diabetic daze because I ate half a gallon of Sour Patch Kids.

Are Sour Patch Kids measured out by the gallon? I'm not sure. They should be.

The point is, I'm down eighteen pounds just in the last three weeks. And I feel so much better physically. I really do.

So I'm grateful for that. And I'm grateful for Justin, even if half the time I resent him and his six-pack-having-sexier-than-he-has-any-right-to-be-meal-prepping-gallon-of-water-carrying-around ass.

---

8. Keeping it real, even typing that makes me want to go get some of those chips. They're just so dang good. I think they're God's favorite chips, too.

Anyway, this is what acceptance looks like.

At least for me.

At this point.

With twelve days left.

IT'S A BEAUTIFUL DAY.
DON'T LET IT SLIP AWAY.

I am driving along I-140 in Tennessee, and the rain is unrelenting. I find my mind drifting. It's funny the things I find myself reflecting on. The Broadway Station is playing on my Sirius XM, and it takes me back. I remember with such vividness December of 2012. It was Christmastime, and it was almost time for the theatrical release of *Les Misérables* starring Hugh Jackman and Anne Hathaway.

I was so excited for this movie. I don't know if you know this about me, but I'm kinda into musical theater. I really like it. So I was *radically* excited about this movie. I even had a daily countdown on my social media.

And I remember this thought I had back then. I was so excited to see this new film adaptation of one of the all-time great musicals in theater history that I had this actual thought: "I would hate it if something happened to me and I died before *Les Mis* came out. That would *suck* if I didn't get a chance to see it."[9]

---

9. The only that that would suck more would be if the producers of the 2012 movie *Les Misérables* decided to cast someone singularly awful—and I mean catastrophically, comically terrible—to play the titular role of Inspector Javert. Someone who sang so poorly that it wasn't just distracting; it made you wonder if you were suddenly watching a Will Ferrell *SNL* sketch. Someone whose singing was, on a purely technical level, abhorrent, and on a purely aesthetic level, more putrid than a red velvet cake made with moldy eggs and rancid oil. Oh, wait, what's that? Did I just describe Russell Crowe's performance? Oh, it seems I have.

I know that sounds petty and stupid, but part of acceptance means admitting that there are some things on this Earth and in this life that I will just miss.

I thought about Uncle Mason. He loved football. He played football when he was in high school, and he loved the Super Bowl. Every part of it. And this year, it just so happened that the Big Game was in his backyard, in his hometown of Las Vegas. I am sure he had plans to watch the game, hang out with some dear friends, and eat some deliciously unhealthy food.

But he missed the Super Bowl.

I got to see the Super Bowl this year. But my uncle did not. I hope to see a lot of Super Bowls. And the chances I'm going to end up missing my share of Super Bowls is pretty low.

But it's not zero.

Acceptance.

While the rain poured over my car, and my windshield wipers struggled to push the water away, I thought about other things I would miss, if I were to leave this Earth.

You know that moment, right before you open a box of pizza? And you pull that first piece of pizza out, and the cheese stretches to meet you, and you see the soft steam rising. That moment right before you take the first bite of the first piece of pizza, knowing you have *an entire pizza* just waiting for you.

God, I would miss that.

Or that feeling when you're with close friends, and someone says something that's so riotously hilarious, so perfectly funny, that you start to laugh. And then someone else makes a comment that's somehow, impossibly, even funnier. And you start laughing uncontrollably, and pretty soon, you're laughing so hard that you're laughing at each other laughing, and you forget what you were even laughing about. And laughter is all there is.

God, I would miss that.

Or the feeling of being in a theater. Maybe it's right before the curtain goes up on a Broadway show you haven't seen, or maybe it's a movie that you've got high hopes for, and you don't know how it's going to go, but you cannot wait to see the brilliance of all these incredible artists fleshed out on the screen or the stage in front of you. That feeling of seeing a show or a movie for the first time knowing there will never be another "first time."

God, I would miss that.

Or the feeling of crawling into bed when you're exhausted, and the sheets are just the perfect temperature. Cool and crisp. And you lie there, and let the tiredness wash over you, but you're so happy that you finally get to rest in the cool comfort of your own bed.

God, I would miss that.

Or any championship sports game. NBA Finals. The World Series. March Madness. National Championship. The Olympics. It doesn't matter. They all rock. You have been waiting all day for the event or the game to start, and you've been going back and forth in your head. Who is gonna win? Who will rise to the occasion? Who will emerge as the hero? Who won't? And you don't know, but you can't wait to find out. Will there be a thrilling come-from-behind improbable victory? Will someone lose badly? A kick that sails wide right. A missed rebound. A game-winning buzzer beater?

God, I would miss that.

Getting to make you smile with this brilliant, hilarious, and yet poignant book that was absolutely worth every penny of the suggested retail price of $27.99, unless you're in Canada, where it's more expensive for some reason. Probably a maple syrup tax.

God, I would miss that.

As I drive in the rain, I think about a woman I met at a speaking engagement a few weeks ago. I was sharing about the uncertainty about the outcome of my surgery. This woman was named Ginger, and she was ninety-one years old, which is quite old. And she said, "I'm ready to go now. I feel good. I have full control of my mind and body. I want the Lord to take me now. I'm good with it. I've lived a great life. Let's go."

The room got awkward. Everyone hesitantly applauded, half-heartedly. I remember thinking, "Good for you, Ginger, but I'm not there." I may be at the station, but I'm like, "No, you go ahead. I'll wait for the next train." No thank you, please.

I'm still stuck on *Les Mis*. I'm reminded of the emotional apex near the end of the show when Jean Valjean, now in the winter of his life, stands over Marius, who has fallen asleep along with the other soldiers in nervous anticipation on the eve of the French Revolution. Valjean loves Marius like a son, a love compounded by the fact that he is the beloved of Cosette, Valjean's adopted daughter. Valjean tenderly sings "Bring Him Home," a prayer to God asking Him to spare this young man's life, for his sake and for the sake of Cosette. In the final lines, as his voice soars into an incredibly powerful and yet vulnerable crescendo, Valjean begs God, even offering his own life in place of Marius.

> If I die, let me die
> Let him live
> Bring him home
> Bring him home.

I think about that. God, here's the truth: I'd like to say I'm valiant and brave like Valjean, prepared to leave this life if it comes to that. But I'm not. I'm Marius. I don't want to go. I want to live.

I'm worried, and just want to get home.

GARDEN STATE

One more final thought.

By now, all of you know that I am not only theatrical but also religious. I can't help but think of that moment in the life of Jesus, right before He died, as he was facing death in a grove of olive trees at midnight in the Garden of Gethsemane.

Jesus knows that death is coming, and yet still, He prays:

"My Father, if it is possible, may this cup be taken from me."[10]

There's so much in this one line, and theologians often point to the cruel death, torture, and suffering that Jesus will inevitably face as He is killed by the Roman government.

But as I reflect on it, is it not possible that Jesus, in His humanity, also just didn't want to die? That He didn't want to end His journey here, in the flesh, on Earth. He tells His disciples that He has to go away, and Peter practically begs to go with Him. Jesus knows that Peter cannot follow Him, and He says no. Jesus then says He "eagerly desired" to eat the last supper meal with His friends.[11] In the garden, Jesus begs the disciples to stay up with Him[12] on his last night. It sounds to me like Jesus is trying to live every second to its

---

10. Matthew 26:39.
11. Luke 22:15.
12. See Matthew 26:40.

fullest, right? I mean, to be fair, Jesus does like life so much that even after being killed, He comes back a few days later. Right? That's what I'm trying to say.

As I reflect on my own life, and on Uncle Mason, and what it means to live, I feel like Jesus is showing me what it's like to be fully human. He's facing death, and He knows it.

But He still wants to live.

Even in this messed-up world, Jesus found goodness and real joy and friendship and love and life.

As I sit and reflect on that, it's helpful to me.

Death is coming.

But I want to live.

Both things can be true at once.

Both things.

Life is amazing.

We must not take it for granted.

Live.

CURTAIN CALL

I'm almost at my destination. A few minutes ago, my mother texted me to tell me that Kayla did come over to the house.

I breathed in deeply. Relief and worry, in one sharp inhale.

"How's it going?" I texted, holding my breath.

"It's good, Tyler. It's good," my mom typed back.

"Good?" I responded.

"I know you were worried about tensions," my mother texted, "but when Kayla walked through the door, Nia saw her sister and everything changed."

I exhaled.

I often think about how hard this world can be. How hard we can be on one another. And what a miracle it is that we ever find our way back to love. Whatever emotional distance, whatever pain, whatever hurts separate us, I find hope that they can somehow be dissolved. Sometimes, it's as simple as just seeing one another. Life requires bravery.

Sometimes, simply taking a step toward someone else is the very bravest thing you can do.

It's brave to grieve.

It's brave to forgive.

It's brave to love.

Sometimes, that sounds like crying.

And sometimes, that sounds like laughing.

Or hell.

Maybe it's both.

Yes.

Maybe both.

Tick.

Tick.

Tick.

<Exhale>

God, be near.

Okay, I'm ready now.

CHAPTER 13

I'M HERE

December 24, 9 p.m.
Eastern Standard Time.

Okay. That's not actually the date. That's the opening line from *Rent*. Sorry. I couldn't help myself.

But today is the day.

You've been with me as I counted down to this second surgery through these pages. And here it is.

I can't believe we're here.

I can't believe I'm here.

In a few hours, I will drive to the Vanderbilt Medical Center with my mother. And I will change into some sort of thin, blue medical gown. And as I do, I will look at the long scar that runs from just below my chest all the way past my belly button. This scar will be the same road for Dr. Tan's scalpel this time. I'll be glued and stapled together here—along this same scar line—once again.

In a few hours, I'll say goodbye to my mother as they wheel me into an operating room. And the anesthesiologist will put a mask over my face and tell me to count down from ten to one.

Okay, that's not what actually happens, but when I was a kid, I watched a movie where that's what they did. I remember this so clearly—I was pumped to someday get put under. I just knew that I was going to make it through the whole countdown, and then I'd get to zero, and I'd still be awake, and I'd laugh at the assembled doctors and nurses.

"Haha!" I'd howl triumphantly. "I'm still awake, you suckers!"

This is what I'm thinking about in these predawn hours as I stand in my kitchen, looking at my coffee maker, wishing I could make a cup, but knowing that I can't drink anything before surgery.

If the doctor tells me to count from ten to one later on this morning, I bet that memory will pop up again. And you best believe I'll try to get down to zero. Or maybe this is my brain's subconscious way of fighting against the truth that once that anesthesia does its magic and knocks me out, it's all out of my control.

All of it.

I control nothing.

God, I hope I wake up.

I look at the clock.

Tick.

Tick.

Tick.

I'm having the most random thoughts as I stand around in my kitchen, not preparing my coffee.

Seriously.

Random.

Memories from my childhood. It's like my brain is rehearsing the high points of my life.

So many of these memories are from my home. Las Vegas. Where I grew up. Where I feel safe.

I really do want to share with you some of these stories, but I don't have time. There are things I have, but time is not one of them.

You know what. Skip it. I'm going to tell you one. Who cares? What's my editor going to do? Kill me? And besides, honestly, what else am I going to do? And who knows if I'll ever have a chance to tell you this.

So let's consider this a tribute to the city I love the most: my Las Vegas. Although I have a strange feeling that even if you didn't grow up in Vegas, so many of you probably had something very close to, if not the exact same, experience that I did.

I remember one of the first times, as a child, that I was genuinely afraid. And oddly enough, it happened during one of the glorious highlights of my childhood in Vegas, when once a year, the carnival would come to town.

Mostly, it was pure joy. I am telling you, when you're nine or ten years old, this is the best thing that could happen to your city. A carnival that just *shows up* out of nowhere.

Leggo!

This carnival was always held on the grounds of Nellis Air Force Base. On Tuesday, you'd be driving along and all you would see was a giant empty field or a vast abandoned patch of asphalt, and then, on Thursday, there would be a giant carnival, with food booths and games of chance and Ferris wheels and bright lights and funhouses—all of which just appeared overnight. Like some sort of pop-up farmers market, only with way less healthy food. A carnival to go-go, if you will.

Oh, and this was the place to be for every kid. All of it was a glorious overstimulation, filled with sights and sounds and smells that would forever be etched into your memories.

But the thing I remember the most was the rides.

- The Carousel
- The Tilt-a-Whirl[1]
- The Swings[2]
- And the Scrambler.[3]

All those rides are not just great, they're iconic. Fantastic fun.

But.

But.

None of them are the ride I most remember.

If this were a movie, this is the part where I cue the scary music.

<Scary music plays ominously>

The ride I most remember was the Zipper™.

The Zipper™ towered over all the other rides, the same way Godzilla would tower over a small town in Iowa. The Zipper™ stood alone. It could have been its own carnival. The Zipper™ don't need no cotton candy or no freaking corndogs. The Zipper™ don't need the carnival ring toss. The Zipper™ don't need clowns making balloon poodles. It needed nothing else. It was its own center of gravity. If you don't know what this ride is, please google it now so you can see what I'm talking about.

---

1. A ride where you could use math and physics to perfectly distribute the weight of you and your two friends to make the car whip around faster than Jay-Z's head when Beyoncé first walked by him.
2. Where you climbed into a hard wicker seat attached to a long chain and then a giant pillar rotated around like a giant metal discus thrower getting ready to launch. And—no joke—if you closed your eyes it felt like you were flying. Flying. FLYING! Until a bug slammed into your eye going 100 mph. Or you happened to look up and realize that a simple, rusty carnival U-bolt was all that connected your seat to the machine, and was all that prevented a couple of hundred people from being hurtled off into the Nevada night.
3. This is a ride whose triple triangle arms whirred around, using centripetal force to make your stomach drop on every single pass. Or is it centrifugal force? Do you honestly think I know? I'm not a physicist. All I know is that whoever is on the outside seat was getting squished. So don't sit next to Chunk.

It was terrifying.

A giant metal beast that rose up into the Las Vegas night. It was as though the person who wrote the *Saw* movies decided to redesign the Ferris wheel to bring as much terror to little kids as possible.

And during the ride, the deafening roar of the creaking wheels and gears of the Zipper™ drowned out every surrounding sound of the bustling community carnival.

Every sound, save one.

The screaming.

Oh, my friends, I remember you could hear the screams of the people, locked in their spinning, rotating cages, puncturing the hot summer night air as their cries carried out over the carnival.

The Zipper™ sizes up every man and makes him face his own mortality.

There was a height requirement, of course, to get on the ride. But that wasn't needed. Smaller kids didn't require someone to tell them "Maybe this ride isn't for you." For young ones, just watching the Zipper™ destroy the lives of all in line was enough to drive them to nightmares.

Looking at the Zipper™ was enough.

Riding it?

Hell naw.

It would be like someone from Charles Schwab offering a financial planning seminar to a fourth grader. It's not even on your radar. You know you're not ready for this. It's *way* too adult.

Okay, okay, you guys get the point.

But at a certain age? Well, at a certain age, the Zipper™ called to you. You had to conquer this thing.

So. You would line up, with your friends, each of you with your ride tickets. And then you would hand your ticket to a disheveled man who looked as though he had "been through some things." A man who looked as though he had "seen some things." Y'all know which carnival worker I am referring to.[4] This is not a man who should be trusted to safely and meticulously assemble a complex machine. This is not a man who should be trusted to safely assemble a burrito.

I remember when I rode the Zipper™ for the first time. I was perhaps ten. Maybe eleven. There I was, in line with my friends, pretending not to be afraid by nervously laughing (some things never change, huh?), looking very fly in my 1990 Cross Colors t-shirt, which made me look like an extra in TLC's "Ain't 2 Proud 2 Beg" video, and hoping I would not vomit on said cool t-shirt. Or worse, hoping that one of my friends didn't vomit on me.

Yeah, I remember that anxiety.

That fear.

Yes, I remember it.

As I stand here in my kitchen, I don't know why this is registering as my first memory of fear. I'm not sure why I'm thinking about it. But it was. And I am.

When I started this book (God, that seems like forever ago), I remember telling you that the primary, overriding emotion that I felt moment by moment was fear. In fact, when I started writing this, I thought the whole book would just be one giant memoir of fear, interrupted only by jokes to defuse that fear. I thought the book's emotional state would resemble a ten-year-old me, in line to ride the Zipper™.

---

4. The look in his eyes was equal parts complete and utter disinterest about everyone and everything in his immediate surroundings, mixed with a palpable contempt for life itself, with just a gleam of anarchy mixed in with a dash of nihilism.

But that's not how things turned out. Surprisingly enough, I don't feel that now. That's not the emotion that's currently running through my body. I feel closer to how I felt after I got off the Zipper™ for the first time.

A sense of "Wow, we really made it through."

A sense of "Did I actually just do that?"

A sense of elation and gratitude to be alive.

To still be here.

I already rode this cancer surgery ride. I've already faced my demons. I've already made my peace. I'm okay. I'll tell you this, though. When I started this book, I did not anticipate I would end up learning about...well, everything. And along the way, well, man, I do feel that I've been changed somehow.

I want to be succinct and precise and tell you a list of things I've learned since this journey began, since I started writing this book.

I've learned that sometimes life goes in directions you never wanted or planned. And it hurts. But to move on, we need to lament. Sometimes, because I see everything in my life through the eyes of being a Black man, I end up learning lessons from those who have come before me. And in this case, what a lesson I learned from the mother of Emmett Till. She taught me that I need to have the courage to face the full reality of the situation, no matter how bad it is. Look it right in the eyes. Even if it's the last thing in the world I want to do. It's the only way.

I learned that to lament, I need to feel the full force of the emotions. You can't wall off your heart. That's not how life works. You need to face the emotions. You have to be brave. Even if it means you'll have trauma years later because of the deaths of (fictional) dogs Little Ann and Big Dan.

I learned that as a Black man in the US, I'm lucky to be alive. Not every Black man my age is as lucky as I am. George Floyd. George Floyd. I need to carry that gratitude forward.

I learned that sometimes pain is like a megaphone. It shouts to us. And these pivotal moments can wake you up to realize that you need to change. Also, isolation from others creates distance and distrust of others, and that can warp you. We need one another.

I learned that scars are from wounds, and some scars are physical markers that you have been changed forever. But like my hero John Lewis taught me, that's not always a bad thing.

I learned that catheters suck. This is a lesson I very much wish I did not learn.

I learned that half of the battle of life is realizing that it's going to be difficult. Life may be a "day at the beach," but it's not a day at the beach in San Diego. It's a "day at the beach" like Omaha Beach during D-Day. Life is quite hard, and the sooner I realize that, the sooner I can prepare and stop complaining that the world won't devote itself to making me happy.

I learned that life is people. And time spent with people we love. Prioritize them.

I learned that no matter how politically justified you think you are, you can't really call yourself "religious" or a "Christian" and treat other people like trash. That's not what Jesus lived or taught. And even if some fools try to hijack Jesus, that doesn't mean I have to let them.

I learned that people never forget the way you made them feel. And that even the scent of warm lemon pound cake is enough for me to remember the love of my grandma, incarnated in that sweet, glazed deliciousness.

And I learned from my Uncle Mason that life is too short to

hang on to unforgiveness. As far as it is with you, if you can, if there's any way possible, run to reconcile. Don't wait.

I also learned some things about some people.

I want to start with my mother. I opened up this book in Chapter 1, and flippantly said that the surgery was "touch-and-go." I wrote that, but I didn't know what had actually happened during the surgery. It wasn't until I interviewed my mom for this book that I found out how dire and complex my situation was. I had no idea how bad of shape I was in. It was a lot more than "touch-and-go." I can't imagine the pain or anguish of a parent who has to hear a doctor say, out loud, "We're going to put this device on your child's head to test for brain activity." I can't begin to imagine. I asked my mom why she didn't tell me any of that when I woke up, and she simply said, "There's just some things you don't tell your child."

I love my mom, but I have a new appreciation for her. Being a woman in this world is tough enough, let alone a *Black* woman. The resilience that you have to have. The fight you have to have, just to survive, let alone having to walk along an uncertain path whose end might lead you to losing your only child. I think as you grow older in life and start to truly understand love better, your view of your parents becomes a bit more clear. And for me, I realized that my understanding of my parents was blurry. I didn't understand the depths of love. I didn't see how layered it was. How it never ends. How it somehow, impossibly even, grows. I learned that my mom is not a rock.

She's a mountain.

A *mountain*.

And, Mom, know that I am trying to return the love you've given me, but also know that I know I'll forever be in a deficit. Thank you, Mom. My heart is full. And I'm so glad I'm your boy.

I learned about my dad, as well. I am learning how cruel and difficult the world right now can be, especially for a Black man who walks in this world. My dad has always been stoic, but what maybe I see as detachment isn't that. Maybe it's just the only way he had to survive. He's buried both his mother and (in the last few months) his very best friend. Maybe his inability to cry or emote is just a necessary byproduct of being a Black man from the South at this point in history. But I know this. I know he's worked to make my life easier and safer, so that I don't have to hide or be afraid. His stoicism and steadiness is a form of love—like a sturdy sea wall, holding back so much. More than I know. Or could ever know. And in the process, he's given me the freedom to be the person I was able to become. My dad might not be able to cry, but because of him, I can. Thank you, Dad. For it all. I hope I've made you proud.

I learned about my friends. I also learned that I am not alone. I am far from being alone. I don't know if you remember this from the earlier chapters, but because of my friends, I was able to be seen at Vanderbilt Medical Center. My friends saved my life. This is not hyperbole. They saved my life. Without them, I don't know if I would have even been able to get to the hospital in time. When you are not strong, lean on your people. That is why they are there. With my friends, I am more than lucky. I'm beyond blessed. My friends are one of the very best gifts ever given to me by God. To the people in my life whom I am blessed to call my friends, and you know who you are, I want to tell you, as an only child, I always had this unspoken fear that at the end of it all, because I have no siblings, I might be alone. But I know now I'm not. I know what it means to have brothers and sisters. Thank you. What a rich life I get to live, because of you. My friends. No. My *family*.

One more person I learned about. As some of you might

remember, in my last book, I laid out how deeply dysfunctional and messed up my romantic relationships have been throughout my life. That's well documented. But along the way as I wrote this book, cancer wasn't the only thing that was introduced into my life. I met someone new. Her name is Jen, and, friends, I'm sorry you didn't get to meet her sooner. Honestly, I had no idea how to introduce a romantic interest into this book. "Oh, hey, I'm dating someone and it's not a dumpster fire. No! It's actually going pretty great." And part of me leaned away from saying all that, because, frankly, there was just too much to say. Sometimes, some things are just too special. If you remember, in Chapter 8, I talked about a trip I took to New York City, to see my friends. It was during that trip that I met Jen. And in the course of this cancer diagnosis (and writing this book), I not only met Jen, but fell for her. Hard. If you remember, I talked about the joy of taking a vacation and the wonder of traveling to beautiful places. That was all thanks to Jen and her friends, who are now my friends, urging me to live. And live I did. Thanks to her. Have I apologized clearly enough yet? Probably not. Jen, I could have written a whole chapter about you—hell, a whole book—about what I learned from you. What joy you have brought me. The fact is, your fingerprints are on every chapter of this book because you helped me learn the lessons from every single chapter. And you taught me another lesson, one that every single one of us needs to hear now and then: that you never know what might be just around the corner. And of course, the greatest lesson I learned from you is that I really and truly must be sexier than Denzel to have landed you. You're welcome.

Oh. And there's one more person I have to acknowledge. Someone I didn't even know before I started writing this book, but someone who has become quite important to me over the past six months.

And that's you.

So before I go, I wanted to thank you for walking through this journey with me. You're still here, at the end of this, and I'm honored that you'd take the time out of your story and spend so much time in mine. I've tried to be as vulnerable as I could, but you did something pretty remarkable as well. You made the decision to stick with me and listen. To choose closeness. To choose proximity. To listen to me as I poured out my fears, wrestled with my doubt, and talked for far too long about the medical state of my penis.

Our world is noisy and filled with distractions. It's a brave thing to take the time to listen to someone else. To create the space for another person to share their life is a gift.

When I started this book, I didn't know if I'd be able to drop the humor and be real. I knew that I was using humor as a mask. And even now, the fact remains, I'm still the LeBron James of jelly jokes. But now, after all that we've shared, I don't feel like I need to hide. I can just *be*. And face it. I think this is probably because of the shared experience of writing this book for you and alongside you. Even if I don't know you personally. But it's my hope—my wish, actually— that someday I get a chance to sit down with you and hear your story. To give you the gift that you've given me of listening. I know a place with great biscuits.

I guess what I'm trying to say is going through anything challenging or difficult can be a very lonely experience. Going through cancer? The loneliness can be suffocating. But because of you, I feel less alone. Because of you, I can breathe. Honestly, I thank God for you. I mean that.

I also need to make sure to say something to my fellow members of the Worst Club On Earth, aka people reading this book who have been given a cancer diagnosis. In my first book, my main topic was about my race—my Blackness if you will. I was hoping, writing that book, that Black folks would feel seen. But this book is different. Like I've said before, cancer doesn't respect race or gender or socio-economic class. It's like automated calls about your car's extended warranty—it attacks everyone. At any rate, to those of you reading this who are suffering, or in recovery, I hope that something I wrote made you feel seen. Because you are. I see you. Actually, I take that back. I hope that no one who reads this book, or ever will read this book, ever has cancer. But I know, statistically, that's just unlikely. So to you, my Cancer Fight Club, I hope you can see this book as a love letter and words of encouragement to you.

I mention this because I know, for me, never before in my life have I found myself so often seeking out encouragement in everyday places. I find myself hunting for it. Trying to find tidbits here and there.

A while ago, I saw a clip from *The Late Show with Stephen Colbert* where Colbert interviewed the quirky, peculiar, and captivating Jeff Goldblum. Colbert asked him, in light of the state of the world and how overwhelming the bad news about things can be, how he maintained his sense of hope.

Goldblum, in typical Goldblum fashion, put his finger to his temple and recited a passage from the Irish playwright George Bernard Shaw. Because of course he did.

What he said was remarkable. It sounded like a finely tuned hip-hop lyric. And I've found myself thinking about the quote that he had memorized:

This is the true joy in life, being used for a purpose recognized by yourself as a mighty one. Being a force of nature instead of a feverish, selfish little clod of ailments and grievances, complaining that the world will not devote itself to making you happy. I am of the opinion that my life belongs to the whole community and as long as I live, it is my privilege to do for it what I can. I want to be thoroughly used up when I die, for the harder I work, the more I live. I rejoice in life for its own sake. Life is no brief candle to me. It is a sort of splendid torch which I have got hold of for the moment and I want to make it burn as brightly as possible before handing it on to future generations.

Bars. And I'm unsure if I should thank Jeff Goldblum or Stephen Colbert or George Bernard Shaw. I guess all three?

All right.

So I hear my mother stirring in the other room. Soon, she'll be up, getting ready to take me to the hospital.

I feel an overwhelming sense of gratitude that she's here.

Not just here.

But *here.*

Here.

If you haven't figured this out about me by now, nearly everything reminds me of a Broadway musical, and that word "here" is no exception. This time, it's *The Color Purple.* It began as a book, then was made into a movie, then into a hit Broadway play, and most recently, a pretty incredible movie musical. This story follows the heartrending journey of Celie, who endures unspeakable pain after unspeakable pain, year after year. You wonder, with empathy, "Dear Heaven. When will things turn for this poor girl? When will the pain stop? Can she ever be whole?"

Toward the end of the musical, Celie sings a soliloquy called "I'm Here"—which is the emotional epicenter of the entire show.

Celie starts by listing the people she knows loves her, who give her strength. And then, almost as though she is being pulled out of the pain of life by some invisible power, she sings about the good things she has. Things that even the cruelest parts of life could not take from her.

> Got my hands doing good like they s'posed to
> Showing my heart to the folks that I'm close to
> Got my eyes though they don't see as far now
> They see more 'bout how things really are now.

I went and saw the Oprah Winfrey–produced movie by myself, in a movie theater in Las Vegas over Christmas. And I'm telling you, Fantasia Barrino (who plays Celie) does not merely *sing* this song. It erupts from her. Fantasia hurls this song at you, and every lyric feels like a body punch from Apollo Creed. It forces you into the back of your seat with a power that a hurricane would be envious of. She sings—at the end of the song—that she is thankful for every day, including the days that are easy and the days that are difficult.

And it's then we realize something so deeply cathartic. Celie's growth as a character…

All of our growth as humans…

…comes from both the trials and the joys of life.

Both.

In the story, one of the characters, Shug Avery, tells Celie that she believes that it angers God if a person walks by the color purple in a field without stopping to notice and admire it. Her point is that the color purple is a surprise, a stunning, arresting color that should not be possible, a regal, beautiful spark of joy in nature that simply ought not be there.

And yet, there it is.

There is purple in this life.

And to Shug, it's proof of God and His intimate care.

Purple is also the color used to represent Celie, who is a beautiful spark of color and hope, even though she absolutely should not be. In her final song, Celie sings, in essence, "This is how I choose to live, in light of all that I have been through."

This moves me.

If Celie's hope can't be crushed, if her determination to love, despite all she has endured, cannot be tamped down, then maybe mine can't be, either.

So here I am.

And I'm left, this morning, feeling hope.

I see purple.

Everywhere.

I realize that, surprisingly, I have an absolute abundance of hope. It's so interesting to me that after everything I've walked through in this book—everything *we've* walked through—I sit here and look at the world through the lens not of fear, but of hope.

I'm not afraid anymore.

<Exhale>

And this? This hope?

Well.

This changes everything.

A TONY AWARD–WORTHY ONE-ACT SCRIPT ABOUT MY BRAIN AFTER MY SURGERY

And now, ladies and gentlemen, a simple one-act play that I wrote about what it might have been like for my body post-surgery. Please enjoy responsibly.

BRAIN:
<Light on. We see BRAIN, lying askew, amid small smoldering fires and wafting smoke in the quasi-wreckage of something that looks very much like the bridge of the Enterprise. Alarms are ringing in the distance. Slowly, BRAIN stirs, turning over and eventually getting to his feet. He appears to be both injured and groggy.>

Great Scott! I must have blacked out. How long was I out? *<Shaking head>*

Comm systems on. Attention, everyone, this is your captain speaking. Stand by for a complete system check. Arms, legs, report in.

LEFT ARM:
Check.

RIGHT ARM:
Check.

RIGHT LEG:

Check.

LEFT LEG:

Check.

BRAIN:

Hands are operational?

LEFT ARM:

Fingers are wiggling, sir.

BRAIN:

All right. So far, so good. Vision. Hearing. You guys online?

HEARING:

Both ears working, sir. All inputs normal and functioning.

BRAIN:

Vision. Both inputs working for you?

VISION:

Eye, eye, Captain.

<snickers>

BRAIN:

F#$%ing knock it off, vision. This isn't the time for jokes. Okay, toes. You guys able to go wee wee wee all the way home?

TOES:

Big toe systems go, Captain.

BRAIN:

Okay, let's go internal. Lungs.

LUNGS:

Breathing normal, sir.

EYES:

Well, to "air" is human.

BRAIN:

Dammit, eyes, if you don't knock it off with the bad puns, I'm going to have left index finger poke you like a Stooge so hard, we'll be wearing an eye patch like Captain Jack Sparrow, you understand me??

EYE:

<crickets>

BRAIN:

Okay, heart?

HEART:

Everything moving as expected.

BRAIN:

Okay, kidneys.

RIGHT KIDNEY:

Here, Captain.

BRAIN:

Good. Left kidney?

<silence>

Left kidney? Left kidney, report in.

<silence>

Can someone ping left kidney and tell her to report in?

GALLBLADDER:

I'm trying to reach her, Captain. Nothing.

BRAIN:

What do you mean there's nothing? Left kidney. Left kidney, come in.

<static>

APPENDIX:

I don't have a visual, sir.

BRAIN:

What do you mean you don't have a visual?

APPENDIX:

There's nothing where she used to be, sir.

BRAIN:

Kidneys don't just disappear one day. They're not like appendixes.

APPENDIX:

Wait, what?

BRAIN:

Never mind. Seriously, where is left kidney?

RIGHT KIDNEY:

He's gone, sir. Just vanished.

BRAIN:

Organs don't just vanish. They're not like planets in *Star Wars*. It has to be here somewhere.

RIGHT URETER:

Sir, I can't reach left ureter, either. We were together all up the bladder, and then we branched off and there's nothing. He's gone, too.

BRAIN:

Dear God. We lost a kidney.

HEART:

What are we going to do?

BRAIN:

Run all systems through right kidney. We can still scrub all metabolic waste of the blood through him, and send it out of here through the bladder.

EYE:

Well, that's a relief.

BRAIN:

Was that a urination joke, eye? Was it? Because so help me I will give myself a stroke and shut down your optic nerve before you can read the big E on the eye chart.

<BRAIN ponders the loss of LEFT KIDNEY and begins to go into an eleven-minute left kidney–centric rendition of "Bring Him Home" from Les Misérables.>

THE TEN BEST FICTIONAL DOGS
OF ALL TIME

LAST PLACE: Cujo from *Cujo* by Stephen King
Cujo is a 200-pound Saint Bernard who chases a bunny into a cave and gets bitten by a bat carrying the rabies virus. He then goes on a murderous rampage, killing his owner, a police officer, and some nice people from Maine. Maybe the worst pet ever. Okay, maybe he's the worst fictional dog ever. But he's so bad that he's making the best list. Bad dog, Cujo! Bad dog!

SECOND-TO-LAST PLACE: Clifford from the Clifford the Big Red Dog children's book series
Clocking in at more than twenty-five feet tall, this dog might seem like fun, but it's unclear how his family was able to afford him. Based on breed and size, I estimate that Clifford would need roughly a ton of food per day. That's two whole cows' worth of meat per day.[1] The going cost of beef right now is about $8.50 per pound of finished, processed meat, so that's $8,500 per day for food. Let alone water. You'd need to live next to a major waterway, like a river or lake. And we haven't even gotten into the logistics of dealing with the excrement. Ugh…this gives "please clean up after your pet" a whole new meaning. That whole "just wrap the little baggy around your hand and pick it up" trick is *not* going to work here. Ain't a trash bag in the world designed for this sh*t. And you best pray to God that Clifford doesn't pull a Cujo and chase a bunny into a cave with rabid bats, or we'll have to call out the National Guard.

10. Scooby-Doo
One of the great cartoon characters ever and arguably the most recognizable dog on this list. So why such a low ranking? Well,

---

1. https://inkopious.com/blogs/articles/taking-care-of-clifford.

I'll tell you. Scooby hangs out way too much with that lazy stoner Shaggy. Also, for being a canine, this dog sure is a fraidy cat. Just a coward, through and through. Scooby is a Great Dane, which means he is more than six feet tall on his hind legs. Just a giant. But you get one elderly real estate developer dressed up in a rubber mask and this dog gets more scared than a white person when the topic of "reparations" gets brought up. Points deducted for always running away. Zoinks. Scooby-Doo better, amirite?

9. Buddy from *Air Bud*

This dog gained fame after it is discovered that he could put a basketball in the basket using his face. In the big final game in this film, Buddy's final stat line might look pedestrian (five assists, two steals, two free throws, and four field goals), but those numbers don't tell the whole story. If you examine the advanced metrics (a sentence I can't believe I just typed), it appears that Buddy shot more than 80 percent when his owner, Josh, passed him the ball.[2] For reference, Steph Curry, the greatest shooter of all time, clocks in at 49 percent.[3] And we haven't even gotten to plus-minus and true defensive rating. Yes, Buddy does head-butt an opposing player's crotch, which we're pretty sure is a flagrant two, but Bud did what it took to win. And, as we'd see in the sequels, Buddy is the Bo Jackson of canine athletes, finding success in American football (*Air Bud: Golden Receiver*), soccer (*Air Bud: World Pup*), and baseball (*Air Bud: Seventh Inning Fetch*). What a versatile athlete. Legen. Dary. I say we bring Air Bud into this Jordan/LeBron debate. A dog being the GOAT?!?! This is exactly the kind of story we need right now. Points slightly deducted for peeing on the court so much.

---

2. Thanks to writer Rajat Suresh for this analytics insight. "Actually, Air Bud Sucks at Basketball," Mel. https://melmagazine.com/en-us/story/air-bud-sucks-at-basketball.
3. "Actually, Air Bud Sucks at Basketball," https://melmagazine.com/en-us/story/air-bud-sucks-at-basketball.

8. Toto from *The Wizard of Oz*

As a Cairn terrier, Toto is the smallest dog on this list. Toto is cute riding around in the basket of that bike and all, but beyond serving as a metaphorical link back to home for Dorothy, this tiny canine doesn't really do anything. But bonus points for pulling back the curtain to reveal the scam that is the Great and Powerful Oz. Also, extra points for being a part of one of the most iconic lines in movie history ("Toto, I have a feeling we're not in Kansas anymore") and for serving as the name of a great eighties band who blessed the rains down in Africa.

7. Hooch from *Turner and Hooch*

Has there been a better use of slow motion in the history of cinema than the scene of Tom Hanks and Hooch shaking their jowls in the car? I think not. Bonus points for having an all-time great dog name *and* for entering into detective work, despite no formal training. Double extra bonus points for valor and saving Tom Hanks because *that man is a national treasure.*

6. Benji

This is probably too retro for some of you, but Benji is the gold-standard classic dog for Gen-X kids like me. Benji was the star of a half dozen feature films in the late seventies and early eighties. Benji, who looked a bit like a cute mini-Chewbacca, was always solving problems and helping people, including single-handedly rescuing children from a band of kidnappers (*Benji*, 1974) and (checking notes) traveling to Greece to make sure top-secret scientific advances didn't fall into the hands of a double-agent (*For the Love of Benji*, 1977). Fun fact: the actual dog who played Benji was a homeless mutt, rescued from a shelter in Beverly Hills, became a movie star, and eventually was studded out to breed other movie star dogs. Kind of a rags-to-bitches story. I said what I said, people!

5. Sam from *I Am Legend*

Samantha is a German shepherd and the only companion of Will Smith during a zombie apocalypse. Samantha doesn't just protect Will Smith and help him with hunting, she's his only source of emotional connection—unless you count the mannequins that Will sometimes talks to, and I definitely do not. After Sam is infected by the zombies, Will has to kill her in one of the most heartbreaking scenes in movie history, basically becoming the modern version of *Old Yeller*. Bonus points for Sam saving Will Smith's life when he's caught in a zombie trap. Points deducted for being a dumb dog and chasing a deer into a building full of zombies and making Will Smith go in there.

4. Brandy from *Once Upon a Time in Hollywood*

It's unclear if Brad Pitt's character is so cool because of Brandy, or if Brandy is cool because of Brad Pitt. Brandy is the slender, strong pit bull terrier who elicits massive jealousy from every guy watching the film (because she gets to hang out with Brad Pitt) and massive jealousy from every woman watching the film (because she gets to give lots of smooches to Brad Pitt). In one of the most graphic and awesome moments in the film, Cliff (Brad Pitt's character) and Brandy kill a bunch of insane, homicidal goons sent by Charles Manson. And Cliff's weapon is a can of Brandy's dog food! Slight deduction for reinforcing the stereotype that pit bulls are a dangerous breed. Slight bonus for saving acting beauty Sharon Tate. Who just rewrote history? Who did? That's a good girl!

3. Balto from *Balto*

This animated dog gets extra points because he's based on a real-life Siberian husky who led a team of sled dogs that delivered life-saving medicine during a deadly outbreak of diphtheria in 1925.[4] These dogs

---

4. "Balto," Wikipedia. https://en.wikipedia.org/wiki/Balto.

went through 600 miles of ice in five days to save the people of Nome, Alaska, from…uh…I'm not really sure what diphtheria is. Oh, man! I just googled it! It basically destroys healthy tissue in your lungs and then the dead tissue forms a thick, gray coating that builds up in the throat or nose and has a 30 percent mortality rate. Nasty! Anyway, there was only one airplane in the region that could deliver the medicine, but its engine was frozen solid and wouldn't start. So these dogs delivered medicine to Nome from Anchorage and saved 20,000 people. Here's how tough that trek was: afterward, to reward the dogs, they let them live in ease at a zoo in Cleveland, Ohio. When Cleveland is your idea of an ideal retirement, you know you've been through hell and back. Balto is the bravest dog on this list. Bonus points for the fact that in the animated film, Balto is voiced by Kevin Bacon. Double bonus points for getting his own statue in Central Park.

2. Lassie and Snoopy (tie)

No dogs have entered the American consciousness more than these two. Just icons. Lassie saved Timmy so many times, you began to wonder if Timmy had a death wish. Bonus points for long, flowing hair. Let's face it, folks: Lassie is the Fabio of canines and I ain't even mad about it. Double bonus points for being able to effectively communicate huge amounts of information via barking.

> LASSIE: <bark>
> OWNER: What's that, girl? Timmy is trapped under a tree down by the crick and the water level is slowly rising?
> LASSIE: <bark>
> OWNER: And be sure to invest in gold futures because of market uncertainties?

Snoopy is just everywhere. No other dog on this list has a giant balloon featuring their likeness every year in the Macy's Thanksgiving

Day Parade. Also, Snoopy's laugh is one of the greatest sounds in the entire world.

1. Little Ann and Big Dan (tie, first place)

These two are just awesome. Big Dan was muscled and broad-shouldered—the brawn of the operation, bold and aggressive. Little Ann, though slighter, was the brains. Together, these two save Billy's life multiple times from legitimately terrifying threats. They win dog shows. They win a national hunting competition. These two dogs reveal themselves to be smarter than most of the general population of the state of Oklahoma. They are so great, they could have run for office and become the first-ever dual canine governors of Oklahoma. Points deducted for being so stupidly named, but if you think about it, that's not really their fault, now, is it? Bonus points for being the *best dogs* in the *history of mankind*.

ACKNOWLEDGMENTS

Mom and Dad, it's such a blessing to have you here to walk with me through these stories. I thank God for you every single day.

Jennifer Lynn King, you continue to be a gift to the whole world. It's amazing and so inspiring to watch. You are all over these pages. I will never be able to thank you enough or come up with the right words to express how much of a gift you have been to me.

Shannon, my ride or die, still. Thank you.

Sara, the way this all falls apart without you. Thank you for keeping it all together.

The Sobeckis, you are my favorite part of the weekend.

Mike and Erin, don't ever leave me again. Ever. Thanks.

The Curetons, my soul's brother and sister.

The Wrights, no matter the time, space, or place, you are my family. Always.

The Crawfords, love y'all with everything.

Tisha, look how far we've come, cousin. Hug those grown-arse kids for me!

Uncle Jimmy and Aunt Mel, I miss you every day. Kemah, your ongoing strength is everything.

Elysha and Cathleen, I'll text you later.

Broken Frame brothers, you know who you are and you know what it is.

James and Dawn, what a ride this has been. I thought I told you that we don't stop!

Praise for
This Changes Everything

"A scary, funny, moving, and inspiring story from a man who deserves cancer less than almost anyone I know." —Jimmy Kimmel

"Tyler Merritt approaches cancer, a subject that is scary for all of us to talk about, with grace and humor, just like everything in his life. This whole book feels like one long, wonderful conversation with a friend. Sometimes you have to laugh, and sometimes you have to get real. That's life. *This Changes Everything* gives me all the feels. We're lucky to have Tyler's voice in the world!" —Trisha Yearwood

"How Tyler has gone and made a book about living with cancer so funny I'm not sure I'll ever really understand. What I do know is that I'm better for leaning into his story. Laced with deep heartfelt moments and stories that can only be told by a man who has become comfortable in his own skin, I'd recommend *This Changes Everything* to anyone who needs a reminder at how beautiful this life truly is." —Anthony Anderson, actor, producer, activist, health advocate, philanthropist

"Tyler Merritt is a national treasure, and *This Changes Everything* is a thoughtful, beautiful, and heartwarming tribute to this wonderful thing called life—as only Tyler can tell it." —Joy Reid

"Tyler takes us on an unimaginable journey through his cancer diagnosis, treatment, and life afterwards, with sage wisdom and unparalleled humor. We are reminded of what truly matters in life—forgiveness, gratitude, and the true meaning of optimism. Through his raw and honest storytelling, Tyler gives us a new perspective on our own struggles and triumphs. Prepare to be moved, and forever changed by Tyler's powerful story." —Heather Locklear

"First of all, I recognized all of the musical theater references Tyler thought he was so sneakily throwing at me! I may have even caught myself singing along to a few. Listen, I just didn't want *This Changes Everything* to end. It's filled with so much love for us, the reader. Somehow even after walking through cancer, Tyler's outlook on this complex life remains uplifting and awe-inspiring. Serious at some points and incredibly funny in others, I cannot wait for you all to read this book."

—Kristin Chenoweth, Emmy- and Tony Award–winning actress and *New York Times* bestselling author

"A heartfelt, laugh-out-loud book about nearly dying and what it means to really live."   —actress/host Yvette Nicole Brown

"I accidentally met Tyler in NYC four days after he found out this surgery was inevitable, and fell in love with him because who could help it? I've only known this Tyler, the one in these exact pages, and he is as marvelous as you think. *This Changes Everything* is a love letter to life. This book will help you understand why I introduced him to my kids and gave him my heart."

—Jen Hatmaker, four-time *New York Times* bestselling author and Tyler's girlfriend

"Tyler Merritt is an artist who can show you a picture, break it back down to a molecular level, and show you layer by layer how he became the work of art that he is today. And facing his own fears, then boldly regurgitating them for us in this manuscript, Tyler puts words to the internal battles and shows us that reckoning with our own mortality can often increase our own vitality."

—Roy Wood Jr., former *Daily Show* correspondent

"My favorite thing about Tyler and his writing is how he dances with joy and humor in the fires of discomfort. This line sums up the path we take together in his latest book—'I think most of us dramatically underestimate not only what we could go through, but what we have been through.' And yet, Tyler's writing reminds me that God is play,

ACKNOWLEDGMENTS

My Comcast family, Nakia, and the leadership there, y'all have played a major role in my health journey. Thank you.

And lastly, hello there, haters,
you didn't think I'd come back.
But now that I'm Mr. Thang, now that I'm a zillionaire...
You scan the credits for your name and wonder why they're not there.

ABOUT THE AUTHOR

Tyler Merritt is an actor, musician, comedian, and activist behind the Tyler Merritt Project. Raised in Las Vegas, he has always had a passion for bringing laughter, grace, and love into any community he is a part of. His film credits include Netflix's *Outer Banks*, Disney/Marvel's *The Falcon and the Winter Soldier*, NBC's *Young Rock*, and A24's *The Inspection*, to name a few. Tyler's viral videos "Before You Call the Cops" and "Walking While Black" have been viewed by over 100 million people worldwide, with "Before You Call the Cops" being voted the most powerful video of 2020 by NowThis Politics. He is a cancer survivor who lives in Nashville, Tennessee.